MITIGATING CONFLICT

THE CASS SERIES ON PEACEKEEPING
ISSN 1367-9880
General Editor: Michael Pugh

This series examines all aspects of peacekeeping, from the political, operational and legal dimensions to the developmental and humanitarian issues that must be dealt with by all those involved with peacekeeping in the world today.

MITIGATING CONFLICT

The Role of NGOs

Editors

HENRY F. CAREY
Georgia State University

OLIVER P. RICHMOND
University of St. Andrews

FRANK CASS

LONDON • PORTLAND, OR

First published in 2003 in Great Britain by
FRANK CASS PUBLISHERS
Crown House, 47 Chase Side, London N14 5BP, England

and in the United States of America by
FRANK CASS PUBLISHERS
c/o ISBS, 920 NE 58th Avenue #300
Portland, Oregon 97213-3786

Website http://www.frankcass.com

© 2003 Frank Cass & Co. Ltd.

British Library Cataloguing in Publication Data

Mitigating conflict: the role of NGOs. – (The Cass series
on peacekeeping; 12)
1. Non-governmental organizations 2. Mediation,
International 3. Conflict management
I. Carey, Henry F. II. Richmond, Oliver P.
327'.06

ISBN 0 7146 5430 2 (cloth)
ISBN 0 7146 8406 6 (paper)
ISSN 1367 9880

Library of Congress Cataloging-in-Publication Data:

Mitigating conflict: the role of NGOs/editors, Henry F. Carey, Oliver
P. Richmond
    p. cm. – (The Cass series on peacekeeping, ISSN 1367-9880)
Includes bibliographical references and index.
    ISBN 0-7146-5430-2 (cloth) – ISBN 0-7146-8406-6 (pbk.)
    1. Conflict management. 2. Non-governmental organizations.
I. Carey, Henry F., 1953– II. Richmond, Oliver P. III. Series.
JZ6368.M58 2003
341.5 – dc21   2003004137

This group of studies first appeared in a special issue of
International Peacekeeping [ISSN 1353-3312] Vol.10, No.1 (Spring, 2003)
published by Frank Cass and Co. Ltd.

Printed in Great Britain by
Antony Rowe Ltd., Chippenham, Wiltshire

Contents

Acronyms and Abbreviations

ACBAR	Agency Coordinating Body for Afghan Relief
AHSAO	Afghan Health and Social Assistance Organization
AIA	Afghan Interim Authority
AMA	Afghan Medical Aid
AWC	Afghan Women's Council
AWN	Afghan Women's Network
BINGOs	Big International, Nongovernmental Organizations
CCW	Convention on Conventional Weapons
CIDA	Canadian International Development Agency
CDO	Centar za Dramski Odgoj [Centre for Drama in Education, Mostar]
CMOCs	Civil–Military Cooperation Centres
CP	Conflict Prevention
CPAU	Cooperation for Peace and Unity
DPRK	Democratic Peoples Republic of Korea
DRC	Democratic Republic of the Congo
DONGOs	Donor Created Nongovernmental Organizations
ECHO	European Community Humanitarian Office
EPLF	Eritrean People's Liberation Front
GDI	Global Development Initiative
HCIC	Humanitarian Coordination Information Centre
HINGOs	Humanitarian International Nongovernmental Organizations
ICC	International Criminal Court
ICRC	International Committee of the Red Cross
ICTR	International Criminal Tribunal for Rwanda
ICTY	International Criminal Tribunal for Yugoslavia
IGOs	Intergovernmental Organizations
INGOs	International Nongovernmental Organizations
LNGOs	Local Nongovernmental Organizations
MAPA	UN Mine Action Program for Afghanistan
MICIVIH	UN/OAS Civilian Verification Mission in Haiti
MSF	Médecins Sans Frontières

NEGAR	Defence of Afghanistan Women's Rights
NGOs	Nongovernmental Organizations
NPFL	National Patriotic Front of Liberia
ODA	Official Development Assistance
OHR	Office of the High Representative
OLS	Operation Lifeline Sudan (UN)
OAS	Organization of American States
OSCE	Organization for Security and Cooperation in Europe
PEACE	Poverty Eradication and Community Empowerment
PHR	Physicians for Human Rights
PrepComs	Preparatory Commissions
QUANGOs	Quasi-Nongovernmental Organizations
RAWA	Revolutionary Association of the Women of Afghanistan
RPF	Rwanda Patriotic Front
SAD	Society of Afghan Doctors
SPLA	Sudan People's Liberation Army
SPLM	Sudan People's Liberation Movement
SRRA	Sudan Relief and Rehabilitation Association
SSIA	South Sudan Independence Army
TPLF	Tigray People's Liberation Front
UEO	Unexploded Ordnance
UN	United Nations
UNDP	United Nations Development Programme
UNFPA	United Nations Fund for Population Activities
UNHCR	United Nations High Commissioner for Refugees
USAID	United States Agency for International Development
VDCs	Village Development Committees
WZB	Wissenschaft Zentar Berlin [Social Science Research Centre, Berlin]

Introduction:
NGOs, Peace and Human Security

OLIVER P. RICHMOND

Since UN peacekeeping and associated forms of international intervention in conflict zones took on a new significance at the end of the Cold War, nongovernmental organizations (NGOs) have also emerged as a vital part of the mechanisms of intervention, both in conjunction with traditional forms of peacekeeping, but more importantly in longer term prevention and peacebuilding tasks. These roles are intended to contribute to the construction of neoliberal, democratic entities in conflict zones, but they also raise a series of questions about the nature of NGO roles, objectives and relationship with the militaries, states and other organizations. Yet, NGOs have become crucial in the social, political and economic issue areas that constitute international-social conflict,[1] particularly in the regeneration of torn and divided societies, restoring infrastructure and providing basic social goods. Indeed, it has often been suggested that NGOs fulfil vital roles that states and their agencies cannot take on. This occurs both in terms of direct involvement with projects in these issue areas, but also in their monitoring and advocacy roles, as many of the following essays illustrate. Just how crucial this contribution has been – its direction, and its longer term impact on conflict zones, as well as what it means for international society and its practices of intervention – have been matters of some debate.

This debate lacks clarity and consensus, and has failed even to come to an agreement on the question of the definition of NGOs. Nor has it arrived at a universal acceptance of how, where, when, and why NGOs may intervene independently or may be employed as subcontractors by states and international organizations, or work in conjunction with peacekeeping operations. Indeed, much NGO participation in conflict zones is *ad hoc* and privately initiated and managed through funds coming from international sources. Such private actors have gained both a sort of legitimacy and have become vital to efforts to end and transform conflict. This has occurred with limited acceptance within policy circles. The UN Secretary-General and UN Secretariat have

regularly pointed to their significance (and shortcomings). In response
to the Cold War inadequacies of limited forms of peacekeeping and
diplomacy,[2] a niche has emerged for greater NGO participation; at the
same time expectations have increased as to their effectiveness in the
context of the far more complex roles ascribed to them.[3] Thus, as a
new agenda has arisen for international peacekeeping so too has the
role increased for NGOs in peace processes and peacebuilding. Equally
significant are the problems arising out of demands for more effective
relationships between NGOs and other actors involved in conflict
zones, including the militaries and international organizations. NGOs
offer possibilities for more effective involvement in dealing with
conflict and raise significant questions about the role, regulation and
organization of humanitarian intervention and peace processes.

This volume analyses how NGOs become involved in preventative
diplomacy, in peacemaking, peacekeeping and peacebuilding. NGOs
have proliferated enormously, becoming integral to international
governance and law, as amply depicted in the literature. However,
apart from examining humanitarian assistance functions, scholars have
largely ignored how NGOs have become systematically integrated into
peace processes, as mandated by international law, as well as facilitated
by the often coherent and effective NGO contributions. A particularly
startling gap in the enormous NGO literature is how states and state-
based intergovernment organizations (IGOs) have provided, or been
pressured to provide, avenues of participation for NGOs, and how
NGOs in turn have endeavoured to constrain states in whether and
how they use force against states and against their own people. NGOs
have also induced states, through legal and political processes, to
interact with domestic civil societies before, during and after armed
conflict by representing societal groups and monitoring results.
Networks of NGOs are endeavouring to develop new peace norms and
to monitor compliance in both the use of force, the negotiation of
conflict, and the development of new institutions. Little has been said
on these complex developments, which requires focusing on how
NGOs have tried to modify the behaviour of actors in international
politics towards a more pacific and democratic ethos and to create
opportunities for dialogue, consultation and monitoring.

Towards that end, this volume eschews the usual scholarly
utopianism about NGOs, adopting a more critical appraisal of the
opportunities and constraints they face. States have often tried to
manage, constrain and create NGOs to serve their own agendas in
peace processes, have exploited factions in the NGO networks, and
have undermined the myth of a powerful international civil society.

NGOs are worthy of study, not because they are omnipotent, but because they are increasingly involved in peace processes, taking on roles that states cannot perform or do not want. The rise of civil society, in large part through NGOs, needs to be studied for its limits, as well as its contributions to existing and evolving peace processes.

Scholars have offered various NGO typologies. Thomas Weiss and Leon Gordenker have posited four types of NGOs. Their orthodox NGO is 'a private citizens' organization, separate from government but active on social issues, not profit making and with transnational scope. They further cite three 'significant deviations' which have less autonomy from the government, but which comprise a large percentage of what are commonly referred to as NGOs, but which should be distinguished from them. For example, the QUANGO is a 'quasi-nongovernmental organization' (such as the Nordic, Canadian and some US NGOs, as well as the ICRC), with relative autonomy which generally decreases as reliance on government funding increases. QUANGOs include government contractors, providing expert services (for example, the International Rescue Committee). Third, DONGOs are donor-created NGOs for particular purposes, such as development and humanitarian emergencies (examples include de-mining in Afghanistan and the UN Fund for Women). Finally, and hardly considered by Weiss and Gordenker, is the GONGO, a 'government-organized, nongovernmental organization...a front for administration activities', especially found in the former USSR but also the United States.[4]

How to categorize non-state actors is a matter of some debate, even using this typology. For example, what are non-state actors such as the National Endowment for Democracy, the National Science Foundation, or the Asia Foundation – QUANGOs, GONGOs and/or DONGOs? The category can also change over time. Catholic Relief, the International Rescue Committee and CARE, for example, have been heavily dependent on US financing. Yet, CARE, which is based in Europe and began as a post-World War II relief organization, is considering adopting a 'rights-based' approach towards assistance to the needy, an organizational transition which would require less dependence on government financing. Among other NGO typologies, Weissberg has outlined different NGO functions, such as documentation, lobbying, dissemination and political activism in analysing effects on human rights.[5] Ropp, Risse and Sikkink have analysed life cycle stages and government responses.[6] Others regard NGOs as instruments of cultural hegemony, for example dependent on the Ford Foundation or USAID and favouring civil and political rights over economic, social and cultural rights.

While NGOs have interacted with states for decades, the 1990s was a time of enormous change, and required a particular focus on how NGOs have or could enhance a new generation of peace activities, from prevention to peacebuilding. The 'new agendas' for peace entail a multiplicity of roles that often require 'deep' intervention in aspects of governance, humanitarian aid and development, which have increasingly become part of the international communities' agenda in dealing with conflict. Yet these developments have also been heavily contested, as some of the essays in this collection illustrate.

International humanitarian law provides a legal context in which NGOs operate. This was originally brought into prominence with the Hague Conventions of 1899 and 1907 and the Geneva Conventions of 1949 which provided protection for war victims, and then through the UN General Assembly's Nuremberg Principles in the early 1950s. UN Security Council Resolution 688 in 1992 demanded protection for humanitarian NGOs in Iraq in the context of Operation *Provide Comfort*.[7] This resolution insisted that Iraq allowed humanitarian intervention to protect and assist the Kurdish population, coordinated by the US and with the agreement of the UN.[8] On the other hand, Resolution 808 (22 February 1993) established an ad hoc international tribunal to prosecute those indicted for committing crimes against humanity, reaffirming the reprioritization of human rights enforcement as crucial in humanitarian intervention. Controversially, this development was heralded as indicative of a change towards a 'human security' ethos in which humans rather than states become the referents of security. In this context NGOs provide an important bridge between the local and the global, public and private, and so may facilitate the broader forms of prevention, peacemaking, peacekeeping, and peacebuilding that are now required.

The status of international NGOs has also been controversial. It has shifted and clarified as shown in their encroachment on the UN General Assembly, and indeed in the Security Council (often through the use of Rule 39) since the ICRC became a UN observer in 1990.[9] Peter Willets points out that the 'strongest evidence that NGO rights have become established...is the way in which NGOs can often gain access to intergovernmental proceedings even when the political climate turns against them'.[10] This has developed to the extent that international NGOs may now have become a third category of subject in international law, along with states and international organizations.[11]

Further controversy has been raised by the question of what motivates NGOs, and what are their overall objectives. As outlined above, an increasing focus on issues pertaining to human security, and the emerging role therein of NGOs has been crucial in the context of what has been termed a 'late Westphalian environment'.[12] There has been an increasingly normative reaction to both local and international politics, relating to the wider existence of political communities, an 'international society' and a 'global civil society'. It is in this late-Westphalian context that NGOs derive their legitimacy, at both the local and global level. As former UN Secretary-General Boutros-Ghali pointed out, NGOs provide access to a global civil society, which they themselves have been instrumental in highlighting and promoting. Space has often been provided for their activities by second-generation, multidimensional peacekeeping activities which have emerged since the end of the Cold War. The search for new approaches implicit in *An Agenda for Peace*, including preventive diplomacy and the UN's wide utilization of broader forms of peacekeeping and peacebuilding to stabilize conflicts, saw the realization that the NGO community can play a relatively greater, if not vital, role in the context of a broader understanding of security.[13] Boutros-Ghali wrote: 'If UN efforts are to succeed, the roles of the various players need to be carefully coordinated in an integrated approach to human security.'[14] As Andrew Natsios has argued, the emergence of numerous centres of power ranging from the civil to the global has in part prompted this change of emphasis.[15] This is particularly the case as NGOs have access to local civil societies and their authority structures.[16] In some cases, NGOs may now substitute for local government and encourage the development of civil society.[17] The increasing legitimization of NGOs at the local, state, regional and global level means that their agendas are more widely propagated; it also means that domestic civil society has a linkage with global civil society, as NGOs are legitimized in international organizations including the UN. NGOs are relatively unencumbered by sovereign concerns and are themselves relatively free from claims to sovereignty, which enables them to work in normative frameworks untainted by official, state and systemic interests.

NGOs offer the flexibility, expertise, rapid responses and commitment in local environments necessary to provide essential services, and they have the capacity to inform and mobilize opinion.[18] Criticisms of NGO activity in complex emergencies have been put forward, such as the erosion of regional and local self-help capacities, state sovereignty and the possibility that NGOs may actually aid one of the disputants indirectly.[19] On the other hand, NGOs can try to empower parties to deal with conflict constructively, monitor and lobby for human rights and the protection of minorities, and enact capacity-building and protective measurements for disadvantaged or endangered groups. On balance, NGOs can play an important role in the creation of 'peace constituencies'.[20] Humanitarian NGOs may be manipulated in conflict environments by disputants, as Abiew and Keating have argued.[21] Yet this is an indirect offshoot of their concern with normative issues like justice and human freedoms and rights. The problem is to retain the advantages of their unofficial status without incurring the wrath of sovereign actors which fear interventionary practices becoming institutionalized upon their territory, as well as guarding against the corruption of NGOs themselves. Natsios is probably right to argue that, despite all of the problematic debates surrounding the development and role of the NGO sector, the evolving international system will continue to demand expanded roles for NGOs.[22]

It is important to note that among NGOs a consensus appears to be emerging that their activities are likely to be more effective if they operate in a multidimensional and 'multitrack' framework in which local actors, external NGOs, governments and international organizations undertake complementary actions.[23] Such multi-dimensional approaches, however, require concerted and consistent coordination and a commonality of objectives. As reflected in the essays in this volume, it is here that a major theoretical dispute is located, in which NGOs, agencies and state-centric actors contest the concept of security and its related norms in international politics.

In the context of a growing acceptance of the transnational nature of contemporary international relations, of globalization and of grassroots contributions via a global civil society, a debate has emerged indicating that NGOs have a particular capacity to assist in establishing human security. Yet this assertion is the target of pragmatic arguments that NGOs can have a role in state-rebuilding as long as they are monitored and controlled by intergovernmental institutions and their member states, and of normative arguments that a global civil society has now transcended state control and represents a cosmopolitan desire for human security. The notion of human security in particular has been attacked on the grounds that as a nodal point for directing state, IGO and NGO activity, it obfuscates the kind of prioritization that is required to preserve state security and stability.[24] Thus, the dynamics of a familiar dispute – between independent, transnational actors, disillusioned with the ability of states to provide security for the marginalized, and the state-centric belief that margins must be sacrificed in order to preserve order and security more generally – become clear. Nevertheless, human security has emerged as a compelling alternative to the more traditional notion of state security.

Both versions of security imply different conceptions of international relations, of the responsibilities of state and non-state actors, of the nature of the international system, and of what kind of ethical order is viable. Yet, while such debates preoccupy policy and academic communities, NGOs continue to raise funding and work in the field to ameliorate the impact of political, social or economic 'abnormalities' and other disasters, using human security as their key referent. Ultimately the debates about human security constitute a dual attempt: to move away from the purely rational approach of state security and to incorporate the diverse elements that are involved into a theoretical understanding of security. The problem here might be that, as Yuen Foong Khong argues, this may lead to a paralysis of our ability to provide security, comparing it to 'speaking loudly about human security but carrying a Band-Aid'.[25] This is clearly an important criticism in the context of the role of NGOs and their increasing use as subcontractors.

Thus, the evolving role of NGOs in conflict zones opens up important areas for research and debate. How should NGOs be differentiated and what are the legitimate objectives of NGOs? Can and should their activities be regulated? How can their activities be coordinated with other NGOs, agencies, organizations and states? What are their relations with donors? How should NGOs be protected in the field? What sorts of norms should NGOs import into civil societies riven by conflict?

Many of these issues, themes and problems are explored in greater depth in the following essays. The first section examines relevant thematic issues, including the relationship of NGOs with peacekeepers and peace support operations, their role with respect to human rights, their role in conflict prevention, their potential in delivering aid, and in relation to crimes of sexual violence.

In the first of these contributions, Karin Aggestam provides an important critique of the conflict prevention debates. The major question she examines is to what extent scholarly work offers new insights into the *problematique* of conflict prevention. In this context she argues that NGOs are increasingly becoming vital actors in international relations, though there exists a cooperative as well as a competitive interplay between different modes of conflict prevention by NGOs and IGOs in the context of debates about conflict prevention. Francis Kofi Abiew examines how NGOs have assumed an increasingly significant role alongside the rapidly developing multilateral peacekeeping operations since the end of the Cold War. He points out that the activities of NGOs, particularly those involved in development, humanitarian relief and human rights, now cut across all phases of the peacekeeping process requiring a clearer understanding of their different roles. Ironically, the military want a greater synergy while NGOs want to preserve their impartiality. He proposes that such incompatibilities require the drafting of a voluntary code of practice on NGO–military consultation processes in order to enhance the efficiency of comprehensive peace operations. This is a key issue in that coordination between NGOs, agencies, officials and militaries has proved to be extremely problematic. Michael Schloms then turns to an examination of the potential of aid agencies as peacebuilding actors. He notes that the nature of intrastate conflicts and the political manipulation of humanitarian aid in the 1990s have led to the popular postulate that humanitarianism has to be included as an instrument for peacebuilding efforts. Subsequently he criticizes the heterogeneity of humanitarian actors and concludes that their contribution to peacebuilding can only be limited.

The next three contributions highlight problems inherent in the role of NGOs. Charlotte Ku and Joaquín Cáceres Brun argue, somewhat paradoxically, that neutrality as practised by the ICRC is both a liability in terms of its performance as a humanitarian relief organization, yet it is also the ICRC's greatest asset. As humanitarian operations have shifted from aiding victims to protecting persons, the question has arisen as to whether neutrality can remain a viable practice. This touches upon a crucial difficulty in the literature on third party intervention in relation to actors' motives and the plausibility of neutrality in highly politicized conflict environments. In the next contribution Felice Gaer looks at the relationship between human rights NGOs and peace missions. She argues that the current literature on human rights in field operations is superficial and has failed to address the specific role of those who contributed to the conceptualization of these missions (that is, persons from human rights NGOs and their impact on the many aspects of the missions). Yet the dependency on these resources has been far more significant than international agencies have been willing to acknowledge. Today, peace operations in Kosovo, East Timor and Sierra Leone, among others, contain important on-site human rights components. All of these programmes have, from the beginning, been heavily dependent upon human rights NGOs – both international groups and those located in and near the country in which the UN programmes are located. Finally, Frances Pilch analyses the efforts of selected NGO's with a human rights focus (especially women's advocacy groups) in raising public consciousness, providing expert opinion and information, prosecuting victims, and influencing the development of legal jurisprudence for sexual violence in armed conflict.

The second section focuses on the problems encountered in the role of NGOs in particular case studies including Bosnia and Herzegovina, Africa and Afghanistan. Each case study deploys somewhat different methodological strategies, perhaps more suited to the grassroots work of NGOs in civil society. Bronwyn Evans-Kent and Roland Bleiker focus on the role of NGOs in the reconstruction of civil society in Bosnia and Herzegovina. They argue that whether in the initial phase of emergency relief or in the latter, more complex and lengthy reconstruction of civil society, NGOs have taken over a number of key tasks that state or multilateral actors are either reluctant or unable to provide. By examining the CARE Welcome Project and the Project Firefly in the context of postconflict reconstruction in Bosnia and Herzegovina, they scrutinize both the potential and the limits of NGO contributions to peace settlements and long-term stability. While their ability to specialize and to reach the grassroots level is of great practical significance, the contribution of NGOs to the reconstruction of war-torn societies is often idealized. NGOs remain severely limited by often ad hoc funding sources, as well as the overall policy environment in which they operate. Unless these underlying issues are addressed, NGOs will ultimately become little more than extensions of prevalent multilateral and state-based approaches to post-conflict reconstruction.

Wafula Okumu examines the role of the international community in humanitarian crises in Africa. He argues that Humanitarian International NGOs (HINGOs) may have been manipulated into participating in the economies of war in African conflicts and discusses possible ways in which this can be avoided. A peace support partnership is required between the military and civilian police, development, democratization and human rights agencies.

Mahmood Monshipouri argues that in post-conflict societies, NGOs are crucial in combatting the sources of insecurity affecting people and communities on the one hand and advancing nationbuilding, on the other. In particular, NGOs are central to building peace in Afghanistan. In his view, peacebuilding is inseparable from the broader context of reconstruction, and conflict resolution must be seen as a central goal of development policy.

The final essay by Larry Taulbee and Marion Creedmore focuses on the particular experience of a relatively small NGO in the field. The Carter Center has undertaken a remarkably broad range of initiatives with the active participation of President Carter. They focus on four projects, two successes and two considered short-term failures, to assess the strengths and weaknesses of the Carter Center's influence. For the most part, the contributors to this volume accept that the democratization of intervention in conflict zones, with the development of the role of NGOs in conjunction with more traditional actors, is a positive development. However, many contributors also point to the many technical, normative and political difficulties that have arisen as their role has expanded, either because NGOs themselves have sought more responsibility and more space in which to operate or because they have been delegated tasks by IGOs, states and other organizations. These contradictions clearly need further investigation in order to develop more effective and multidimensional responses to conflict in the field on the part of NGOs and the many actors they are associated with. This volume, we hope, contributes to these emerging research agendas.

NOTES

1. See Hugh Miall, Oliver Ramsbotham and Tom Woodhouse, *Contemporary Conflict Resolution*, Cambridge: Polity, 1999, pp.77–8.
2. For a discussion of this see, among many others, Oliver P. Richmond, *Maintaining Order, Making Peace*, Basingstoke: Palgrave, 2002, esp. chs 1 and 2.
3. Boutros Boutros-Ghali, *Supplement to Agenda for Peace*, A/50A/60-s/1,3, Jan. 1995, para.81.
4. T.G. Weiss and L. Gordenker, 'Pluralizing Global Governance: Analytical Approaches and Dimensions', in Weiss and Gordenker (eds.), *NGOs, the UN and Global Governance*, Boulder: Lynne Reinner, 1996, pp.20–21.
5. Laurie S. Wiseberg, 'Human Rights Nongovernmental Organizations', in R.P. Claude and B.H. Weston (eds.), *Human Rights in the World Community: Issue and Action*, Philadelphia: University of Pennsylvania Press, 1992, pp.372–82.
6. Thomas Risse, Stephen C. Ropp and Kathryn Sikkink (eds.), *The Power of Human Rights: International Norms and Domestic Change*, New York: Cambridge University Press, 1999.
7. Francois Debrix, *Re-Envisioning UN Peacekeeping*, University of Minnesota Press, 1999, p.191.
8. Oliver Ramsbotham and Tom Woodhouse, *Humanitarian Intervention in Contemporary Conflict*, Polity Press: Cambridge, 1996, p.81.
9. Peter Willets, 'From "Consultative Arrangements" to "Partnership": The Changing Status of NGOs in Diplomacy at the UN', in *Global Governance*, Vol.6, No.1, 2000, p.196.
10. Ibid., p.205.
11. Risse et al. (n.6 above), 206.
12. For more on this debate in the context the UN's role regarding peace see Edward Newman and Oliver P. Richmond, eds., *The UN and Human Security*, Basingstoke: Palgrave, 2001.
13. David Held, *Democracy and the Global Order*, Cambridge: Polity, 1995, pp.266–86.
14. Supplement to *Agenda for Peace*, A/50A/60-s/1,3, Jan. 1995, para, 81.
15. Andrew S. Natsios, 'An NGO Perspective', in I. William Zartman and J. Lewis Rasmussen, eds., *Peace-Making in International Conflict: Methods and Techniques*, Washington DC: United States Institute of Peace Press, 1997, p.338.

16. Pamela Aall, 'Nongovernmental Organisations and Peace-Making' in Chester Crocker, Fen Osler Hampson, with Pamela Aall (eds.), *Managing Global Chaos,* Washington DC: USIP, 1996, p.434.

17. Ibid., p.436.

18. See Carnegie Commission on Preventing Deadly Conflict, *Preventing Deadly Conflict, (Final Report),* Washington DC, 1997, p.114.

19. See Eftihia Voutira and Shaun A. Wishaw Brown, *Conflict Resolution. A Review of Some Non-Governmental Practices: A Cautionary Tale,* Uppsala: Nordiska Afrikainstituet, 1995.

20. See John Paul Lederach, 'Conflict Transformation in Protracted Internal Conflicts: The Case for a Comprehensive Framework', in Kumar Rupesingh. ed., *Conflict Transformation,* Basingstoke: Macmillan, 1995, pp.201–22.

21. Francis Kofi Abiew and Tom Keating, 'Strange Bedfellows: NGOs and UN Peacekeeping Operations', *International Peacekeeping,* Vol.6, No.2, 1999, p.93.

22. Natsios, (n.15 above) p.343.

23. Miall et al. (n.1 above) p.119. See also L. Diamond and J. McDonald, *Multi-Track Diplomacy: A Systems Approach to Peace,* Washington, DC: Kumarian Press, 1996; K. Rupesinghe, *General Principles of Multi-Track Diplomacy,* London: International Alert, 1996.

24. See Yuen Foong Khong, 'Human Security: A Shotgun Approach to Alleviating Human Misery?' in *Global Governance,* Vol.7, No.3, 2001, pp.231–6.

25. Ibid.

Conflict Prevention:
Old Wine in New Bottles?

KARIN AGGESTAM

The notion of conflict prevention (CP) has a general appeal to most scholars within conflict research. It implies that we might be able to avoid destructive conflicts through external intervention before any major violent actions have taken place. The notion of conflict prevention tends to be launched as a new phenomenon both in theory as well as in practice. One of several reasons why CP has received new and extensive attention in the last ten years is the increasing number of internal conflicts in comparison to interstate wars. Internal conflicts have resulted in state collapse and humanitarian catastrophes such as gross human rights abuses, ethnic cleansing and large groups of internally displaced people and refugees.

Yet, despite the many books and articles on CP there are surprisingly few critical analyses of the present state of research. This article therefore seeks to make a critical assessment of the research on CP. How is CP defined and operationalized? Does there exist a general understanding and knowledge about contemporary conflicts and of CP especially? In what ways does the research offer new insights to the prevention of conflict? Since research on CP is assumed to be policy-relevant, this article also addresses the question of theory and practice. Does a greater emphasis on the prevention of conflict mirror any major alteration in the practice and management of conflict? What roles and activities do nongovernmental organizations (NGOs) exercise and play in the prevention of conflict? In what way do states, intergovernmental organizations (IGOs) and NGOs interact in CP, and what are the potentials as well as limitations of such cooperation?

Theory: Conceptual Confusion?

In 1992, former UN Secretary-General Boutros-Ghali called for conflict prevention in *An Agenda for Peace*.[1] Today, there is a vast amount of literature on CP and the field of research is multifaceted. Unfortunately, it has not contributed to a greater in-depth understanding of the phenomena. Most of the studies are empirically oriented and lack explicit theoretical frameworks and operational definitions. Traditional diplomatic strategies tend to be reconceptualized and renamed without any real change of substance and content. There is a whole array of concepts that refer to CP, such as 'blind prevention', 'complex prevention', 'direct prevention', 'structural prevention', 'preventive diplomacy', 'preventive engagement' and 'preventive deployment'. However, it remains obscure what prevention actually stands for. Moreover, prevention contains diverse understandings and norms of strategies. Although most scholars agree on the need to develop and enhance an international norm system of preventing conflict, they tend to avoid the fact that there exist divergent and often competing understandings of CP.[2]

To structure the discussion, I have adopted two commonly used categories of CP, namely direct and structural prevention.[3] Structural prevention focuses primarily on the underlying causes as to why conflicts arise in the first place. Such an approach includes a long-term engagement and commitment. It attempts to address social, political and economic structures, such as political and democratic institution building or economic and social development, which may inhibit conflict escalation. Structural prevention is first and foremost concerned with internal conflicts and actions that are centred on how to prevent state failure and collapse as well as how to reconstruct economic, political and social structures in a post-conflict situation. Consequently, this approach argues for a long-term involvement of CP and an in-depth understanding of the contextual dynamics of specific conflicts. It is therefore less concerned about timing and identification of a particular phase of conflict escalation per se.

Direct prevention has a more limited agenda. The emphasis is placed largely on short-term strategies and interaction of the conflicting actors and third parties. This approach is guided by a pragmatic ambition of prevention without any comprehensive prescribed formula.[4] The primary goal is not to resolve all outstanding issues of disputes but rather to control and remove the imminent causes to violent escalation both within and between states. As a consequence, the timing of preventive actions is mostly centred on the pre-conflict phase and less on the phases after violence has broken out or the post-conflict situation. Hence, CP is more narrowly defined than structural prevention and does not include economic development.

Preventing What? Diagnosis, Understanding and Prediction of
Conflict

The diagnosis and knowledge of conflict dynamics are critical
prerequisites of efficient CP since most conflicts are contextually
bounded. Prediction has never been the strength of social sciences and
in CP it would require long-term monitoring of structural factors and
extensive knowledge of how underlying sources of conflict interact
with more immediate political dynamics. Today, the civilian
populations constitute the majority of war victims. The distinction
between combatants and non-combatants is no longer valid. The
disputing parties are both state and non-state actors, hence questions
about recognition and identification of non-state actors become
particularly troublesome. The political, military and economic
asymmetry between state and non-state actors also has consequences
for various efforts to prevent and resolve conflict peacefully. This
requires, according to Andy Knight, Mary Kaldor and others, a new
proactive understanding of security that addresses failed and collapsing
state structures and massive human rights abuses.[5] Yet, many studies on
CP are primarily focused on *how* to prevent conflict rather than on in-
depth analysis of the causes and characteristics of contemporary
conflicts. Conflict is viewed as a general phenomenon, which ranges
from interstate, civil, resource and nuclear wars to state-sponsored
terrorist campaigns.[6] As a result, attention is largely placed on the
'preventer', that is, activities of third parties rather than the 'target' of
prevention.

   If we assess more closely the two approaches of direct and
structural prevention discussed above, they differ on a number of issues
regarding their understanding of contemporary conflict, which have
several implications on the selection of preventive strategies. Direct
prevention is dominated by a strong focus on the 'preventer', which
according to Raimo Väyrynen is the biggest flaw in the voluminous
literature as CP is a contingent action.[7] Since the goal of CP is
pragmatic, that is, to treat rather than cure conflict, the main aim is to
contain escalation and the spread of conflict. Structural prevention is
focused on 'cure' rather than 'treatment.' Conflicts are recognized as
extremely complex to resolve, without any clear beginning or end.
Hence, there is no predictable linear pattern of causes and effects,
which limits the predictability of efficient preventive strategies.[8]

Practice: Alteration in the Management of Conflict?

The major challenge for the international community is, as discussed above, how to manage communal, ethnic and internal conflicts, which tend to be more intractable than interstate conflicts. The increasing complexity and the occurrence of human catastrophes, such as ethnic cleansing and gross human rights abuses, are the main reasons why CP is a 'buzzword' for both practitioners and academics, though at the same time CP has been described by some scholars as a 'pipe-dream', containing false assumptions about conflict.[9]

In practice, states and IGOs have come to dominate CP. The UN is an obvious player, exercising a critical leading role in the prevention of conflict since it generates international legitimacy and symbolizes what is often referred to as the international community. The UN Secretary General Kofi Annan has, for example, declared that the goal is to create a worldwide culture of CP in which human rights take priority. Mary Robinson, the UN High Commissioner for Human Rights has underlined that the focus should be placed on the implementation of international norms and standards that are universal and indivisible as there still exists a huge gap between aspiration and reality.[10] However, traditional tools of diplomacy and conflict management frequently referred to in direct prevention, such as mediation, peacekeeping or sanctions, are often state-oriented and limited in time. These strategies are also more reactive than proactive, primarily aimed at influencing the external incentives of the disputing parties.[11] Since the dynamics and characteristics of contemporary conflicts differ from traditional interstate conflict, they have also been of limited use and at times even counterproductive. Kaldor, for instance, argues that 'conflict resolution from above', such as elite-based negotiations, has resulted in several unfortunate outcomes, including giving public legitimacy to individuals who are criminals responsible for grave human rights abuses.[12] Consequently, many calls have been made about the necessity to rethink strategies of international intervention in contemporary conflicts. The following section will therefore focus on the growing number and significance of NGOs in the international arena. In what ways have they contributed to the development of CP and altered the international management of conflict?

The Role of NGOs in Conflict Prevention

NGOs refer to a wide range of formal and informal associations and activities. There is subsequently barely any agreement about what NGOs as a whole stand for. They are part of worldwide networks, which are forged through a variety of links between professional, commercial, religious, research, human rights, environmental and education bodies, only to mention a few. The revolution in communication and information technology has enabled NGOs to cut across national boundaries through loosely organized transnational coalitions formed according to a particular vision of society. NGOs are therefore not value-neutral but they do tend to present ethical judgements as impartial and universal standards. Many NGOs take a strong interest in preventive actions and in strengthening global society. At the same time, NGOs are connected to and dependent on their home governments in ambivalent, cooperative and at times contentious relations.[13]

Most of the contemporary conflicts concern state–society relations, in which victims of war are primarily civilians. This is one major reason for the increasing relevance of NGOs in CP, in particular, human rights and other advocacy groups, such as Amnesty International; humanitarian relief organizations such as the International Committee of the Red Cross (ICRC); associations promoting socio-economic development, such as Oxfam; and groups supporting conflict resolution techniques, such as the Carter Center in Atlanta.[14]

NGOs are often the first actors to become aware of the risks of conflict escalation and tend to be the ones who remain in conflict areas the longest. Early warning is an essential part of CP and focuses on gathering, interpreting and communicating information about specific and potential conflicts. It aims to create a network of people and associations to monitor conflicts while at the same favouring and supporting preventive solutions on grass root levels through empowering peacemaking. NGOs may, for example, facilitate communication channels, foster peaceful dialogues between disputing parties, and counter hate propaganda.[15] NGOs may also provide documentary evidence and specific case materials on human rights abuses to relevant international institutions.[16]

Structural peace building includes a whole range of activities such as human rights education, developmental assistance, and the (re)construction of political and democratic institutions. These processes may, for example, be supported by NGOs through election monitoring as illustrated by the Council of Freely Elected Heads of Government led by Jimmy Carter.[17] NGOs also play increasingly important roles in the growing number of human rights missions and have become integral parts of the second/third generation of peacekeeping in post-conflict settings. Finally, NGOs have become significant actors in economic development, particularly in the last ten years as the West's official development assistance (ODA) in general has seen major cut backs and/or has been relocated to NGOs. This trend of 'privatization' is partly based on the assumption that development assistance will become more efficient. Activities by NGOs are believed to be more participatory, flexible, innovative and effective while less expensive than governmental agencies. For example, it is easier for NGOs than for governmental agencies to link development aid to ethnic reconciliation.[18]

(Inter)Governmental–NGO Relations: Competition or Cooperation?

Since the end of the Cold War, we have been witnessing a trend where governmental aid in general is increasingly being channelled through NGOs. Development assistance is turning private in form while staying public in purpose. Also many IGOs are 'contracting out' development work and humanitarian relief and assistance to NGOs. According to Mark Duffield, this seems to have become the West's favoured response to political crises and violent conflicts. He concludes that this privatization has led to a 'new aid paradigm', which includes a stronger focus on welfare, relief, people-centred development and general support for civil society and democratization. It may, however, also be viewed as an attempt to 'internalize' and contain the effects of political crisis and conflicts within unstable regions.[19]

This development has been criticized especially concerning the implications for CP. First, it is argued that the privatization of world politics tends to de-politicize CP, which ultimately is value-laden. The activities of NGOs and developmental strategies are often framed as 'technical' problems and as an apolitical tool in the management of conflict. Thus, the 'de-polarization' of NGOs risks focusing on technical and not political solutions. However, others argue that the trend of privatization of world politics is part of a new policy agenda of neo-liberal economics and western liberal democratic theory. NGOs in this interpretation come to symbolize everything that governments are not, that is, unburdened with large bureaucracies, flexible and open to innovations, faster at implementing development efforts and quicker to respond to grassroots needs. If the problem is framed in such a way, it might be argued that the functions of NGOs are politicized and directed not only on the basis of the target groups' needs, but also on the interests of external third parties.[20]

Second, some critics argue that the essence of what makes NGOs attractive might be undermined by the fact that several of them receive more than half of their funding from government sources. Changing funding arrangements might encourage NGOs to develop fundraising tactics and rivalry in an unregulated and fiercely competitive aid market. The implication of such activities is a tendency to dramatize conflicts and emphasize emergency work while undermining the potential for improved coordination between NGOs.[21]

Third and most important, critics question the assumed causal link between economic development and foreign aid as an integral part of CP. Stephen Stedman points to the lack of a direct relationship between foreign aid and CP. He asserts that such a view suffers from economic and ecological determinism, assuming that the shortage of resources causes violent conflict and therefore the solution must be to increase aid. However, contrary to the general assumption about cost-efficiency, CP might in the end prove more costly and long term.[22] As a result, the competition over scarce resources between various CP strategies, such as between peacekeeping and socio-economic activities as seen in the UN could increase.[23]

The Possibility and Limitation of Cooperation

The prospect of increasing cooperation between states, IGOs and NGOs in CP depends to a great extent on the existence of some kind of shared understanding of war and peace generally and CP specifically. However, there exists a general division between direct and structural prevention. The first is mostly associated with a state and actor oriented approach, including short-term, pragmatic and traditional methods of conflict management, whereas the latter emphasizes a structural approach, which attempts to address underlying causes to conflict and where NGOs tend to be more engaged. To give an example, the UK Department for International Development refers to CP as 'conflict handling', which encompasses conflict readiness, prevention and mitigation, but excludes ambitions of conflict resolution.[24] The distinction may be traced to a general dualism that also exists in conflict theory, often referred to as conflict management/track one (official) and conflict resolution/track two (unofficial). Conflict management is focusing on strategic interaction where third parties intervene impartially without moral judgement. The unofficial approach strives towards resolving human needs, enhancing human rights and democratic institutions. Third parties are not able to negotiate and compromise on these issues and thus, cannot be morally neutral in conflict. The differences between the two approaches have increased since the end of the Cold War because normative issues such as justice and morality have become more important and increasingly acceptable in the international arena as an integral part of any peace settlement.[25] According to Frost, this tension expresses a dividing line between supporters of a transnational civil society and a Westphalian state system.[25] There are a number of scholars who view these two approaches as incompatible, whereas others argue that they can complement each other in efforts to prevent and resolve conflict.[27]

In practice, there exists an interdependence between states, IGOs and NGOs from economic, political and social relations around the globe. This (inter)governmental–NGO relationship is described by some as one more of convenience than of a 'passionate romance'. Each side remains distrustful and uncomfortable about working together, partly because they differ (and at times compete) in their understandings of peace and consequently in CP approaches, and partly because they speak to different constituencies.[28] There are, for example, many governments who evaluate information emanating from NGOs as inaccurate and unbalanced because NGOs are considered to have their own agendas, which do not conform to the views held by many governments. This 'credibility problem' becomes particularly troubling at times of early warning issued by NGOs.[29]

Still, there is widespread acknowledgement and an expressed need among states, IGOs and NGOs to pool resources and improve coordination in order to meet the challenging task of preventing contemporary conflicts, which are bound to be at the core of twenty-first century diplomacy. For instance, there is an obvious need to mainstream CP in such areas as information gathering and contingency planning of preventive actions. The UN has attempted to centralize functions and improve interagency flow of interaction and coordination mechanisms with NGOs through the establishment of the UN Department of Political Affairs. Yet it has failed to design comprehensive strategies to prevent failed and collapsing states.[30]

In sum, (inter)governmental–NGO cooperation in areas of CP can best be described as ad hoc. Institutionalization is still lacking or exists in an embryonic state. There is clearly a need to develop norms and institutional capacity for the prevention of internal conflicts. Some analysts argue for the establishment of an international prevention regime, which would contain an ethical code of what CP entails. Such a regime would be able to respond early with operational warnings based on shared and coherent standards of interpreted information and mobilized resources of both states, IGOs and NGOs.[31] Yet, it needs to be recognized that CP is and will continue to be a highly contested process not only between (inter)state agencies and NGOs but also among states in the North and in the South.

Conclusion

This essay has sought to give an assessment of the present state of
research on conflict prevention and to discuss in what ways it expresses
any alteration in the management of contemporary conflicts. Both
research and practice contain a wide array of definitions and strategies,
which tend to result in a confused picture of the exact meaning of CP.
Two approaches of CP have been discussed at greater length, namely
direct and structural prevention, which hold a number of divergent
views about prevention as well as in their understandings of conflict.

The research exhibits a number of weaknesses. First, many studies
avoid providing exact definition and operationalization of the concept,
or presenting explicit theoretical frameworks for empirical analyses,
which consequently do not result in any substantial cumulative
knowledge about CP. Second, it is difficult to distinguish in what ways
the field of research contributes to any new insights to the management
of conflict since CP is used interchangeably with such general notions
as conflict management, conflict resolution and peacebuilding. Many
scholars list for instance a whole set of strategies to prevent conflict,
but these are rarely new. Also there seems to be little theoretical and
methodological awareness of the implications of these strategies and
how they might produce counterproductive results. One reason for this
is that there is generally a strong emphasis on *how* to prevent
(strategies) rather than any in-depth elaboration upon *what* is to be
prevented (knowledge about conflict).

If the research is supposed to be of policy relevance this becomes
particularly troublesome since it is unable to establish a causal chain of
variables and predict conflict escalation. At the same time, prediction
is one of the most difficult tasks of social sciences and as argued by
Alexander George, neither should it be our main goal.[32] As an attempt
to bridge the gap between theory and practice, the emphasis should
rather be placed on the *diagnosis* of conflict. It means on the one hand
that CP needs to be context-specific since no predictable linear pattern
of cause and effect can be established. On the other hand, evaluations
of various strategies in different conflicts may be analysed and
compared as a way to make some kind of conditional generalization
and to discuss plausible scenarios. However, the importance of time
and timing should be underlined in such discussions, that is, the
problem of both the timing of preventive strategies as well as their time
span.

In the analysis of CP in practice, the roles and activities of NGOs
have been given particular attention. NGOs have become important

actors in many international arenas and in the various modes of CP as most contemporary conflicts concern unstable state–society relations with great implications for civilians. Two activities have been highlighted in this article, namely early warning and structural peace building. Early warning in particular is a critical contribution of NGOs to the practice of CP since they often hold vital information, which improves the capacity of diagnosis. At the same time, NGOs suffer from a credibility problem, partly because (inter)state agencies and NGOs tend to hold different imperatives of peace and what ultimately is to be understood as preventive actions. Yet, the activities of NGOs often take place in collaboration with states and IGOs, which expresses an interdependent nature of relations between these actors. For example, states and IGOs are today increasingly 'contracting out' and channelling development aid through NGOs.

In sum, conflict prevention is a problematic analytical concept and resembles mostly a new label with an old content. CP should nevertheless be viewed as an expression of engagement in promoting a normative agenda and an international culture of conflict prevention. There is today a strong drive for normative concerns about such issues as human rights, justice and democracy in which NGOs constitute a driving force. Greater collaboration and coordination between states, IGOs and NGOs through a transnational framework is not only desirable but a necessary prerequisite if we are to improve our capacity and efficiency in addressing contemporary conflicts.

NOTES

1. Boutros Boutros-Ghali, *An Agenda for Peace: Preventive Diplomacy, Peacemaking and Peacekeeping*, New York: United Nations, 1992.
2. See, for example, Annika Björkdahl, *From Idea to Norm. Promoting Conflict Prevention*, Department of Political Science: Lund University, 2002. Michael B. Brown and Richard N. Rosencrance (eds.) *The Cost of Conflict Prevention and Cure in the Global Arena*, Lanhman, Boulder, New York and Oxford: Rowman & Littlefield, 1999; Carment, David and Albreht Schnabel (eds.) *Conflict Prevention: Path to Peace or Grand Illusion?* Tokyo: United Nations Press, 2001; Michael S. Lund, *Preventing Violent Conflicts. A Strategy for Preventive Diplomacy*, Washington DC: United States Institute for Peace, 1996.
3. See, for example, Peter Wallensteen, 'Preventive Security: Direct and Structural Prevention of Violent Conflicts', in Peter Wallensteen (ed.) *Preventing Violent Conflicts: Past Record and Future Challenges*, Uppsala: University Department of Peace and Conflict Research, 1998, p.35.
4. Raimo Väyrynen, 'Preventing Deadly Conflicts: Failures in Iraq and Yugoslavia', *Global Society*, Vol.14, No.1, 2000, p.6.
5. W. Andy Knight, 'Towards a Subsidiarity Model for Peacemaking and Preventive Diplomacy: Making Chapter VIII of the UN Chapter Operational', *Third World Quarterly*, Vol.17, No.1, 1996; Mary Kaldor, *New and Old Wars: Organized Violence in a Global Era*, Stanford: Standford University Press, 2001.

6. See, for example, Michael Lund, 'Underrating Preventive Diplomacy', *Foreign Affairs*, Vol.75, No.4, July/August, 1995; Peter Wallensteen, Birger Heldt, Mary B. Anderson, Stephen John Stedman and Leonard Wantchekon, *Conflict Prevention through Development Co-operation*, Uppsala University: Department of Peace and Conflict Research, Research Report No.59, 2001.
7. Kalypso Nicolaidis, 'International Preventive Action: Developing a Strategic Framework', in Robert I. Rotberg, ed., *Vigilance and Vengeance: NGOs Preventing Ethnic Conflict in Divided Societies*, Washington, DC: Brookings Institution Press, 1995, pp.27–31; Väyrynen (n.4 above), p.10.
8. Jonathan Goodhand and David Hulme, 'From Wars to Complex Political Emergencies: Understanding Conflict and Peace-Building in the New World Disorder', *Third World Quarterly*, Vol.20, No.1, 1999, pp.18-24; Because of the problem of prediction, Nicolaidis (n.7 above, p.26) argues for 'blind prevention' that is independent of prediction. It should be focused on preventing the reoccurrence of conflict in post-conflict phases, relying on institutionalized rules, norms and procedures that are applicable to all conflicts. Blind prevention should include rapid standing operating procedures and resources, which are to be activated once violence has broken out.
9. Väyrynen (n.4 above), p.32.
10. Mary Robinson, 'The Next Human Rights Agenda: Preventing Conflict', *New Perspectives Quarterly*, Vol.16, No.5, Fall, 1999, pp.23–8.
11. Nicholaidis (n.7 above), pp.38–9.
12. Kaldor (n.5 above), pp.10, 91, 119.
13. Lund (n.2 above), pp.178–9; Andrew Natsios, 'NGOs and the UN System in Complex Humanitarian Emergencies: Conflict or Cooperation', *Third World Quarterly*, Vol.16, No.3, 1995, p.458; John Stremlau, *People in Peril Human Rights, Humanitarian Action, and Preventing Deadly Conflict*, New York: Carnegie Commission, May 1998, pp.54–6.
14. See further, Carnegie Commission on Preventing Deadly Conflict, *Preventing Deadly Conflict: Executive Summary of the Final Report*, Carnegie Corporation of New York, December 1997, p.32; Mary B. Anderson, 'Humanitarian NGOs in Conflict Intervention', in Chester A. Crocker and Fen Osler Hampson with Pamela Aall, *Managing Global Chaos: Sources of and Responses to International Conflict*, Washington DC: United States Institute of Peace Process, 1996, p.344.
15. Nicolaidis (n.7 above), pp.60–65.
16. Emily MacFarquhar, Robert I. Rotberg, and Martha A. Chen 'Introduction', in Robert I. Rotberg (ed.), *Vigilance and Vengeance: NGOs Preventing Ethnic Conflict in Divided Societies*, Washington, DC: Brookings Institution Press, 1995, p.6.
17. Vikram Chand, 'Democratisation from the Outside in NGO and International Efforts to Promote Open Elections', *Third World Quarterly*, Vol.18, No.3, 1997, pp.546–50; Ian Smillie, 'NGOs and Development Assistance: A Change in Mind-Set?, *Third World Quarterly*, Vol.18, No.3, 1997.
18. Mark Duffield, 'NGO Relief in War Zones: Towards an Analysis of the New Aid Paradigm', *Third World Quarterly*, Vol.18, No.3, 1997; Nicolaidis (n.7 above), pp.60–64; Smillie (n.17 above), pp.564–71.
19. Duffield (n.18 above).
20. Ibid.; Natsios (n.13 above), pp.444–6; Dan Smith, 'Legitimacy, Justice and Preventive Intervention', in Wallensteen et al. (n.6 above), p.262.
21. Smillie (n.17 above), pp.563–9; An illustrative example is the Swedish Christian aid organization, *Lutherhjälpen*, which recently appealed in an advertisement campaign for funds in order to prevent a starvation catastrophe in southern Africa. The picture chosen for the ad is a starving child, hanging in a bag, to be weighed. The black and white picture, shown in profile, was taken in Sudan four years ago. Several Swedish NGOs reacted against the advertisement, accusing *Lutherhjälpen* of presenting an over-dramatized picture, which portrays and stigmatizes the African continent as weak, passive and vulnerable. According to some analysts, this type of fundraising is described as 'pornography of poverty'. Smillie, p.569.

22. Stephen John Stedman, 'Alchemy for a New World Order: Overselling "Preventive Diplomacy"', *Foreign Affairs*, Vol.74, No.3, 1995.
23. Nicolaidis (n.7 above), pp.27–31.
24. Goodhand and Hulme (n.8 above), p.15.
25. Pauline Baker, 'Conflict Resolution Versus Democratic Governance: Divergent Paths to Peace', in Crocker, et al. (n.14 above), pp.565–7; compare Michael Lund 'Not Only When to Act, But How: From Early Warning to Rolling Prevention', in Wallensteen (n.3 above), p.161.
26. Mervyn Frost, 'Ethical Aspects of Combat in New Wars', Paper presented at British International Studies Association, Bradford 18–20 December 2000.
27. See, for example, John Burton, 'Conflict Prevention as a Political System', in John A. Vasquez, James Turner Johnson, Sanford Jaffe and Linda Stamato, eds., *Beyond Confrontation: Learning Conflict Resolution in the Post-Cold War Era*, Ann Arbor: The University of Michigan Press, 1995; Ronald J. Fisher, 'Pacific, Impartial Third-Party Intervention in International Conflict: A Review and an Analysis', in Vasquez et al.
28. Natsios (n.13 above), p.413.
29. Carnegie Commission (n.14 above), p.10; Felice Gaer, 'Reality Check: Human Rights Nongovernmental Organisations Confront Governments at the United Nations', *Third World Quarterly*, Vol.16, No.3, 1995; Lund (n.2 above), p.108; Nicolaidis (n.7 above), pp.34, 65; Stremlau (n.13 above), pp.54–6.
30. Carnegie Commission (n.3 above), pp.10–12; Natsios (n.13 above), pp.415–16; Stremlau (n.13 above), p.53; Wallensteen et al. (n.6 above), p.50; Nicolaidis (n.7 above), pp.23–5.
31. Aall (n.14 above); Lund (n.2 above); Nicholaidis (n.7 above); Kaldor (n.5 above), pp.88, 148, calls for a cosmopolitan approach, based on a political consciousness that is placed in a global context, which is to be attentive to democratic accountability and equality of all human beings. She believes that there already exists a partial cosmopolitan regime through several layers of governance of IGOs, social movements and NGOs that operate according to a set of accepted rules and norms, although lacking mechanisms to enforce cosmopolitan norms and human rights.
32. Alexander George, *Bridging the Gap: Theory and Practice in Foreign Policy*, Washington DC: United States Institute of Peace Press, 1993.

NGO–Military Relations in Peace Operations

FRANCIS KOFI ABIEW

The last decade of the twentieth century and the beginning of the twenty-first century have brought about notable changes in dealing with new security challenges. The demand for multifunctional/ multidimensional peacekeeping which encompasses both traditional peacekeeping and new tasks has increased dramatically in the post-Cold War era as the number of latent and internal tensions spilled over into violent conflicts and their attendant complex emergencies. By the mid-1990s, the International Committee of the Red Cross (ICRC) intimated that the human costs of conflicts and complex emergencies were overwhelming the international community's ability to respond.

International response in the form of multi-task, multi-component UN peace operations of recent years thus assumes critical importance.[1] Designing these operations to create space in which peace processes can take root, however, has not been easy and has engendered mixed results. The trend towards coordination and integration of tasks in peace operations was reflected in Boutros-Ghali's *An Agenda for Peace*.[2] Furthermore, the *Report of the Panel on United Nations Peace Operations* – the Brahimi Report – has given impetus to the debate on cooperation between various agencies involved in complex peace missions.[3] This need for cooperation in peace missions involving attempts at settling conflicts rather than simply policing ceasefires has been reflected in the considerable body of literature on the subject-matter by commentators such as Thomas Weiss, Hugo Slim, Michael Pugh and Pamela Aall, to name a few. As a result, civilian and military personnel are working closer together in the same theatre of operations due to a strong demand for coherence of approach. Contrary to expectations, however, the various military and civilian actors have not always necessarily acted jointly or in concert to achieve the desired aims of sustainable peace. Several areas of tension still exist between the two groups. To date the international community is still grappling with these issues.

It is in this context that this essay explores some relevant considerations pertaining to humanitarian NGO–military relations in contemporary peace operations.[4] It argues that, given the complex nature of contemporary conflict management and resolution involving military and non-military activities, only a well-planned and coordinated combination of civilian and military measures can create the conditions for long-term stability and peace in divided societies. First, it briefly discusses the differences within and between international military forces and humanitarian NGOs, and their respective roles in peace operations. Any initial steps in developing a complementary approach between both actors need to clarify their respective roles. Second, it examines various factors impeding effective NGO–Military cooperation in peace operations with a view to overcoming those barriers. Lastly, it offers suggestions for improvement of NGO–Military relations in peace missions.

Over the past decade or so, an expanded role for NGOs in peace operations has occurred. This development has taken place in the midst of declining development assistance budgets by western governments, which has seen greater reliance on NGOs in relief operations and the delivery of development programmes.[5] If this trend continues, NGOs will in the foreseeable future be indispensable partners alongside the military in peace operations, given their ability to forge long-term relationships within divided societies.[6] Today, the conventional wisdom is that while military means may be employed in attempting to control violent conflict and create a secure environment necessary for rebuilding divided societies, these measures have to be supported, supplemented and closely coordinated with civilian instruments if peace missions are to achieve the goal of restoration of peace and stability.

The dynamics of previous complex emergencies which saw limited need for civil–military interaction, partly because of concerns over 'mission creep' on the part of the military (and an uneasiness on the part of NGOs working with military forces) have given way to the recognition that supporting civil implementation has become a *sine qua non* for successful missions. The intense field experience of the past few years has tended to reveal the fact that effectiveness of contemporary peace operations will depend on the collaboration of military and civilian actors.

Perhaps, it is important to be cognizant of the fact that although there are clear differences of approaches between the military and NGOs, there are differences both within international military forces and within the humanitarian NGO sector. The military is not monolithic or a homogenous body. There are disparities in military capabilities, configuration, competence and levels of professionalism even among northern militaries, and between northern and southern militaries. Some nations' militaries are better than others, and are better suited for specific tasks than others. There is a wide spectrum of traditions and cultural characteristics exhibited by military forces of various nations involved in a complex emergency. To a greater or lesser extent, these characteristics may reflect national agendas that may differ subtly from international opinion. The composition of UN multinational military forces, for instance, deriving from different national forces such as Canada, Britain, France, Belgium, the United States, India, Pakistan, Bangladesh, Nigeria and Ghana, to mention a few, can sometimes prove to be a weakness. Thus, the recognition of differences within the military sector is vital. In light of the foregoing, it is not surprising that NGOs are reluctant to sign up to cooperate with all, or even any particular military forces under all conceivable circumstances.[7]

Important differences among NGOs in size, mandate, capacity and levels of professionalism affect efforts to alleviate human suffering.[8] A taxonomy of NGOs might distinguish these organizations according to their relationship with local, national and international groups. Such a listing might, for example differentiate between local (LNGOs), international (INGOs), and state-sponsored or government-created nongovernmental organizations (QUANGOs). Thomas Weiss and Leon Gordenker note that as much as 90 per cent of financial support for NGOs emanates from the governments of rich countries.[9] Existing research shows that different types of NGOs are influenced by different sets of interests and concerns which in turn shape the mandates and operations of the organization. It is, however, beyond the scope of this essay to develop such a taxonomy. This essay's reference to and use of NGOs is based primarily on the activities of big INGOs operating in the arena of humanitarian relief, since these organizations have been the most active in conflict situations. While the more generic term NGO is used here, the reader should be aware of these distinctions among various types of NGOs. Examples of some of the big international NGOs operating in humanitarian relief include: CARE, the International Committee of the Red Cross, World Vision International, Oxfam, Médicins Sans Frontières, Save the Children Federation, Catholic Relief Services, International Rescue Committee, and InterAction (a coalition of NGOs based in the United States). Some of these organizations specialize in responding to humanitarian crises, while some focus their efforts and resources on relief and development. NGOs determine their missions, mandate, and write their own charters and principles. The upshot of this is the freedom they have, which they are determined to maintain. This means, according to Slim, that 'any consensus across the NGO sector about a mission and mandate will often be variable and cast in the broadest terms. It can seldom be assumed that every NGO will be singing the same song in a given situation. Such independence has important consequences for the civil–military relationship and may make NGOs unpredictable and even tempestuous partners.'[10] Thus, it is imperative that both the military and NGOs put their respective houses in order as a necessary condition for improved relations.

Today's complex emergencies inevitably suggest performance of specific military and civilian tasks. At the policy level, new relationships have been forged between the international security community and humanitarian actors. Military personnel from various countries have become engaged in humanitarian politics, while NGOs involved in global security and conflict resolution have also taken up issues relating to humanitarian affairs.[11] This fusion of security/humanitarian policy has, at the operational level, seen overlapping roles being performed by the military and NGOs as described by various UN Security Council Resolutions.

Apart from purely military tasks such as the provision of a secure environment for the affected civilian population either through disarming belligerents, restoring public order, or enforcing peace agreements, the military normally play a supporting role in helping NGOs provide relief assistance. They protect relief supplies particularly in unstable situations where armed groups may attempt to engage in banditry or in the diversion of those supplies in order to deny aid to their adversaries. Somalia and the Sudan provide examples where several NGOs discovered that over 80 per cent of food supplies were lost as a result of misappropriation or theft. NGOs' attitudes towards such diversions however differ, often creating a potential source of tension. In the words of Daniel Byman, 'major NGOs often don't want to shoot people for taking the food that they brought', the reason being an implicit acceptance that a proportion of their aid will go to the combatants.[12] Such an attitude however presents a conundrum of continuing instability and poses challenges for the overall security environment, since relief channelled to these very groups goes to sustain the war effort. To make sure that relief reaches the affected populations, the military may also secure warehouses, convoy routes and various distribution points. Furthermore, the military may also provide security for NGO personnel. NGOs working without military protection often encounter dangerous situations.

Instances of NGOs being attacked abound. It is however, difficult to protect NGOs where their personnel are normally scattered in a conflict zone. NGOs are often reluctant to consolidate their activities because they want to maintain close contact with the local population.[13] In Kosovo, the dilemmas of armed protection once again came to the fore. There seems to be a presumption that armed protection of NGOs is undesirable since it makes their work more difficult if not dangerous, in addition to compromising their neutrality.[14] Military forces may also be engaged in de-mining, demobilization, election monitoring and the implementation of peace accords. These functions overlap with NGOs that are engaged in similar processes.

Last, in exceptional circumstances, military forces may also be directly involved in the distribution of assistance. NGOs, tend to resent this, and understandably so, given the real danger that their humanitarian principles and objectives are likely to be compromised since military operations are framed by a political agenda and not by the humanitarian imperative. As Pugh notes: 'military personnel are not ideally suited to humanitarian work; they lack training, expertise and appropriate policy configurations for building local capacities and accountability to local populations; above all, military acts are inherently political and usually connote partisanship – in contrast to traditional humanitarianism, which is idealized as morally autonomous and not politically conditioned or imposed'. On the other hand, he continues, 'It is infeasible simply to rule out military involvement in relief.'[15]

NGOs are involved at the grassroots level in the short-term provision of relief – such as food, water, sanitation equipment, medicine, shelter, human rights monitoring – and in capacity-building, and conflict resolution. They are engaged in long-term projects in support of economic and social reconstruction and development, and in reconciliation processes that help communities become self-sustaining. NGOs provide early warning of looming conflict and help in the mobilization of international support for action in conflict zones.

Relations between the military and NGOs are problematic when they both operate outside of their 'comfort zones' in peace missions. Political, humanitarian, security, socio-economic, legal, and other issues cannot be separated into watertight compartments and are inextricably linked. Thus, they both need each other and an understanding of how the other operates.

Yet there are numerous barriers or impediments militating against a harmonious relationship. A widely noted challenge relates to the proliferation and heterogeneity of civilian actors involved in recent missions which tends to create a host of problems. The sheer number of humanitarian NGOs often makes it difficult to have an overview of their activities, let alone coordinate them. This proliferation of NGOs has resulted in a growing coordination challenge. Reports indicate that in 1994 some 250 NGOs were operating in the complex emergency in Goma, and about 175 in Kigali. A similar number currently operate in Kosovo. While the plethora of NGOs allows for implementation of an array of services and the provision of aid, this development also leads to poor standards of provision and management, in addition to exacerbating conflict by fuelling wartime and post-war economies.[16] Coordinating the activities of these NGOs 'could be likened to herding cats'. Each NGO has its own specific area of interest and expertise.[17] While they bring a wide range of competence to the field, some are highly effective and others are simply not. Attempts by military authorities to control and coordinate their work are sometimes resented. The impressions formed by the military of the work of the less competent ones also tends to colour the perception of the whole spectrum of NGOs as incompetent and their operations as disjointed or uncoordinated,[18] tending towards more competition rather than collaboration. In Somalia, many NGOs started operations after the military intervention, lacking experience and knowledge of the country, or even knowing what had taken place before their arrival. The result was poor coordination partly stemming from unwillingness to consult those with knowledge of the situation. The inclination on the part of the NGOs was to 'do their own thing'.[19] The competition for high visibility, fund raising requirements, and media coverage makes it difficult for NGOs to agree on a common strategy. The consequences of this competition suggests not only that coordination with the military is highly unlikely, but that there are also profound implications for the overall effectiveness of peace missions.

Another impediment to civil–military cooperation stems from the mutual lack of familiarity and the new roles that they are playing both jointly and severally. Military forces have made very little effort to engage NGOs. They lack an understanding of the different hierarchies, charters, distinctions and modes of operation of NGOs, and a lack of recognition that what works with one NGO may not work with another. Byman maintains that this lack of knowledge is institutional. This is the case, since the knowledge gained from the limited contact by the military with NGOs is not retained. The practice with the US military, for instance, is that only civil affairs officials, who are mainly reservists, regularly work with NGOs. Thus, obtaining the relevant knowledge before a crisis erupts, when the reserves are less likely to be deployed, is difficult. There is also a corresponding ignorance of the military on the part of NGOs. Military organization, hierarchies and capabilities are often poorly understood. The result is that NGOs often make unrealistic demands on the military.[20] The problem is also compounded by the fact that NGOs are often suspicious of the military and vice versa. Cedric Thornberry notes how, in recent missions, NGO workers tend to be much younger than their military counterparts, and this age difference can sometimes reinforce perceived differences of approach.[21]

Closely related to the lack of familiarity is the common refrain and recurrent theme about differences in organizational cultures between the two communities. Both NGOs and the military are in agreement that cultural incompatibility is at fault and often one of the primary obstacles to effective cooperation.[22] In many ways, as Slim maintains, 'military and humanitarian organizations find themselves as much connected as separated by the common roots in war', and the perceived nobility both of dying for your country and of saving lives; a major difference, however, is that while the military find it easy and morally acceptable to be humanitarian occasionally, the reverse of NGOs taking part in military activities is much less likely.[23] Joëlle Jenny encapsulates the differences: 'An army and a humanitarian organization work with fundamentally different rationales. While soldiers respond to clear lines of command, sets of rules and operational orders, aid workers are generally independent minded and retain considerable decision-making power at field level.'[24] Military officers working with local authorities have been reluctant to cooperate with NGOs, an inherent mistrust that stems from the very different institutional cultures. NGOs are less hierarchical than the military and are under no obligation to take instructions from people outside their group, and so there is more freedom of action which they cherish. This makes it difficult for the military to engage in any sort of cooperative arrangements with NGOs. A possible consequence might be the tendency by the military to think they can provide better quality aid.

Some military personnel act in a hegemonic manner towards the NGOs, typified by the attitude: 'only we understand the security situation'. This attitude is counterproductive as the military are often less knowledgeable about the cultural, social and political realities of the situation in the target society.[25] Tamara Duffey drives home the point: 'The operations in Somalia exposed serious organizational culture differences between the military and the diversity of civilian agencies.'[26] For NGOs, it is easy for any sort of cooperation to be resented as 'encroachment'.[27] Brigadier Cross's example of Kosovo, where military-led meetings were instinctively viewed with suspicion by NGOs who expected those meetings to be highly structured and for 'orders' to be given, is particularly instructive. Not surprisingly, many NGOs stayed out of those meetings or were reluctant participants, and throughout the NGO community there was a noticeable determination not to be controlled or commanded. The end result was that military resources were not optimally utilized.[28] The reluctance of NGOs to cooperate with the military, according to Nicholas Stockton, stems from cultural and practical reasons. He argues that the NGO community harbours a tradition of embattlement with authority, especially authority in uniform, and this has profound implications for any successful degree of cooperation. Practically, the military tend to monopolize media coverage, which NGOs resent because of a perceived loss of fundraising.[29] A military agenda may also be perceived as overshadowing a humanitarian one. During the Australian-led intervention in East Timor, many NGOs raised concerns regarding the dominance of security issues to the exclusion of humanitarian ones in the early stages of the mission planning.[30]

Problems have arisen in the context of a reluctance of NGOs dealing with the military because of the perception of compromising their security, impartiality, neutrality, or even because of a mistrust arising from previous experience.[31] In operational terms, NGOs are apprehensive that the use of the military to protect relief supplies and personnel might have the opposite effect: the turning of humanitarian facilities and staff into perceived enemies, and therefore, targets.[32] One of the large NGOs that had operations in Albania encountered a situation subsequently in Angola which compromised its operations in that country because Angolan rebels had seen the NGO working in a refugee camp where NATO forces were also present. In no uncertain terms the NGO was told, 'We don't trust you; you're with NATO'.[33] In Somalia, the attempt to apprehend the warlord Mohammed Aideed was viewed by his supporters as the US and UNOSOM taking sides in the conflict. Consequently, NGOs feared that this loss of neutrality would make them targets, which was borne out with the attack on World Vision personnel by militias as an expression of displeasure with the US-led enforcement action.[34] In the wake of the Rwandan genocide, NGOs refused to allow UNAMIR to lend support to their efforts or needs, often claiming to have enough experience in dangerous situations that they did not need the UN's help or protection.[35] Moreover, NGOs have also expressed fears of being co-opted into a 'new Cold War strategy whereby the national interests of a dominant power define the operations of the day – meaning that NGOs could become a non-military extension of a new structure for great power interests working beside or through the UN'.[36] In general, NGOs have more reservations working with the US military than with those of smaller powers, because the US military is often seen as having a political agenda, hence working with US military forces risks being seen as US pawns.[37]

Mike Aaronson has also highlighted from Save the Children's perspective, what is termed the 'new reality' of humanitarianism that attempts to bring political, military and humanitarian objectives within the same framework. For him, that represents a real danger that humanitarian aims and principles will be compromised as a result of which the capacity to alleviate suffering will be reduced.[38] Given the Brahimi Report's conclusions on the need for a robust force posture and a sound peacebuilding strategy which implies that the UN must now be willing to take sides, one should not lose sight of the fact that the more assertive a peacekeeping force becomes, the more likely it is to confront or engage rogue forces. In such circumstances NGOs will have to be seen as distinct from the military. NGOs must weigh the advantages of short-term cooperation with the military against the possible consequences of long-term alienation since they often remain long after military forces have departed. The perils of close association with the military have led NGOs to distance themselves, wherever possible, from military operations. Overall, NGOs' insistence on impartiality, neutrality and independence have served as a stumbling block to any long-term planning with the military.

NGOs are often unwilling to share information, not only among themselves but also with the military. Although, they are forthcoming with information concerning the needs of suffering people, they are reluctant to share other sensitive information with the military. They will not for instance give information on the host government, fearing it might jeopardize their operations in terms of access to crisis areas. Some NGO personnel are concerned that the military seeks information that goes beyond the immediate crisis. On the other hand, the military will not share information with NGOs due to operational secrecy, for example, on issues relating to deployments and capabilities.[39]

More effective peace missions will require minimizing or overcoming these problems that currently plague military–NGO relations. The utility of broader cooperation and coordination between military and civilian actors is becoming more widely recognized in the international community.[40] Yet, coordination itself is a value-laden concept. For some, it implies 'control', while others resist being bogged down by interminable layers of bureaucracy.[41] Cooperation is a relatively weak concept for the military, but it has stronger meaning for NGOs. From the British military perspective for example, cooperation is more about consensus and heading together in an agreed direction than about strict coordination and command, to achieve a comprehensive approach based on complimentary capabilities.[42] The definition of cooperation is 'working together to the same end', while coordination is defined as 'bringing together (various parts etc.) into a proper or required relation to ensure harmony or effective operation'.[43] These definitions are simple enough and relatively straightforward in their application to the military/NGO context in terms of achieving mutually workable relations. As Peter Viggo Jakobsen suggests, civil–military relations mean 'creating an effective partnership with civilian agencies and NGOs based on mutual respect and coordination by consensus and not command'.[44] Thus, both the military and the NGOs need to understand why they are involved in a particular peace mission and they can only improve cooperation and collaboration through flexibility and building trust.

Despite efforts to address issues of cooperation and coordination, it seems to be the case that either lessons have not been learned or indeed few lessons have been learned, or as Weiss bluntly puts it, 'Perhaps too many lessons have been learned periodically'.[45] In any case, the problems discussed above still exist. It has been suggested that this may be due in part to the fact that ad hoc improvements made at the working level, largely by personalities involved in the field, have not translated into policy and institutionalized in higher offices.[46] Civil–Military coordination is important and should be seen as part of the overall strategy to enhance the effectiveness of peace missions. NGOs will have to demonstrate that preserving their independence does not mean the duplication of work in certain areas and leaving gaps in others.[47] The creation of an NGO coordination body to discuss a common programme of action, to act as the centre for information exchange, and first point of contact for NGOs arriving in a particular crisis situation, should be encouraged as a way of consolidating their operations.[48] NGOs need to constantly re-examine their performance in the context of ongoing efforts aimed at developing a comprehensive code of conduct conveying their missions, objectives and operating procedures more clearly to the military, such as the initiative taken by the ICRC.[49] In addition, agreement should be sought among NGOs on modalities of civil–military cooperation with a view to encouraging greater unity of effort in theatre as part of a new partnership, given the 'new reality' integration of humanitarian, political and military activities. It has been suggested that the Steering Committee on Humanitarian Response, which is a coalition of large international NGOs that informs the UN about NGO policies, would be a suitable forum to examine these issues.[50]

For military forces, streamlining and harmonizing operational plans and goals of potential troop-contributing nations, for example, on what constitutes adequate protection of civilians, should be undertaken where possible at the start of a mission. A detailed development of a field manual for use by military contingents of various nations for each peace mission should be a step in the right direction to avoid confusion over operating principles. It is encouraging that the United Nations Department of Peacekeeping Operations is currently developing a training programme including mission-specific preparations for military forces.

Another consideration for better coordination in closing the gap regarding cultural differences is that, at a minimum, the military should ensure familiarity with relevant NGOs that play leading roles in peace missions. A concerted effort through the organization of conferences, identifying and conducting joint exercises, training, planning and offering courses examining civilian–military relations in military educational institutions should be encouraged.[51] This will lead to an improvement of the overall awareness of NGOs' concerns and capabilities and vice versa. It will ensure familiarity with each other at the pre-deployment stage and will foster predictability, given the difficulties of the military in comprehending the diverse nature of humanitarian action in peace missions.[52] Ultimately, such joint initiatives may result in the development of common standards of good practice within and between the military and NGOs' operations.[53]

In order to avoid duplication, it is important to define and clarify the roles and responsibilities of the various actors engaged in complex emergencies. This will go a long way in enhancing who is best for what job. Achieving maximum effectiveness from any federated response suggests the need for a clear division of labour. Discussions could start both within and outside of the UN regarding an 'inventory' of activities carried out by the various actors, analysing where their functions overlap or conflict, and how these could be improved.[54]

The UK Ministry of Defence Civil–Military Co-operation philosophy recognizes with regard to early engagement with civilian organizations that 'each organisation needs an appreciation of the values and principles which motivate and guide the activities of others, and the mandates under which each of them operate. Fostering this greater understanding should reduce the suspicion and resistance to cooperation that sometimes surface during operations'. To this end, prospects for any enhanced collaboration should be complementary and based on a clear understanding and respect for each other's mandates and operating principles. Ultimately, as Koenraad Van Brabant asserts relating to different mandates: 'Agencies have to recognise that the underlying humanitarian mandate is the same: save lives, reduce suffering and try to restore local capacities. The work of different agencies is therefore inherently complementary.'[55] The creation of institutions to promote familiarity would go a long way in helping cooperation during a crisis.

To overcome lack of coherence across the entire range of operations in the field, possibilities for cooperation will require the exchange of information at all levels, building on the awareness and understanding established prior to deployment. The need to know what can and cannot be achieved, what will and will not be undertaken, by whom and under what circumstances will be important factors in the attempt at having the desired impact on complex emergencies. This communication imperative has already resulted in work on the coordination of information being undertaken in the NGO community. The Humanitarian Co-ordination Information Centre (HCIC) set up in Kosovo as a centre for data sharing available to all organizations and agencies is one such example. As Ann Fitz-Gerald and Fiona Walthall note: 'It provides information on who is doing what, where and when and provides visibility to empower the doers.'[56] This helps in the categorization of information and the development of common standards. The need for the military to become involved in initiatives such as the HCIC will assist in the provision of overall clarity over the role of all actors and those whom they are trying to help.[57]

In recent years the military, for its part, has sought to improve its relationship with NGOs through the evolution of Civil–Military Co-operation Centres (CMOCs) or other coordinating mechanisms. Liaison officers have been attached to the leading NGOs in the field. These developments have facilitated interaction between the various actors by working together and building personal relationships. Although these cooperation centres have had a mixed record in bringing together the military and NGOs, they can be improved and serve as useful models for future operations.[58]

Conclusion

The primary task in securing peace today is one of assisting in the long-term political and social transformation of war-shattered societies. Comprehensive peace operations thus need to address not only the immediate military and humanitarian concerns, but also the longer-term tasks of state building, reforming the security sector, strengthening civil society and promoting social reintegration.[59] These tasks can only be effectively implemented through a well-coordinated system involving both the military and NGOs. Although significant differences do exist between these actors hindering closer relationships in the field – a reflection of their respective missions, expectations, perceptions and professional ethos – this should not be, as Brigadier Tim Cross observes, a battle between 'bloody hands' and 'bleeding hearts'.[60] Working separately in an uncoordinated manner is likely to lead to undermining each other, with substantial implications for bringing about peace in divided societies. Understanding and accepting these differences and moving forward through familiarization with each other, planning together, communicating, and an appropriate division of labour regarding roles and responsibilities, will go a long way towards improving the ability to adequately respond to complex emergencies. Flexibility on both sides will be the key to further progress.

NOTES

1. The tripartite division of peace operations referred to here includes: peacekeeping defined as the containment, moderation or termination of hostilities through the medium of an impartial third party; peacemaking which is action designed to bring parties to a resolution of conflict and end to their dispute; and, peacebuilding which is the post-conflict action to strengthen or solidify a political settlement to avoid a relapse to conflict. Peacekeeping emphasizes tasks such as security and deterrence, normally associated with military forces. Peacemaking includes such processes as fact-finding, facilitation, negotiation, mediation, provision of good offices, or other third–party mechanisms, and normally carried on by diplomats. Lastly, peacebuilding is less well defined, but characterized by a wide variety of tasks ranging from reform of the military to societal reconstruction. These missions are either multilateral in nature as in UN operations; regional as in NATO operations, or bilateral as carried out by two countries. For detailed discussions see for example, Alexander Woodcock and David Davis (eds.), *Analysis for Peace Operations*, Clementsport, NS: Canadian Peacekeeping Press, 1998.
2. See *Agenda for Peace: Preventive Diplomacy, Peace-Making and Peacekeeping*, New York: United Nations, 1992, para 82, and the *Supplement to the Agenda*.
3. See *The Report of the Panel on United Nations Peace Operations*. See also, The World Bank and the Carter Center, 'From Civil War to Civil Society', 19–21 Feb. 1997 conference proceedings report, July 1997, cited in Dayton Maxwell, 'Facing the Choice Among Bad Options in Complex Humanitarian Emergencies' in Max

Manwaring and John Fishel (eds.), *Toward Responsibility in the New World Disorder: Challenges and Lessons of Peace Operations*, London and Portland, OR: Frank Cass, 1998, p.179.

4. CIMIC (Civil–Military Co-operation) is a term widely used to characterize the management of this type of civil–military interface. This terminology is current both in NATO and the UN. The NATO definition of CIMIC is along the lines of a partnership between civil and military organizations in support of the military mission. For NGOs, this is seen as a military concept. The inherent danger of CIMIC is that it could lead the military to go beyond the performance of its (military) mandate and focus more on humanitarian activities than on peace and security functions. The UK Ministry of Defence, for example, is considering the adoption, with minor changes, of the UN definition. CIMIC is defined as: 'The relationship of interaction, co-operation and co-ordination, mutual support, joint planning, and constant exchange of information at all levels between military forces, civilian organisations and agencies, and in-theatre civil influences, which are necessary to achieve an effective response in the full range of operations'. See UK MOD, *Civil Military Co-operation (CIMIC) Philosophy Document*. This definition thus is along the lines of support for the long-term comprehensive solution to a crisis. The concepts and procedures of Canadian CIMIC doctrine, for example, are drawn largely from American Civil-Affairs (CA) doctrine with minor differences. Canadian doctrine emphasizes cooperation over direction; a reflection of Canada's greater experience with peacekeeping. See DND, Civil–Military Co-operation in Peace, Emergencies, Crisis and War, Canada, 1999. Cited in Sean Pollick, 'Civil–Military Co-operation: A New Tool for Peacekeepers', *Canadian Military Journal*, Vol.1, No.3, autumn 2000, p.11. For an outline of what CIMIC is not, see for example, J. Rollins, 'Civil Military Co-operation (CIMIC) in Crisis Response Operations: The Implications of NATO', *International Peacekeeping*, Vol.8, No.1, Spring 2001, p.123. See also, Stuart Gordon, 'Understanding the Priorities for Civil–Military Cooperation (CIMIC)', *The Journal of Humanitarian Assistance*, 13 July 2001, www.jha.ac/articles/a068.htm ; Alexander Woodcock and David Davis (eds.), *Analysis of Civil–Military Interactions*, Clementsport, NS: Canadian Peacekeeping Press, 1999. It should be noted that the term CIMIC is still dogged by a plethora of definitions and concerns. A degree of caution should therefore be exercised when referring to CIMIC.

5. For a fuller discussion of the increased role of NGOs in peacekeeping and peacebuilding operations see Francis Abiew and Tom Keating, 'NGOs and UN Peacekeeping Operations: Strange Bedfellows', *International Peacekeeping*, Vol.6, No.2, Summer 1999, p.89; Andrew Rigby, 'Humanitarian Assistance and Conflict Management: The View from the Non-Governmental Sector', *International Affairs*, Vol.77, No.4, 2001, p.957.

6. Research by Joanne Macrae focusing on the Netherlands and the UK, suggests, however, that some donor governments have retreated from this 'chequebook approach to relief' since the mid-1990s for a variety of reasons, not least in response to perceived political pressure for greater 'visibility'. Cited in Mike Aaronson, 'NGOs and the Military in Complex Emergencies: The New Realities – The NGO Perspective', Paper presented at Wilton Park Conference, 23 April 2001, pp.3–4.

7. See Hugo Slim, 'The Stretcher and the Drum: Civil–Military Relations in Peace Support Operations', *International Peacekeeping*, Vol.3, No.2, 1996, pp.126–28; Ted Van Baarda, ' A Legal Perspective of Cooperation between Military and Humanitarian Organizations in Peace Support Operations', *International Peacekeeping*, Vol.8, No.1, Spring 2001, p.99; Mike Bryan, 'Observations on Wilton Park NGO Conference Report', Wilton Park Conference, April, 2001.

8. For various definitions of NGOs see for example, Thomas Weiss and Leon Gordenker (eds.), *NGOs, The UN, and Global Governance*, Boulder: Lynne Rienner Publishers, 1996, pp.18–21; Pamela Aall, 'NGOs, Conflict Management and Peacekeeping', *International Peacekeeping*, Vol.7, No.1, Spring 2000, p.124.

9. Weiss and Gordenker, ibid., p.31.

10. Slim (n.7 above), p.128.
11. Ibid., p.129.
12. Daniel Byman, 'Uncertain Partners: NGOs and the Military', *Survival*, Vol.43, No.2, summer 2001, p.99.
13. Ibid.
14. Michael Pugh, 'Civil–Military Relations in the Kosovo Crisis: An Emerging Hegemony?', *Security Dialogue*, Vol.31, No.2, June 2000, p.236.
15. Ibid., p.230.
16. Ibid., p.235. But see Slim (n.7 above), pp.127–8.
17. Christopher Bellamy, 'Combining Combat Readiness and Compassion', *NATO Review*, Summer 2001, p.10.
18. Pollick (n.4 above), pp.6–7.
19. Tamara Duffey, 'Cultural Issues in Contemporary Peacekeeping', *International Peacekeeping*, Vol.7, No.1, Spring 2000, p.156.
20. Byman (n.12 above), p.106.
21. See Cedric Thornberry, 'Peacekeepers, Humanitarian Aid, and Civil Conflicts', *The Journal of Humanitarian Assistance*, 3 June 2000, p.3, www.jha.ac/articles/a002.htm.
22. Meinrad Studer, 'The ICRC and Civil–Military Relations in Armed Conflict', Paper presented at Wilton Park Conference, April 2001, p.11.
23. Slim (n.7 above), p. 124; see also, ibid. Although Slim also acknowledges 'despite apparently similar organizational behaviour, international humanitarian organizations tend to be made up of people who have profound reservations about militarism'.
24. Joëlle Jenny, 'Civil–Military Cooperation in Complex Emergencies: Finding Ways to Make it Work', *European Security*, Vol.10, No.2, Summer 2001, p.27.
25. Duffey (n.19 above), p.156.
26. See, ibid.
27. Gordon (n.4 above), p.8.
28. Tim Cross, 'Comfortable with Chaos – Working with the UNHCR and the NGOs: Reflections from the 1999 Kosovo Refugee Crisis', Paper presented at Wilton Park Conference, April 2001, p.21.
29. Cited in Gordon (n.4 above), p.8.
30. Ibid.
31. See Thomas Weiss, *Military–Civilian Interactions: Intervening in Humanitarian Crises*, Lanham: Rowan & Littlefield Publishers, 1999, p.3.
32. Romeo Dallaire, 'The Changing Role of UN Peacekeeping Forces: The Relationship between UN Peacekeepers and NGOs in Rwanda', in Jim Whitman and David Pocock (eds.), *After Rwanda: The Coordination of United Nations Humanitarian Assistance*, London: Macmillan, 1996, p.207.
33. Ted Van Baarda (n.7 above), p.103.
34. Byman (n.12 above), p.104. It is precisely the sort of situation Gordon reminds us about when he states: 'humanitarian action alongside an enforcement force may...be perceived as being utilized by politicians to legitimize military action and overcoming controversies relating to mandates and legality. This may also prejudice the willingness of members of the humanitarian community to become part of an integrated structure'. Gordon (n.4 above), p.8.
35. See Dallaire (n.32 above), pp.210–11.
36. Ibid., p.207.
37. Byman (n.12 above), p.105.
38. See Aaronson (n.6 above), p.5.
39. Byman (note 12 above), p.105.
40. For a discussion on the developing experience and doctrine of civil–military collaboration or cooperation see Koenraad Van Brabant, 'Understanding, Promoting and Evaluating Coordination: An Outline Framework', in D.S. Gordon and F.H. Toase (eds.), *Aspects of Peacekeeping*, London and Portland, OR: Frank Cass, 2001, p.156. See also, Bruce Jones, 'The Challenges of Strategic Coordination: Containing Opposition and Sustaining Implementation of Peace Agreements in Civil Wars', *IPA*

Policy Paper Series on Peace Implementation, June 2001, New York. For a useful discussion on models of cooperation and coordination which is beyond the scope of this work, see for example, Gerald Hatzenbichler, 'Civil–Military Co-operation in UN Peace Operations Designed by SHIRBRIG', *International Peacekeeping*, Vol.8, No.1, Spring 2001, pp.117–21; Ted Van Baarda (note 7 above), pp.107–12.

41. Jon Bennett, 'Coordination, Control and Competition: NGOs on the Front Line', in Jim Whitman and David Pocock (eds.) (n.32 above), p.136.

42. Cited in 'NGOs and the Military in Complex Emergencies', *Summary of Wilton Park Conference*, 23–26 April 2001, p.7.

43. *Concise Oxford Dictionary*, 8th edn., Oxford: Clarendon Press, 1991.

44. Peter Viggo Jakobsen, 'The Emerging Consensus on Grey Area Peace Operations Doctrine: Will it Last and Enhance Operational Effectiveness?', *International Peacekeeping*, Vol.7, No.3, Autumn, 2000, p.42.

45. This judgement is based on ongoing research by Brown University's Humanitarianism and War Project reviewing institutional performances and adaptations in post-Cold War crises. See Thomas Weiss, 'Learning from Military–Civilian Interactions in Peace Operations', *International Peacekeeping*, Vol.6, No.2, Summer 1999, pp.115–18.

46. This was noted by the conference organizers at Cranfield University's Department of Defence Management and Security Analysis and the Joint Doctrine and Concepts Centre in the UK, at a conference on the Kosovo experience held in May 2001, that brought together experts, practitioners, policymakers and academics to explore issues involved in moving towards an integrated approach to complex emergencies.

47. Jenny (n.24 above), p.30

48. These coordination bodies have worked well in practice in such places as Thailand, Ethiopia, and in Mozambique as a way around dealing with the sheer number of NGOs that are engaged in complex emergencies. See Bennett (n.41 above), pp.143–5.

49. The introduction of the Code of Conduct for the International Red Cross and Red Crescent Movement and NGOs in Disaster Relief (1994) and the accompanying Humanitarian Charter (SPHERE 2000) are initial steps at developing a beneficiaries charter and minimum standards in humanitarian response. For a further exposition on the effectiveness of codes of conduct regarding NGOs, see Warren Lancaster, 'The Code of Conduct: Whose Code, Whose Conduct', *The Journal of Humanitarian Assistance*, June 2000, pp.1–9, www.jha.ac/articles/a038.htm.

50. See for example, Peter Bell and Guy Tousignant, 'Getting Beyond New York: Reforming Peacekeeping in the Field', *World Policy Journal*, Vol.18, No.3, Fall 2001, pp.41–6.

51. For a detailed discussion of these issues see for example, Ann Fitz-Gerald and Fiona Walthall, 'An Integrated Approach to Complex Emergencies: The Kosovo Experience', *The Journal of Humanitarian Assistance*, August 2001, pp.1–7, www.jha.ac/articles/a071.htm.

52. This recognition of broader planning should be given priority in preparations prior to deployment in peace missions. See Walter Clarke, 'Waiting for the "Big One": Confronting Complex Humanitarian Emergencies and State Collapse in Central Africa', in Manwaring and Fishel (eds.) (n.3 above), p.95.

53. Slim (n.7 above), p.139.

54. Bell and Tousignant (n.50 above), pp.45–6.

55. Van Brabant (n.40 above), p.144.

56. Fitz-Gerald and Walthall (n.51 above), p.4.

57. Ibid., pp.4–5.

58. For examples of activities carried out by these centres see Aall (n.8 above), pp.133–4; Pollick (n.4 above), p.9.

59. Espen Barth Eide, 'Peacekeeping Past and Present', *NATO Review*, Summer 2001, p.8.

60. Cross (n.28 above), p.iii.

Humanitarian NGOs
in Peace Processes

MICHAEL SCHLOMS

The ambiguity experienced by aid agencies in intrastate conflicts in the 1990s triggered much criticism and debate. Discussions focused on two main issues: the necessity of linking aid to peacebuilding, and the understanding and standards of humanitarian action.

The peacebuilding debate stems from the aftermath of aid missions (including in Sudan, the African Great Lakes region and Sierra Leone), when critics claimed aid supported war instead of peace. As a reaction to this criticism it was claimed that if aid agencies wished to 'do no harm', they would have to strengthen a society's 'capacities for peace'.[1] Supporting those forces that bring peace thus offered humanitarian NGOs 'a new moral banner to march behind' that 'serves to re-legitimise an arena of aid that has been blamed for fuelling conflicts, prolonging wars and standing neutral in the face of genocide'.[2] Basically, this argument states that 'the new world clearly needs a new humanitarianism'.[3]

The assumption that aid agencies – especially NGOs – dispose of 'comparative advantages' in peace processes further supports the idea of coordinating aid and peace efforts. Through their work, aid agencies gather local expertise, develop links to local actors, get direct access to war-torn populations and are often respected by all parties as an impartial and neutral actor.[4] The establishment of durable peace in post-conflict situations – the concept of peacebuilding – depends on factors such as the expertise of local actors, structures and access. In other words, peacebuilding 'involves a shift of focus away from the warriors, with whom peacekeepers are mainly concerned, to the attitudes and socio-economic circumstances of ordinary people'.[5] Thus, the characteristics of aid work make aid agencies appear as significant actors in the implementation of peace. In particular in the field of 'low-level peacebuilding' where humanitarian organizations 'have the resources to carry out the activities necessary for reintroducing a sense of security which may promote sustainable peace'.[6]

The second debate concerns the nature of humanitarianism surrounding issues such as the relation between aid and politics, the standards of action, the conditionality of aid and the accountability of humanitarian NGOs. Many of the issues discussed are directly related to the role of humanitarianism in conflict and peace processes. In terms of the objectives pursued by humanitarian action, for instance, 'the principles debate has to frame questions which challenge the extent to which peacebuilding activities should occupy humanitarian agencies'.[7]

The proposal to use aid in order to strengthen peace processes, however, largely ignores the discussions within the humanitarian movement. Intergovernmental organizations and international aid donors such as the UN and the European Union are strongly in favour of a peacebuilding/aid-coalition. Essentially, it is argued that the complexity of intra-state conflict requires a maximum of coordination and a common approach that embraces a wide range of actors, including aid agencies. The European Commission noted in 1996 that '"peacebuilding" must be an intrinsic element of development cooperation strategies'. Furthermore, 'relief actions should, apart from their primary objective of saving the lives of victims, take account of the longer term objectives of reconstruction and development'.[8]

Empirical evidence suggests that the inclusion of humanitarian aid into peacebuilding strategies faces three problems. First, the evaluation of aid efforts casts doubts upon whether the principles of humanitarian action are compatible with the objectives pursued by peacebuilding. Second, coordination remains a critical point. As Leon Gordenker and Thomas Weiss conclude, 'the different values and operating styles between NGOs and intergovernmental organizations, along with the NGOs' ferocious insistence on maintaining independence, probably preclude any far-reaching harmonisation of efforts'.[9] Third, evaluation reports frequently demonstrate 'a major gap in agencies' understanding of the context in which they were intervening'.[10] This lack of analysis further hinders a comprehensive and effective engagement of aid in peace efforts.

This essay discusses the compatibility of humanitarian action and peacebuilding. When do aid and peace efforts coincide and when do they conflict? It analyses the prerequisites for a humanitarianism/peacebuilding coalition and refers to the findings of the debate surrounding humanitarianism. It will be shown that the requirements aid has to comply with in order to play a peacebuilding role touch the most controversial points of the humanitarian debate. Furthermore, the theory that humanitarian NGOs have to play a peacebuilding role takes for granted what is highly contested among the NGOs themselves.

Prerequisites for a Humanitarianism/Peacebuilding Coalition

The linkage between aid and peace efforts can be achieved in two possible, mutually complementary, ways. Peacebuilding can be seen as the final phase of a 'hand-over-process' that begins with relief aid, leads to rehabilitation and development efforts, and ends with the construction of sustainable peace. In addition, peacebuilding can be regarded as an integrated approach that requires any actor, including humanitarian NGOs, to integrate peacebuilding efforts at every stage of engagement.

Both strategies require humanitarian NGOs to cross three hurdles if they are to play a peacebuilding role. First, their objectives have to be compatible with the goals pursued in a peacebuilding process. Second, aid agencies have to be willing to cooperate with political actors for the sake of a common goal. And third, any peacebuilding engagement requires the capacity to analyse the context in which peacebuilding activities are to take place. The objective of peacebuilding is 'to reassemble the foundations of peace and provide the tools for building on those foundations something that is more than just the absence of war'.[11] As opposed to peacemaking and peacekeeping, which aim at establishing negative peace (i.e. the absence of war), the objective of peacebuilding is positive peace built 'around such ideas as "harmony", "cooperation" and "integration"'.[12]

This positive peace is to be achieved by addressing the underlying causes of a conflict, namely 'economic despair, social injustice, and political oppression'.[13] Accordingly, peacebuilding tools include economic rehabilitation, the provision of equal access to basic goods, and the abolition of dominance. Evidently, peacebuilding to a certain extent means democratization, since democracy 'not only opens the space for nonviolent political competition, but also helps to sustain the balanced distribution of power that underpins the peace process'.[14] Humanitarianism has to share these goals if it is to play a significant peacebuilding role. It must be willing to undertake long-term projects that address the root causes of violence by aiming at structural changes. Democratization cannot be achieved without touching on both the recognition of the needs of civil society and governance issues. Peacebuilding is thus, fundamentally, a political endeavour and 'should not be confused with regular, longer-term development programmes'.[15] Consequently, humanitarian NGOs included in peacebuilding processes have to be conscious of the political impact of peacebuilding in general and, in particular, to their specific impact in this regard. Advocates of an aid/peacebuilding coalition highlight the economic and political impact aid can have in war-torn societies. James K. Boyce, for instance, argues that 'aid affects not only the size of the economic pie and how it is sliced, but also the balance of power among competing actors and the rules of the game by which they compete...the political impacts of aid can help to decide whether the peace endures or war resumes'.[16] The question arises, how far do humanitarian organizations agree with such an assessment of their work and mandate? Furthermore, and more generally, we have to take a closer look at how humanitarian agencies perceive their relation to politics.

The final hurdle aid agencies have to cross as peacebuilding actors derives from the characteristic of peacebuilding as a 'comprehensive learning process'.[17] Any actor involved in peacebuilding efforts has to shape their engagement according to the specific context, since 'there are no set patterns or models applicable to every conflict'.[18] A wide range of factors (regional settings, group interests, peace initiatives and own failures in the past) has to be taken into account in order to develop and revise a peacebuilding strategy. Therefore, humanitarian NGOs engaged with peace processes 'should be aware of socio-economic disparities and gender-related issues; understand the prevailing disparities and security environment; and be able to analyse and build upon local strengths and coping mechanisms'.[19] In short, without identifying the causes and dynamics of a conflict it is impossible to pave the way to peace. Additionally, it is often argued that the need to analyse and learn is closely related to the nature of post-Cold War conflicts.[20]

As noted above, empirical evidence suggests humanitarian NGOs do not meet the fundamental preconditions that would allow them to play a role in peacebuilding processes. We will therefore have to discuss whether the very nature of humanitarian action is incompatible with the prerequisites of peacebuilding, or whether in some circumstances, aid and peace do coincide.

Objectives of Humanitarian Action

Humanitarian aid or humanitarian assistance can be defined as 'the provision of basic requirements which meet people's needs for adequate water, sanitation, nutrition, food, shelter and health care'.[21] Does this mean that aid also pursues the goal of positive peace? In fact, it already appears problematic to assume that humanitarian aid accepts any goal that goes beyond the direct alleviation of suffering. Generally, one could argue that the most fundamental principle of humanitarian aid – humanity – focuses on the same ideal as does the pursuit of peace:

human well-being. The driving force behind humanity is compassion and concern for the person in need. One tradition within humanitarianism claims that 'compassion is not a means to an end but an end in itself'.[22] Evidently, such a conviction – an 'ethics of commitment' in Max Weber's terms – contravenes any effort that aims to include aid into a phalanx of actors pursuing a common goal. Aid, one could argue, is an act in itself that cannot be measured or judged by the effects it engenders. What counts instead is the humanity that lies in the act of giving.[23]

This argument is highly contested within the debate surrounding humanitarianism. The assumption that aid is an act in itself is blamed for representing a 'sentimental, paternalistic and privileged discourse of philanthropy and charity'.[24] Instead, some advocate a shift towards a rights-based approach that highlights a perceived commonness between humanitarian and human rights philosophy. In such a perspective, aid could accept a goal that lies outside the act of giving as long as it improves the respect of individual freedom and rights.

It is not our intention to decide which of these approaches is right or wrong or more appropriate to describe the motives of humanitarian action. It has just to be noted that the willingness of humanitarian actors to pursue the goal of positive peace as part of a peacebuilding approach cannot be taken for granted.

As mentioned above, peacebuilding addresses issues of social injustice and political oppression. In view of the role aid should play in such an endeavour, Mary B. Anderson states that 'aid workers should try to identify local capacities for peace and connectors and design their aid programs to support and reinforce them'.[25] This 'do-no-harm' approach paves the way to linking aid to peacebuilding processes. It is, however, criticized for surpassing the resources and mandates of aid agencies. Instead of expanding their agenda, some authors argue, aid agencies should focus on the alleviation of human suffering only. Aid agencies are advised to be modest in their objectives 'to ensure that priorities are set according to needs'.[26]

Humanitarian NGOs are split along these lines. The willingness among humanitarian NGOs to provide structural change through projects that go beyond the immediate alleviation of suffering and saving of lives (educational, employment, agricultural rehabilitation projects and so on) clearly differs. One group of agencies highlights relief aid as the classical task of humanitarianism and claims that immediate threats to human lives require immediate action. The other underlines the necessity to provide sustainable aid through more development oriented interventions. In part, the controversy between and within humanitarian NGOs surrounding relief and development has reached heights of vehemence hardly comprehensible to outsiders.[27]

It could be argued that the distinction between relief and development in the field is artificial. Additionally, one could say that all humanitarian NGOs – including those labelling themselves 'relief agency' – actually undertake longer-term rehabilitation and development projects. Both arguments are true. However, aid approaches are designed from case to case. The French section of Médecins Sans Frontières (MSF), for instance – an agency strongly critical of the development approach – spends a considerable portion of its finance (about 38 per cent) on mid- and long-term missions.[28] This type of project, however, is undertaken in countries where either no emergency situation can be detected (for example, Cambodia, China, Peru) or where this kind of project goes along with emergency relief (South Sudan). In North Korea, MSF failed to establish emergency relief programmes and – after they were asked to become involved in pharmaceutical rehabilitation – decided to leave the country.

However artificial the distinction between relief, rehabilitation, and development might be, humanitarian NGOs pursue differing objectives depending on their history, values and convictions. In a study on British aid agencies, Hugo Slim and Isobel McConnan conclude that a distinction has to be made between organizations that seek to restrain war and mitigate its consequences on one side, as opposed to those who above all adhere to the value of social justice.[29] These objectives may or may not be compatible with peacebuilding. The willingness to provide societal change through long-term projects as an important prerequisite for peacebuilding cannot be taken for granted.

Typologies of NGOs, as described by Weiss and Gordenker for example, refer to their organizational structure and financial resources as the main distinctive features.[30] However, with regard to the different sets of objectives pursued by aid agencies the differentiation, as proposed by Nicholas Leader, appears to be more useful because it refers to the activity field and ethical framework as distinctive features: 'Very broadly, it is possible to locate most humanitarian agencies on an idealised spectrum, with, at one end, preventative, community-based, partner-orientated, faith-based, developmental, food delivery agencies, and at the other, emergency, objective/scientific, operational, curative, secular, "health" agencies'.[31]

In terms of compatibility of objectives, the types of NGOs characterized by Leader as faith-based, development oriented, 'food agencies' appear to be the most appropriate partner in peacebuilding strategies. The US Institute of Peace comments on the role of faith-based NGOs: 'The peacebuilding agendas of these organizations are diverse and range from high-level mediation to training and peace-through-development at grassroots levels. While a direct approach to peacemaking is often effective, very often peace can be promoted most efficiently by introducing peacebuilding components into relief and development activities'.[32] Medical relief aid agencies inspired by a secular ethical framework, however, will most likely not be prepared to accept any other criteria than immediate humanitarian needs.

Coordination of Humanitarian Action with Politics

Aid cannot promote peace on its own but has to be part of a wider strategy that includes political and governmental actors. As a result, 'we must take conflict for granted and integrate humanitarian action and development with politics'.[33] Thus, the inclusion of humanitarian action in peacebuilding efforts requires that humanitarian agencies be willing to cooperate with those actors traditionally involved in peacebuilding – political and governmental actors. An agency's willingness to cooperate with political actors is primarily determined by its understanding of neutrality. Its perception of its own neutrality defines an aid agency's position towards politics and political actors. Not surprisingly, 'the most significant discussions, disagreements, confusions and conceptual developments have been around the idea of neutrality'.[34]

The willingness to cooperate with political actors for peacebuilding objectives appears incompatible with the traditional concept of neutral humanitarianism. In a classical understanding of neutrality, aid must not take sides and it must remain equally distant from all parties and actors involved. In other words, neutrality requires aid to 'check that the economy is not benefiting in any significant way: more "do no good" than "do no harm"'.[35]

A further well-established principle of humanitarian action – independence – hinders any subordination to political goals and institutions. Any compromise made at the expense of the principle of independence poses a risk to the main task, which is the alleviation of suffering. Thus, in this perspective peacebuilding is seen as a noble goal that should be achieved by others and not by humanitarian NGOs. An illustration of this relates to North Korea where the promotion of peace as an objective by humanitarian NGOs is highly contested among the aid agencies involved. In spite of South Korean NGOs claiming to include the terms 'reconciliation" and 'peace' in the final report of an international NGO meeting, no such passage is to be found in the final draft.[36] Western NGOs successfully argue that these terms imply a political engagement which has to be kept away from humanitarian action.

The principle of neutrality has lost much of its absolute validity among humanitarian NGOs. The basic rule that aid workers should refrain from taking sides in a conflict is still widely accepted. More importance is attached – by a number of agencies – to a common strategy and to cooperative efforts with political and governmental actors. Nevertheless, even if one ignores the alleged incompatibility of the 'do no harm' approach with the principles of neutrality and independence, still one question remains unanswered. Does the willingness to cooperate with politics go along with a political consciousness that sees humanitarian action as being part of a wider, political strategy?

Since the beginning of academic reflection on humanitarian aid, the debate has focused on the relation between humanitarianism and politics. Further discussion regarding this connection has become redundant: 'Saying that humanitarian action is political is like saying orange is a colour, true, but not very illuminating'.[37] Aid agencies, however, do not describe their work as political, nor do they openly claim to be political actors. This is illustrated by Jean Pictet's often quoted description of the International Committee of the Red Cross (ICRC) that 'like a swimmer, is in politics up to its neck. Also like the swimmer, who advances in the water but who drowns if he swallows it, the ICRC must reckon with politics without becoming a part of it'.[38] Herein lies an important area of potential ambiguity, since aid is linked by two 'dependency relationships' to the donor (financial resources) and to the recipient (access, staff safety).[39]

Some considerable differences concerning aid agencies' political perception become evident when it comes to the delicate issue of speaking out about human rights violations witnessed by aid workers. Often discussed in relation to the principle of neutrality, this issue illustrates, to a certain extent, how far a humanitarian actor thinks of himself as non-political, that is, as working in a sphere that is distinct from politics. In fact, the practice of not denouncing human rights violations is often justified by an agency's conviction that humanitarian work is non-political. Furthermore, it is argued that such work is carried out by non-political actors whose function it is to provide help to the needy without getting involved in politics. Aid agencies that do not share this conviction are often criticized for being human rights organizations rather than humanitarian agencies.

In sum, the classical principles of neutrality and impartiality potentially collide with the requirements of peacebuilding. An evaluation study of humanitarian coordination in Angola stresses that 'if the Humanitarian Coordinator becomes more directly involved in political negotiations his/her impartiality and neutrality may be more easily questioned, and it is the very neutrality and impartiality of humanitarian activities that allows humanitarian negotiations and facilitations to commence at all'.[40]

Importantly, NGOs that distance themselves from the principle of neutrality such as the 'sans-frontièrisme' branch of humanitarianism do not mean to move closer to politics. In contrast, emphasizing their independence is their main goal. They state that 'the literal application of neutrality awards the stronger and may entail that one becomes an accomplice of human rights violations'.[41]

The political environment in the recipient country plays a crucial role as far as coordination between aid agencies and political or governmental actors is concerned. After analysing attempts of aid missions in Cambodia, Ethiopia and Uganda that aimed at providing structural long-term improvements, Joanna Macrae laid down one basic condition for success: 'the recipient state must be able to function as a state, able to make and execute policy and to maintain security'.[42] In post-Cold War reality, however, this condition is rarely met.

Lack of Analysis and Limits to Learning and Accountability

As noted earlier, aid agencies have to understand the political environment in which they act in order to address the problems and obstacles they are confronted with in their humanitarian work. The capacity to analyse the political context of aid, however, is often described as the weak link in humanitarianism. The aid agencies' tendency to think of themselves as in some ways non-political has often been criticized and equated with political naivety.

Two basic observations can be made that suggest a lack of analysing capacity among humanitarian NGOs. First, it is the very nature of humanitarianism to be reactive. Unlike a private company that sells a specific product and is able to actively influence the demand through marketing strategies or technological innovations, giving aid is purely a response to the needs of a population. Therefore, humanitarian staff have to cope with fast-evolving ad hoc situations that hardly leave time for reflection. This evidently limits the capacity to learn from own experience.

Second, high staff turnover is a characteristic of the vast majority of aid organizations. Usually, expatriate staff are employed only for a certain period of time in a given mission.[43] It is hard to find senior aid workers who have spent all their working lives in one single organization. It seems to be common practice for workers to try out agencies until they find the organization that best suits their own expectations. Consequently, for those who have a critical view of an agency's approach it is often more convenient to leave the organization than it is to try to achieve some change within the agency. It goes without saying that both factors – the high staff turnover as well as the loss of unsatisfied and critical personnel – have a negative impact upon an organization's learning capacity.

In addition, NGOs often argue that every crisis is unique. To a certain extent, this point is legitimate. However, each crisis involves a similar set of aid institutions (United Nations, Red Cross, NGOs) that have to deal with a similar set of problems and obstacles, that is, denial of access, manipulation of aid, and so on. In some cases, the parallels between situations are particularly striking. As Larry Minear observes: 'The manipulation of belligerent and criminal elements of the refugee camps in eastern Zaire in 1994 was a rerun of problems unaddressed in Cambodian refugee camps along the Thai border years before'.[44] Generally speaking, similar problems of humanitarian action reoccur whenever aid is given in a highly politicized environment. Ignoring similar precedent cases means that aid agencies have to reinvent the wheel.

The 'overemphasis on the idiosyncratic'[45] does not, however, add weight to an operational approach designed to cope with the particular necessities of every crisis. A certain inappropriateness of aid projects is often identified in evaluation programmes. Ian Smillie, for instance, states that 'inappropriate blueprint-type reconstruction and rehabilitation programs continue to abound, in part because of the absence of institutional learning'.[46] Evaluations of humanitarian activities in Kosovo conclude that 'once again "foreign" humanitarian workers arrived ill-equipped in terms of their socio-political and cultural knowledge of the conflict-affected populations'.[47]

From a humanitarian perspective, the capacity to learn has no marketing appeal. On the contrary, minimal administrative costs are seen as a big plus among donors and thus, among aid organizations as well. A case study on humanitarian action in Afghanistan concludes:

> Greater emphasis on finer conflict analysis, on more sophisticated forms of interaction with conflict entrepreneurs, on skilful

negotiations, on strategic co-ordination, on local peacebuilding and the like, requires not only highly qualified staff but is also intensive in staff time investment. Yet budget considerations remain inspired by a now outmoded 'commodity logic' that allocates staff expenses to 'overhead' and seeks to keep 'overhead' to the absolute minimum.[48]

The lack of learning processes cannot only be related to the nature of humanitarian work, nor can the absence of learning processes be entirely blamed on a structural lack of capacity – a lack of willingness also seems to play a role. The unwillingness to dedicate financial resources in order to store and diffuse knowledge – at least in part out of respect for donors – hints at the fundamental obstacle to learning processes inside humanitarianism: the perception of responsibility.

With regard to the general characteristics of humanitarianism much has been written on the lack of accountability of aid agencies.[49] In fact, openly questioning the success of an aid project means putting future funds at risk. Any doubt that is expressed with regard to a certain practice or approach potentially weakens an agency's position towards donors. Unlike private companies that are obliged, first and foremost, to meet the demands of their clients, the survival of aid agencies does not depend on the decision of their beneficiaries. The capacity to learn from past experience is decisive to the survival of a business company. The same incentive cannot be found in humanitarianism. In contrast, 'unlike most market-oriented firms (which rely on consumer feedback to modify and improve their product or service), humanitarian organizations seek to discourage consumer feedback'.[50] In the first place, humanitarian organizations see their responsibility as accountability to their donors. As a result, the inclusion of humanitarian work into peacebuilding strategies depends to a certain extent on the establishment of new procedures of accountability in order to strengthen learning mechanisms.

A recent trend towards the evaluation of humanitarian assistance can be observed. This proliferation of 'lessons learned units', however, does not go along with the introduction of new procedures of accountability. On the contrary, this development – that largely originated from donor pressure after the experience in the Great Lakes region – has led to further strengthening humanitarianism's accountability to the donor. Moreover, the lack of institutional learning mechanisms, as outlined above, is not addressed by these evaluation studies, since these studies are mainly executed by external agencies. In some cases these might be helpful, but the establishment of learning mechanisms inside the organizations is not achieved.

Finally, beside the question of how organizations learn, the question of what they learn is equally crucial. Evaluations so far concentrate on analysing experience gained in the field and tend to ignore the organizational frameworks and procedures of aid agencies. Moreover, most of the evaluation efforts focus on the operational, technical side of humanitarian work. In other words, information is gathered without creating knowledge. Knowledge in the sense of 'embedding the results in private images and shared maps of the organization'[51] means to analyse the operational experience in relation to the normative framework of an aid agency, to the principles of action.

In fact, few agencies discuss and question their principles of action on the basis of past experience. In his analysis of the willingness of aid agencies to discuss issues of principles, Leader observed that some agencies 'were on the whole more interested in, and articulate about, issues of humanitarian principles and often took the lead in the development of the mechanisms under discussion'; others 'were less concerned with, or interested in, the mechanisms'.[52] In sum, the issue of accountability lies at the heart of the lack of learning capacities of humanitarian NGOs. Accountability and transparency are undermined by the perception of aid as a self-justifying cause. In this respect, the understanding of aid as an act of compassion or religious duty hinders the establishment of learning mechanisms.

Conclusion

The debate surrounding the inclusion of aid into peace processes widely assumes that such a linkage is primarily a matter of practical coordination. The discussion concerning humanitarian aid, however, reveals that more fundamental factors have to be taken into consideration. Three major conditions for the inclusion of humanitarian NGOs into peacebuilding strategies have been discussed that aid agencies theoretically have to fulfil:

- The objectives of humanitarian action need to include the abolition of structural violence and the promotion of positive peace by means of mid- and long-term rehabilitation.
- NGOs must be willing to cooperate with political and governmental actors (the perception of humanitarian aid agencies' role in politics needs to be clarified).
- Humanitarian organizations need to be willing to analyse, and moreover be capable of analysing, the political environment in which aid is to be given.

The analysis of the nature and behaviour of aid agencies has led to two main findings. First, considerable differences among humanitarian organizations have been revealed that concern each of the criteria mentioned above. Humanitarian NGOs are often referred to as a 'community', suggesting a homogenous group sharing the same approaches and principles. But the perceptions of the aims and purposes of humanitarian aid, the environment, and the history of humanitarian action differs to an extent that does not allow one to speak of a common identity. Marked differences, therefore, seem to be the striking feature among aid agencies. It goes without saying that the heterogeneity characterizing humanitarian organizations renders it difficult to identify a common conceptual basis, allowing for a systematic link between humanitarianism and peacebuilding. Furthermore, neither the faith-based development-orientated type nor the secular, medical relief-orientated type of NGO appears to be an appropriate agent in peacebuilding activities. If an agency fulfils some conditions it will very likely not satisfy others. Political consciousness seems to be linked to a strict conceptualisation of neutrality and independence hindering any institutional cooperation with governmental actors. The goal of structural change does not coincide with a political consciousness and a sufficient capacity to analyse the political context of a crisis. An aid agency that primarily seeks to restrain violence and to promote peace, that is willing to provide structural and societal change, that is prepared to cooperate with governmental and political actors for the benefit of a common political strategy and, finally, that is willing and able to analyse the political context of its action, is an illusion.

The second finding is that, to a certain extent, the compatibility of peacebuilding and humanitarian action depends on the context of the crisis. In case of an imminent humanitarian crisis where the immediate survival of population groups is at risk, humanitarian NGOs – especially those with a medical relief mandate – will most likely not be prepared to include peacebuilding objectives in their agenda. In such a situation, aid will primarily focus on the immediate needs of a population in accordance with the most fundamental principles of humanity and impartiality. Refugee crises in the immediate aftermath of armed conflict, for instance, hardly allow for a linkage between humanitarian aid and peacebuilding.[53]

In view of the objectives pursued by humanitarian NGOs, their perception of politics, and their lack of policy analysis, the scaling up from project-based relief aid to policy-based peacebuilding assistance seems to surpass the capacity and willingness of aid agencies. Arguably, the inclusion of humanitarian NGOs into peacebuilding strategies is only feasible in post-conflict situations where a settlement has been enacted. However, the fundamental discrepancies between humanitarianism and peacebuilding exist independently from the phase of crisis management. Moreover, the argument that aid has a role to play in reinforcing the political structures established by a settlement agreement is problematic. Empirical studies suggest that the success of aid in terms of structural impact depends on the existence of functional, legitimate public institutions. In other words, a functioning political regime positively influences aid, not *vice versa*.[54] Aid can therefore hardly play a peacebuilding role in crises marked by social disruption, permanent insecurity and collapsed statehood. Paradoxically, the role of humanitarian NGOs in peace processes is very limited, particularly in those conflict situations that gave rise to the proposal of bringing humanitarianism and peacebuilding together.

NOTES

1. M.B. Anderson, *Do No Harm: Supporting Local Capacities for Peace through Aid.* Cambridge, MA: Local Capacities for Peace Project, Collaborative for Development Action, 1996 and *Do No Harm: How Aid Can Support Peace – or War,* Boulder and London: Lynne Rienner, 1999.
2. F. Fox, 'New Humanitarianism: Does it Provide a Moral Banner for the 21st Century?', *Disasters,* Vol.25, No.4, 2001, p.275.
3. Ibid., p.288.
4. See J. Egeland, 'Peacemaking and the Prevention of Violence: The Role of Governments and Non-Governmental Organizations', *International Review of the Red Cross,* Vol.81, No.833, Mar. 1999, p.77.
5. S. Ryan, *Ethnic Conflict and International Relations.* Aldershot: Darmouth, 1990, p.61.
6. T. Spencer: *A Synthesis of Evaluations of Peacebuilding Activities Undertaken by Humanitarian Agencies and Conflict Resolution Organizations,* London: Active Learning Network on Accountability and Performance in Humanitarian Action (ALNAP), 1998, p.28.
7. Ibid., p.39.
8. European Commission, *Linking Relief, Rehabilitation and Development.* Communication from the Commission of 30 Apr. 1996.
9. T.G. Weiss and L. Gordenker, 'NGO Participation in the International Policy Process', in Weiss and Gordenker (eds.), *NGOs, the UN, and Global Governance,* Boulder and London: Lynne Rienner, 1996, p.219.
10. Active Learning Network for Accountability and Performance in Humanitarian Action (ALNAP), *Humanitarian Action: Learning from Evaluation.* London: ALNAP, Annual Review Series, 2001 (paras 4.2.8).
11. United Nations, *Comprehensive Review of the Whole Question of Peacekeeping Operations in All Their Aspects ('Brahimi Report'),* New York: General Assembly and Security Council, 21 Aug. 2000, p.3.
12. J. Galtung, 'Twenty-Five Years of Peace Research: Ten Challenges and Some Responses', *Journal of Peace Research,* Vol.22, No.2, 1985, p.145. Also see J. Galtung, 'Three Approaches to Peace: Peacekeeping, Peacemaking, and Peacebuilding', in

Galtung (ed.), *Peace, War, and Defense: Essays in Peace Research*, Vol.II, Copenhagen: Christian Ejlers, pp.282–304.

13. B. Boutros-Ghali, *An Agenda for Peace: Preventive Diplomacy, Peacemaking and Peacekeeping*. New York: United Nations, 1992, paragraph 15.

14. J.K. Boyce, 'Beyond Good Intentions: External Assistance and Peace Building', in S. Forman and S. Patrick (eds.), *Good Intentions: Pledges of Aid for Postconflict Recovery*, Boulder and London: Lynne Rienner, 2000, pp.373–4.

15. J.G. Cockell, 'Peacebuilding and Human Security: Frameworks for International Responses to Internal Conflict', in P. Wallensteen (ed.), *Preventing Violent Conflicts: Past Records and Future Challenges*, Uppsala: Uppsala University and Department of Peace and Conflict Research, Report No.48, 1998, p.206.

16. Boyce (n.14 above), p.367.

17. T. Paffenholz, 'Peacebuilding: A Comprehensive Learning Process', in L. Reychler and T. Paffenholz (eds.), *Peacebuilding: A Field Guide*. Boulder: Lynne Rienner, 2001, p.535–44.

18. K. Rupesinghe, *Civil Wars, Civil Peace: An Introduction to Conflict Resolution*, with S. Naraghi Anderlini, London and Sterling: Pluto Press, 1998, p.139.

19. I. Smillie, *Relief and Development: The Struggle for Synergy*, Providence, RI: Thomas Watson Jr. Institute for International Studies and Brown University, Occasional Paper No.33, 1998, p.54.

20. See H. Slim, 'The Continuing Metamorphosis of the Humanitarian Practitioner: Some New Colours for an Endangered Chameleon', *Disasters*, Vol.19, No.2, 1995, p.112: 'Sophisticated political analysis and negotiation are now a major element of humanitarian practice in complex emergencies. In the past, a certain naivety was considered a useful asset to relief workers, and political ignorance was the bliss in which they thrived on the fringes of many wars and dictatorships.'

21. Sphere, *Handbook*, Annex: Glossary of Key Terms.

22. T. Vaux, *The Selfish Altruist: Relief Work in Famine and War*, London: Earthscan, 2001, p.45.

23. See N. Leader, *The Politics of Principle: The Principles of Humanitarian Action in Practice*, London: Overseas Development Institute, HPG Report 2, Mar. 2000, p.20: 'From the point of view of an absolute morality it could be argued that it does not matter if aid influences a war; humanitarian aid, it could be argued, should be judged by its moral rather than its practical impact, it is simply the right thing to do and that is enough, aid is a value not a policy.'

24. H. Slim, *Not Philanthropy but Rights: Rights-Based Humanitarianism and the Proper Politicisation of Humanitarian Philosophy in War*, Paper presented at Politics and Humanitarian Aid: Debates, Dilemmas and Dissension, Commonwealth Institute, London, 1 Feb. 2001, p.3.

25. Anderson (n.1 above), 1999, p.146.

26. J. Macrae, *Aiding Recovery: The Crisis of Aid in Chronic Political Emergencies*, London and New York: Zed Books, 2001, p.172. Also see C. Götze, *Von der humanitären zur Entwicklungshilfe. Entwicklung, Konflikt, Nothilfe und die ambivalente Aktualität des Kontinuum-Ansatzes*, Berlin: Social Science Research Center (WZB), Discussion Paper (P 99–304), 1999.

27. See, for instance, Vaux (n.22 above), pp.76–81.

28. Médecins Sans Frontières: *Rapport financier. Comptes 2000*. Paris: MSF, 2001.

29. H. Slim and I. McConnan, *A Swiss Prince, a Glass Slipper and the Feet of 15 British Aid Agencies: A Study of DEC Agency Positions on Humanitarian Principles*, Oxford: Disaster Emergency Committee, 1998, pp.3–4.

30. See T.G. Weiss and L. Gordenker, 'Pluralizing Global Governance: Analytical Approaches and Dimensions', in Weiss and Gordenker (eds.) (n.9 above), pp.20–21.

31. Leader (n.23 above), p.42.

32. United States Institute of Peace, *Faith-Based NGOs and International Peacebuilding. (Special Report 76)*, Washington DC: USIP, p.9.

33. A. Donini, 'Asserting Humanitarianism in Peace-Maintenance', *Global Governance*, Vol.4, p.94.
34. Leader (n.23 above), p.19.
35. K. Mackintosh, *The Principles of Humanitarian Action in International Humanitarian Law*, London: Overseas Development Institute, HPG Report 5, Mar. 2000, p.9.
36. *Report of the Third International NGO Conference on Humanitarian Assistance to North Korea: Cooperative Efforts beyond Food Aid, Final Report*, 20 June 2001, Yong In (Republic of Korea).
37. Leader (n.23 above), p.15.
38. Quoted in L. Minear, 'The Theory and Practice of Neutrality: Some Thoughts on the Tensions', *International Review of the Red Cross*, Vol.81, No.833, Mar. 1999, p.66.
39. W.D. Eberwein, *Realism or Idealism, or Both? Security Policy and Humanitarianism*, Berlin: Social Science Research Center (WZB), Discussion Paper (P 01-307), 2001, p.14.
40. N. Ball and K. Campbell, *Complex Crisis and Complex Peace: Humanitarian Coordination in Angola*, New York: OCHA, 1998, p.36.
41. A. Destexhe, *L'Humanitaire Impossible ou Deux Siècles d'Ambiguïté?*, Paris: Armand Colin, 1993, p.209.
42. Macrae (n.26 above), p.158.
43. A study on major French humanitarian NGOs estimates that 40–70 per cent of the personnel leaves the organization after having worked as an expatriate on one project. See J. M. Davis, 'Approche Psychologique de la Médecine Humanitaire. L'Expérience des Médecins Volontaires en Mission Humanitaire à l'Etranger', unpublished dissertation, Université René Descartes Paris V, 1999.
44. L. Minear, 'Learning the Lessons of Coordination', in K.M. Cahill (ed.), *A Framework for Survival: Health, Human Rights and Humanitarian Assistance in Conflicts and Disasters*, London: Routledge, 1999, p.310.
45. Ibid., p.310.
46. Smillie (n.19 above), p.53.
47. ALNAP (n.10 above), para. 3.3.3.
48. K. Van Brabant and T. Killick, *The Limits and the Scope for the Use of Development Assistance Incentives and Disincentives for Influencing Conflict Situations. Case Study: Afghanistan*, Paris: OECD and Development Assistance Committee, 1999, p.6. Several case studies draw a similar conclusion, see A. Taylor and F. Cuny, 'The Evaluation of Humanitarian Assistance', *Disasters*, Vol.3, No.3, 1979, pp.37–42; W. Shawcross, *The Quality of Mercy: Cambodia, Holocaust and Modern Conscience*, New York: Simon and Schuster, 1984; F. Terry, 'Condemned to Repeat? The Paradoxes of Humanitarian Action', Unpublished PhD thesis, Department of International Relations, Australian National University, Canberra, 2000.
49. See, among others, Minear (n.44 above), p.311; Smillie (n.19 above), p.53; Vaux (n.22 above), p.67.
50. M. Walkup, 'Policy Disfunctions in Humanitarian Organizations: The Role of Coping Strategies, Institutions, and Organizational Culture', *Journal of Refugee Studies*, Vol.10, No.1, 1997, p.51.
51. C. Argyris and D. Schön, *Organizational Learning: A Theory of Action Perspective*, Reading, MA: Addison-Wesley, 1978, p.29.
52. Leader (n.23 above), p.42.
53. See Verband Entwicklungspolitik deutscher Nichtregierungsorganizationen (VENRO), *Nachhaltigkeit in der Humanitären Hilfe*, (VENRO-Arbeitspapier No.8). Bonn: VENRO, 1999, pp.2–3.
54. See Macrae (n.26 above), pp.170–72.

Neutrality and the ICRC Contribution to Contemporary Humanitarian Operations

CHARLOTTE KU and
JOAQUÍN CÁCERES BRUN

The emergence of humanitarian operations whose purpose is to protect victim populations in addition to aiding them is presently challenging the well-established and practised principle of neutrality embedded in international humanitarian law. As a leader in the development and practice of international humanitarian law, the International Committee of the Red Cross (ICRC) is deeply associated with the principle of neutrality in its assistance and relief operations. But maintaining this practice of neutrality has become controversial within the humanitarian assistance and relief community, with some organizations implying that maintaining neutrality in instances of gross violations of human rights is tantamount to complicity with those violations. The charges go further to suggest that the practice of neutrality may stand in the way of a permanent and just political solution in a humanitarian crisis. Why then does the ICRC maintain its tradition of neutrality and what contribution does this practice continue to make in today's complex relief operations and peace processes? Can neutrality remain a viable practice in the conflicts and emergencies of the twenty-first century where states may pursue policies of gross violations of human rights against their own people including the elimination of whole groups?

Four episodes of perceived failure to protect victimized populations from the actions of their own governments have caused the international community to reconsider the nature of conflict and to blur the lines between military and humanitarian operations. The four episodes specifically responsible for the conceptual and political shift in the scope of international security are:

Somalia (1992–93) where military forces initially asked to deliver food assistance ended up undertaking a military operation with inadequate preparation and planning, resulting not only in the failure of the missions, but also the loss of soldiers' lives.

Rwanda (1994) where the failure to respond to the humanitarian emergency created an uproar over the inability of the international community to react, as plans were made and carried out by the Rwandan government to destroy its Tutsi population.

Srebrenica (1995) where the UN's failure to ensure the safety of the protected populations in designated 'safe areas' like Srebrenica in the Bosnian conflict precipitated a review of the capacities of peacekeepers to act in a protective role in the face of a determined adversary.

Kosovo (1999) where the ethnic cleaning against Kosovar Albanians by the Bosnian government led to the bombing of Kosovo by North Atlantic Treaty Organization forces without authorization by the UN Security Council.

These episodes have left a legacy that found aid to victims an insufficient response to the crises and led to a view that more had to be done both by governments and by the humanitarian relief organizations.

The blurring of lines between military and humanitarian organizations has led to a reconsideration of peace processes and of key political actors in any given crisis. It has further required a rethinking of the concept of security to include not only the security of the state, but also that of individuals within a state. This changed view of 'victims' in a crisis has expanded the role of some non-governmental relief organizations from providing relief to advocacy for those populations or positions not advanced either by governments or intergovernmental organizations like the UN thereby becoming a factor in creating an enduring and stable political solution.

Several factors contributed to this change:

The development of an international human rights system: Included in the UN Charter in Article 55 as a reaction to the genocide against the European Jewish population by Germany, the international protection of individual human rights has resulted in a world-wide revolution in the status of the individual. Not only is the status and dignity of an individual a matter of general interest to the international community, but it has also increasingly become a matter requiring international action.

The emergence of UN peace operations: As the outgrowth both of the UN Charter's system of peaceful settlement of disputes in Chapter VI and the maintenance of peace and security in Chapter VII, the UN has evolved a range of activities using military forces. These include monitoring and observation tasks, relief operations, and peacekeeping where the purpose of a military presence is to prevent the spread and continued violence until the conflicting parties can arrive at a political solution.

The advent of global communication and focus on the plight of the individual: The 'CNN factor' is often perceived as a factor that stymies robust military operations because of the concern for incurring casualties. But perhaps the more significant impact of the CNN factor is the ability of television viewers today to witness directly the plight of victims through reporting from crises spots around the world. The images of fleeing or otherwise victimized populations have fuelled demands for actions to stop such atrocities. The availability of private organizations with private and government financial resources to provide relief in these situations has created an expectation that something can (and now increasingly the expectation is 'should') be done to stamp out the causes of these atrocities.

As a neutral organization with a long tradition of working with the consent of the relevant governments, can the ICRC remain effective as a relief organization in this new environment of protection? Founded in the nineteenth century to alleviate the suffering caused by armed conflict, the ICRC[1] marked its centennial in 1963. Unique among private voluntary organizations, the ICRC has status under international law.[2] Its work, to serve as a neutral intermediary between parties to conflicts, in order to bring protection and assistance to the victims of war,[3] is based essentially on the Movement's Fundamental Principles of humanity, impartiality, neutrality and independence.[4]

International humanitarian law[5] and UN practice[6] agree on the main characteristics of humanitarian assistance: the obligation of the sovereign state to provide humanitarian assistance and/or to give its consent to ensure that it is provided by humanitarian actors, the right of the civilian population to receive it and the corresponding right of third states, IGOs and NGOs to provide it within certain limits. The International Court of Justice (ICJ), has defined humanitarian assistance as 'the provision of food, clothing, medicine and other humanitarian assistance' and has cited the first and second principles of the Red Cross (to prevent and relieve human suffering without discrimination giving priority to the most urgent cases of distress)[7] as determining the characteristics of such assistance.[8]

The concept of state neutrality[9] has gradually evolved into an international legal practice that comprises a wider set of rights and duties than simple non-belligerent status (non-participation in hostilities). But for the ICRC neutrality stretches beyond security and encompasses ideological and other aspects.[10] In fact, the ICRC attaches a special significance to neutrality, which it sees as (a) one of its attributes, (b) one of the Movement's Fundamental Principles[11] and (c) connected to humanitarian assistance.[12] The principle of neutrality defines its main task – humanitarian assistance – and determines its *modus operandi*: the Movement's Statutes consider the ICRC as a 'neutral institution' and as a 'specifically neutral and independent' institution and intermediary[13] while international humanitarian law describes the ICRC as 'an impartial humanitarian body'.[14] Its conventional and extra-conventional legal bases secure the ICRC's privileges such as the right of access[15] and the right of initiative,[16] but also impose limitations such as the principle of neutrality.

But, even though most humanitarian actors consider themselves neutral,[17] not all of them understand the concept of neutrality in the same way. This may be so because there is no general principle of neutrality and impartiality in general custom and because its various elements (constitutional element, code of conduct, substantive principles, etc.) may vary greatly.[18] Its contents and, above all, its implementation, have been a source of misunderstanding between the ICRC and other humanitarian actors. Other humanitarian organizations may forcefully denounce breaches of human rights and international humanitarian law – an action which the ICRC would take only exceptionally – in situations which in certain cases might even lead them to call for military intervention or, at least, to help build public opinion for such action. According to the majority of humanitarian organizations, there can be no neutrality in cases of grave breaches of international humanitarian law. For example, Médecins Sans Frontières (MSF)

> refuses to wait for the approval of all parties before acting. It insists on the right to speak out in the face of human rights violations. Putting populations in danger first, above political considerations, is engrained as core to our mission – and in this MSF has helped shape the humanitarian movement world-wide.[19]

Can the ICRC maintain credibility as a humanitarian organization in the wake of such sentiments?

Neutrality and Peace-Support Operations

As a result of the changes that have taken place in humanitarian operations and the emergence of a 'military humanitarianism'[20] since 1989, the humanitarian landscape has been altered. Assistance is now provided by political and military actors whose mandates have evolved from those previously limited to providing a secure environment for humanitarian operations to those who now include providing relief. For humanitarian agencies and NGOs, such as the ICRC – whose main task is providing humanitarian assistance to victims of armed conflict in accordance with the principles of humanity, impartiality and neutrality – interaction and, especially, close association with actors in the field who do not operate on the basis of neutrality can pose certain risks not only on the policy level for the humanitarian concept itself but also for ICRC staff in the field.

Recent practice has witnessed an increasing tendency to include assistance to victims of conflict in the agenda of political and military actors whose mandates and roles have evolved in the context of peace-support operations. Such was the case of the Western European Union's *Petersberg Tasks*, which declares that military units of member states could be employed for 'humanitarian and rescue tasks, peacekeeping tasks and tasks of combat forces in crisis management, including peacemaking'.[21] The UN's *Comprehensive Review on the Whole Question of Peacekeeping Operations in All Their Aspects* calls for a more comprehensive approach to peacekeeping missions taking into account their humanitarian aspects.[22] And NATO's Strategic Concept included the new civil and military cooperation doctrine and policy defined as 'The co-ordination and co-operation, in support of the mission, between the NATO Commander and civil actors, including national population and local authorities, as well as international, national and non-governmental organizations and agencies' which recognizes that even though the military will normally only be responsible for security-related tasks and for support – within means and capabilities – of the appropriate authority, where it is not present, or is unable to carry out its mandate or where an otherwise unacceptable vacuum may arise, 'it may be required to take on tasks normally the responsibility of a mandated civil authority, organization or agency until it is prepared to assume them'.[23]

The expansion of these policies into what was until very recently the exclusive realm of humanitarian agencies and NGOs could result in a conflict with the principle of neutrality. This may occur not only because (a) the actors that are called upon to implement such policies are intrinsically non-neutral and (b) assistance through armed force can never be considered humanitarian, but because of its effects on how humanitarian actors will be perceived in the field by parties to conflict when non-humanitarian actors take up their traditional tasks. While it is true that humanitarian action sometimes requires an array of political, military and humanitarian initiatives, when the humanitarian role is assumed by non-humanitarian actors, there is a risk of blurring the divisions which quite clearly must separate strictly humanitarian action from political and even military action, or neutral action from essentially non-neutral action. Not doing so could result in dangerous strategic and operational consequences for those humanitarian NGOs, such as the ICRC, whose legal status and mandates require them to be neutral and whose ability to operate relies on their being perceived as such in all circumstances in order to achieve the ultimate goal of any humanitarian operation – to have access to victims, a purpose that can be facilitated by steadfast adherence to the neutrality principle by all actors involved.

The Protection of Personnel and Loss of Neutrality

One of the issues raised by the difficult relationship between military operations and humanitarian organizations is reflected in the 1994 *Convention on the Safety of United Nations and Associated Personnel*, which does not automatically extend to NGOs the level of protection provided for UN personnel unless a contractual link is established between them and the UN.[24] This clause is the result of the position expressed by the ICRC which stated its desire not to have its personnel afforded the protection established in the treaty, because its application to the ICRC would necessarily imply a fairly close association between it and the UN, a situation which would be complicated further if UN forces were to engage in hostilities. The reasons behind this position are two: ICRC personnel are already entitled to international protection under the Geneva Conventions, and the ICRC would be unable to preserve its ability to fulfil its main task to act as a neutral humanitarian intermediary between parties to conflict if it were granted the same protection provided to UN forces.[25]

The same dilemma faces other humanitarian organizations. MSF asks how it can:

> stay close to the ideal of independence from political forces, of impartiality in conflicts, when the success of humanitarianism has led to an invasion of its sphere by political, military and economic

interests? Today, humanitarianism carries so much emotional and historical weight that it has become a target for manipulation, a smokescreen to conceal entirely self-interested motives. In addition, the 'humanitarian' label is selectively employed. These trends have been obvious in the past year in the very different levels of international response to crises in Kosovo and East Timor, for example, when compared to several places in Africa.[26]

In the context of humanitarian action, neutrality can play such a crucial role that the success or failure of some humanitarian actions has been linked in certain cases to a lack of respect for the principle of neutrality (the violation of the 'code of conduct' that guides action by humanitarian actors) and in others to the attempt to act in strict compliance (the abuse by states of the so-called 'sovereignty clauses' in humanitarian assistance agreements according to their interests).[27]

Efforts to provide relief to Biafra after its break away from Nigeria in the early 1970s was a watershed in humanitarian relief operations when the ICRC, following its practice of neutrality, did not criticize the Nigerian government for its part in starving the Biafrans. The ICRC position caused Bernard Kouchner to resign from the ICRC and to found MSF in 1971 'declaring that the ICRC's silence over Biafra made its workers "accomplices in the systematic massacre of a population"'.[28] A recent survey of humanitarian relief organizations in the United Kingdom revealed that 'neutrality has almost become a 'dirty word'.[29] Other critics see ICRC practice of discretion and silence as reflecting a 'legalistic bias' that 'has shaded into complicity with war crimes'.[30] This tension is even reflected within the ICRC itself where writers like David Forsythe have observed internal divisions between a 'legal culture and a pragmatic operations culture'.[31]

The award of the Nobel Peace Prize to relief organization MSF acknowledged that there were alternatives to neutrality in providing humanitarian relief. MSF founder Bernard Kouchner noted that: 'MSF's work was political from the start. I hope the prize marks the recognition of a type of humanitarian work which fights injustice and persecution, in contrast to traditional organizations'.[32] This perhaps marked the high point of the shift in the humanitarian relief community from the ICRC's tradition of political neutrality and the providing of relief on a needs basis to one of political activism and the providing of relief on a rights basis.

For the ICRC, neutrality affects not only its status but also how it performs its tasks. The ICRC's approach may be equated to the formula: neutrality=confidentiality=trust=access, implying that access to victims – the ICRC's main task – is subject to the parties' prior authorization, which requires gaining their trust based on confidentiality. According to Marco Sassòli and Antoine Bouvier, the ICRC's general approach favours confidentiality, not publicity, cooperation, not confrontation, and access to victims, not investigation of violations.[33] The importance of the 'rule of confidentiality' (which safeguards the legal position of ICRC personnel who might have witnessed human rights law and international humanitarian law violations) has been highlighted by the progressive establishment of several mechanisms to implement international humanitarian law at the international level,[34] and has been expressly admitted by national law[35] and only recently by international law. But the principle of neutrality and its logical consequence, confidentiality, as the best means to assist and protect victims which otherwise might be left unattended or not taken care of, are not to be understood as a synonym for ICRC inaction in case of international humanitarian law breaches and a loophole through which serious violations are going to be silenced.

In fact, the ICRC's neutral attitude towards belligerents and ideologies does not determine its behaviour towards the victims because, under very special circumstances, the rule of confidentiality is subject to exceptions. The ICRC reserves its right to make public statements when: (a) the confidential steps have failed to put an end to major and repeated violations which have been witnessed by its delegates or when their existence and extent have been established by reliable and verifiable sources; (b) going public is in the interest of the persons or populations affected or threatened; and (c) the ICRC considers that the use of a weapon or method of warfare gives rise to an exceptionally grave situation.[36] The rule of confidentiality also guides the standard ICRC working procedure in case of visits to prisoners of war, protected civilians and persons detained for security reasons. The delegates speak with the prisoners of their choice in private and give them the opportunity to exchange news with their families by means of Red Cross messages; they discuss their findings directly with the detaining authorities, submit their recommendations to them and encourage them to take the measures needed to solve any problems of humanitarian concern. The ICRC submits strictly confidential written reports on the delegates' findings to the detaining authorities and in no circumstances does the organization comment publicly on the treatment of detainees or on conditions of detention.[37]

The establishment of the International Criminal Tribunal for the Former Yugoslavia (ICTY), the International Criminal Tribunal for

Rwanda (ICTR), and the International Criminal Court (ICC) has raised the need for a provision safeguarding the legal position of the ICRC's personnel who might witness violations of human rights and international humanitarian law: the importance of the 'rule of confidentiality' has been expressly recognized as customary international law in a landmark decision by the ICTY.[38] Considering whether the ICRC has a confidentiality interest that would entitle it to prevent disclosure of information under conventional or customary international law, it found that:

> The parties to the Geneva Conventions and their Protocols have assumed a conventional obligation to ensure non-disclosure in judicial proceedings of information relating to the work of the ICRC in the possession of an ICRC employee, and that, conversely, the ICRC has a right to insist on such non-disclosure [by said parties and that the] ratification of the Geneva Convention by 188 States can be considered as reflecting the *opinio iuris* of these State Parties, which, in addition to the general practice of States in relation to the ICRC as described above, leads the Trial Chamber to conclude that the ICRC has a right under customary international law to non-disclosure of the Information.[39]

The inclusion of the confidentiality rule in the ICC's Statute has underlined the practical consequences for the ICRC of the implementation of the principle of neutrality. According to the Statute:

> The Court shall regard as privileged, and consequently not subject to disclosure, including by way of testimony of any present or past official or employee of the International Committee of the Red Cross (ICRC), any information, documents or other evidence which it came into possession of in the course, or as a consequence, of the performance by the ICRC of its functions under the Statutes of the International Red Cross and Red Crescent Movement, unless (a) after consultation with the Court the ICRC does not object to disclosure, or otherwise has waived this privilege; (b) the ICRC has made the information public; or (c) independently from the ICRC, the information has been collected from another source.[40]

This provision clearly intends to reinforce the trust that the ICRC must gain from all parties to a conflict. The ICRC's confidentiality approach should not be seen as obstructing justice: considering whether the ICRC's confidentiality interest 'should be balanced against the interests of justice, on a case by case basis, having regard in particular to the importance of the information to the prosecution's case', the ICTY determined that:

> No question of the balancing of interests arises. The Trial Chamber is bound by this rule of customary international law which, in its content, does not admit of, or call for, any balancing of interest. The rule, properly understood, is, in its content, unambiguous and unequivocal, and does not call for any qualifications. Its effect is quite simple: as a matter of law it serves to bar the Trial Chamber from admitting the Information.[41]

For the ICRC, neutrality requires cooperation with actors who may not be neutral or may have a different approach to neutrality. Cooperation with parties to conflict is essential in order to gain access to the victims and most of the time involves negotiations in highly politicized surroundings to reach agreements that will allow the ICRC to exercise its right of access and right of initiative. The ICRC does not judge governmental entities' politics so as not 'to waste its energies in idle diplomatic procedures but so as to gain access to victims in need of help, and these victims are in the power of the States. It is therefore necessary to obtain the required authorization from States and to maintain the relations of confidence essential for continuing co-operation'.[42] The divergent views[43] over the legal status of the prisoners transferred from Afghanistan and detained by US forces at Guantánamo Bay Naval Station have not prevented the ICRC from reaching an agreement with the US allowing the former to exercise its right of access.[44]

The ICRC's relationship with the military is limited to those issues and to an extent that does not compromise the ICRC's neutrality status. According to Meinrad Stauder, the relationship evolves around issues of protection and support. The ICRC has sometimes agreed to put its personnel and assets under the protection of peacekeeping operations and security personnel – the so-called 'technicals' – to guard against petty crime and banditry. Strategically, the ICRC makes use of support when the military takes control over the use of airspace and airport runways, and operationally, through the use of military and civil defence assets, provided that they are placed under the ICRC's direct control, that the conditions offered are conducive to its work and only if no comparable civilian resources are available. Such support from the military is based on a needs-driven, not a resources-driven, policy.[45]

Cooperation between humanitarian actors increased dramatically after a number of UNGA resolutions[46] indicated the need to better coordinate humanitarian aid. The UN has established the Office for the Coordination of Humanitarian Affairs which discharges its functions primarily through the Inter-Agency Standing Committee, a response system for complex emergencies and natural disasters with the participation of all humanitarian partners, including the ICRC. A number of coordination efforts with humanitarian agencies and NGOs also reflect the ICRC's active participation in the improvement of the relationship between relief actors.[47] As practice has shown, the success of these relationships between different actors depends on achieving a better understanding and respect of their mandates.[48]

The ICRC also has specific duties in the implementation of international humanitarian law,[49] limited to the prevention[50] and control[51] of international humanitarian law breaches. Exercising its 'watchdog function' it frequently calls upon all those involved in a conflict to observe international humanitarian law and its underlying principles.[52] How can public denunciations by the ICRC be reconciled with the principle of neutrality? Neutrality is not an end in itself but merely a means to an end so when the welfare of the victims is at stake, humanity is the overriding principle. But the ICRC's participation does not extend to the investigation or repression of such violations,[53] a limitation that has not prevented it from actively supporting the establishment of an international criminal jurisdiction.[54] The ICTY has stated that [the ICTY and the ICRC]

> are two independent international institutions, each with a unique mandate conferred upon them by the international community. Both mandates are based on international humanitarian law and ultimately geared towards the better implementation thereof. Although both share common goals, their functions and tasks are different. The ICRC's activities have been described as 'preventive', while the International Tribunal is empowered to prosecute breaches of international humanitarian law once they have occurred.[55]

The ICRC's implementation of the principle of neutrality has been severely criticized as ineffective and even incompatible with justice when confronted with serious human rights and international humanitarian law violations.[56] Amir Pasic and Thomas Weiss argue that 'Humanitarian efforts have never really been neutral; there is no such thing as "pure" humanitarianism because the distribution of aid always has political ramifications'.[57] But its potential political consequences do not preclude humanitarian action in accordance with the principle of neutrality. In fact, it is precisely in the midst of a political environment where neutrality is most necessary, but only as a means to an end, because humanitarianism is the only subject on the ICRC's agenda. At the same time, according to Minear, neutrality should not be seen as political naïveté: but on the contrary, surviving in the international arena and not being drawn by it, neutrality requires its own form of pragmatism political:

> The real issue, in my judgement, is not whether it is possible for the ICRC to function as a neutral actor in highly politicised landscapes. It is such an actor and it does so function. The critical issue is rather whether its approach is more effective than the route taken by organizations that follow a different paradigm. My own sense is that the ICRC's methodology may indeed correlate more closely with effectiveness, although data to support this judgement remains inadequate and other variables need to be assessed.[58]

And as the experience of NGOs working in North Korea has shown, neutrality is in certain cases *condition sine qua non* to ensure that humanitarian assistance reaches its recipients.[59] The ICTY has admitted that 'on many occasions, and in particular in highly politicised situations, the ICRC is the only humanitarian organization granted access'.[60]

Conclusion

As the cases involving humanitarian intervention increase, so have the number of humanitarian actors with different legal characters, status, and approaches. The character of relief organizations has also changed with many private organizations now receiving large sums of government funds to undertake development as well as relief work.[61] The application of international humanitarian law and the related aid to victims is clear when there is armed conflict between states. But today, humanitarian assistance related to an armed conflict may not be directly related to that conflict alone and may be provided by several organizations, each of which may be pursuing a different mandate (of relief, of development, of reconstruction) and using different approaches – for example, to observe neutrality or not. Humanitarian operations therefore may involve not only the humanitarian operation per se but may also involve political and military action by sympathetic governments. While humanitarian operations can be neutral, military and political activity is generally not, regardless of its humanitarian objectives. At the same time, it is true that all activities within a crisis area have political ramifications whether they are intended or not. This is the case even for the avowedly neutral classic UN peacekeeping that influences eventual political outcomes by 'freezing' a particular conflict situation.

This ambivalence embedded in the concept of neutrality provides a flexible umbrella under which humanitarian organizations have been able to provide relief and assistance. The ICRC has applied the notion of neutrality in its strictest sense – providing aid only after securing authorization from all parties, and not denouncing human rights and international humanitarian law violations except in extreme cases and only when going public was seen as the only means to protect victims against further violations – whereas MSF and other similar organizations do not always expect, ask or wait for authorization and generally forcefully denounce such grave breaches. These differences have led to severe criticism of the ICRC's approach even though critics may not always have taken into account the ICRC's tasks, including the unique role played by the ICRC in the development and implementation of international humanitarian law – a body of law that in some ways paved the way for today's human rights law by addressing the status of individuals under international law.

The rights enjoyed by the ICRC under international humanitarian law are a privilege, but they are balanced by the fact that they are to be exercised by ICRC delegates on the basis of impartiality and neutrality. To assume a different position is thought to jeopardize the ICRC's main role which is to care for the victims of conflict. The ICRC's major asset is acceptance by all parties to a conflict while providing some short-term relief and stability during negotiations for longer-term solutions. This interim role can provide continuity in activities between pre- and post-conflict situations through coordination with the other components of the Red Cross Movement.

At the same time, it may be useful to recall that the ICRC's practices are not static and have changed over time. Building on its long and recognized record of cooperation with governments to bring relief to victims, the ICRC has had a particular advantage in working through channels in order to deliver aid in disaster relief operations. Although more is needed, analysts are optimistic that the ICRC will be able to adapt to new needs. Peter Maclister-Smith wrote:

> The traditional humanitarian activities of the Red Cross fall within a framework of concern for world peace, a mission which

the Red Cross regards itself as entitled to pursue. The original approach of Henry Dunant was not only to respond to human suffering and to mitigate the evils of warfare, but to put an end to war. The realisation, expressed in the Charter of the United Nations, that there can be no true peace when human rights are violated and when inequality, injustice and discrimination prevail, reinforces the view that the discharge of the Red Cross duties of protection, assistance and community service are a contribution to peace. Impartial humanitarian activities and the application of the fundamental Red Cross principles form the basis of this contribution.[62]

If neutrality as practised by the ICRC might be considered a liability in its present-day performance as a humanitarian relief organization, it might also be regarded as the ICRC's greatest asset as the basis for its century-long record of service and world-wide acceptance. If the ICRC remains a neutral institution, limits on its activities are clear. Although the ICRC approach of neutrality may not be adequate to cover all cases of victim protection, there is also little to support the view that the ICRC approach has nothing to contribute to providing relief and protection to victims, preserving a potential role for all political players likely to be needed in any permanent political solution.

Violations of human rights and other crimes can perhaps be most effectively handled by those institutions and bodies of law specifically set up for those purposes. Relief to individuals who have fallen victim to natural disaster or political crisis still appears a viable task as evidenced by the continued donations to and calls for ICRC assistance. The ICRC further remains key to the development of international humanitarian law and to the monitoring of state practice in this area. So for now, humanitarian relief is provided by organizations practising two distinctly different, but equally valuable paths to relieve the immediate suffering of individuals and to provide a safe and secure environment for them. It remains to be seen if adequate relief, protection and political stability can be provided over the long term in this mixed humanitarian environment.

ACKNOWLEDGEMENTS

This essay originated as a paper at the Academic Council on the United Nations System (ACUNS)/American Society of International Law (ASIL) Summer Workshop on Humanitarian Intervention, Windhoek, Namibia, 5–18 August 2001. The authors thank Professor Manuel Pérez González, of Universidad Complutense de Madrid, the ACUNS/ASIL workshop co-directors and the workshop participants.

NOTES

1. Statutes of the International Red Cross and Red Crescent Movement, preamble, arts.3–7.
2. See Christian Dominicé, 'La personnalité juridique international du CICR', *Studies and Essays on International Humanitarian Law and Red Cross Principles in Honour of Jean Pictet*, The Hague: ICRC/Martinus Nijhoff, 1984, pp.663–73.
3. 'Statutes' (n.1 above) arts 5.2(d), 5.3. and 23, of the 1949 Geneva Conventions [hereafter GC], I, 73, 123, 125 and 126; GC III, 14, 59, 61, 140, 142, 143; GC IV, 33 1977 Additional Protocol [hereafter AP] I, common art.3 and 9/9/9/10 common GC.
4. 'Statutes' (n.1 above), preamble and art.5.2(a).
5. Arts.10, 23, 55, 59–61 IV GC, 61–67, 70 AP I and 18 AP II. See also Prosecutor v. Zoran Kupreskić et al., IT-95-16, ICTY Trial Chamber II, Judgement, 14 Jan. 2000, para.519.
6. General Assembly resolutions 43/131 (1988), 45/100 (1990) and 46/182 (1991); 'An Agenda for Peace', UN Doc. A/47/277-S/24111, of 17 June 1992, para.30; Security Council resolutions 688 (1991), 794 (1992), 819 (1993) and 836 (1993).
7. 'Statutes' (n.1 above), preamble, Fundamental Principles of humanity and impartiality.
8. International Court of Justice, *Nicaragua v. US*, Judgement, 1986, paras. 242, 243.
9. See Marion Harroff-Tavel, 'Neutrality and Impartiality: The Importance of These Principles for the International Red Cross and Red Crescent Movement and the Difficulties Involved in Applying Them', *International Review of the Red Cross* No.273, Dec. 1989, pp.536–52; Dietrich Schindler, 'Transformation in the Law of Neutrality since 1945', *Humanitarian Law of Armed Conflict – Challenges Ahead*, in A.J.M. Delissen and G.J. Tanja (eds.), Dordrecht: Martinus Nijhoff, 1991, pp.367–86; Maunce Torrelli, 'La neutralité en question', *Revue Genérale de Droit International Public* Vol.96, No.1, 1992, pp.5–43.
10. Jean Pictet, *Commentary on the Fundamental Principles of the Red Cross*, ICRC, Geneva, 1979, pp.52–60.
11. 'In order to continue to enjoy the confidence of all, the Movement may not take sides in hostilities or engage at any time in controversies of a political, racial, religious or ideological nature'. 'Statutes', preamble (n.1 above).
12. Denise Plattner, 'ICRC Neutrality and Neutrality in Humanitarian Assistance', *International Review of the Red Cross*, No.311, April 1996, p.162.
13. 'Statutes' (n.1 above), arts5.2(d) and 5.3.
14. Common art.3 and arts 9/9/9/10 GC and 5.3 AP I.
15. Arts 126 III GC and 143 IV GC.
16. Common art.3 GC and 'Statutes' (n.1 above), art.5.3.
17. MSF 'observes neutrality and impartiality in the name of universal medical ethics and the right to humanitarian assistance and demands full and unhindered freedom in the exercise of its functions', *The Charter of Médecins Sans Frontières*, accessed at: www.msf.org/about/index.
18. Marc Weller, *The Relativity of Humanitarian Neutrality and Impartiality*, www.jha.ac/articles/a029.htm.
19. MSF International Activity Report 2000, 'The Year in Review', http://web.archive.org/web/20010417174232/www.msf.org/publications/activ_rep/2000/2000review.htm.
20. David Chandler, 'The Road to Military Humanitarianism: How the Human Rights NGOs Shaped a New Humanitarian Agenda', *Human Rights Quarterly*, Vol.23, Aug. 2001, pp.678–700.
21. WEU Council of Ministers, 'Petersberg Declaration', Bonn, 19 June 1992, Pt II, para.4.
22. 'Brahimi Report', UN Docs. A/55/305 and S/2000/809, 21 Aug. 2000. See also follow-up reports, UN Docs. A/55/502, A/55/507, A55/977 and A/56/732.
23. *Military Policy on Civil–Military Co-operation*, NATO Doc. MC 411/1 (2000). See also NATO's *Compendium of Views and Experiences on Humanitarian Aspects of Peacekeeping*, Annex to EAPC(C)D(99)5(revised).
24. Art.1.b (iii).

25. Antoine Bouvier, 'Convention on the Safety of United Nations and Associated Personnel: Presentation and Analysis', *International Review of the Red Cross*, No.309, Dec. 1995, pp.655–6.
26. MSF (n.19 above).
27. 'A Freedom Fighter Speaks', *Newsweek*, 9 Apr. 2001, p.36.
28. Chandler (n.20 above) p.684.
29. Ibid., p.695.
30. Michael Ignatieff, 'International Committee of the Red Cross (ICRC)' in Roy Gutman and David Rieff (eds.), *Crimes of War: What the Public Should Know*, New York: W.W. Norton, 1999, pp.202–4.
31. David P. Forsythe, 'Humanitarian protection: The International Committee of the Red Cross and the United Nations High Commissioner for Refugees', *International Review of the Red Cross*, No.843, Sept. 2001, p.693.
32. As quoted in Chandler (n.20 above) p.695.
33. Marco Sassòli and Antoine A. Bouvier, *How Does Law Protect in War?*, ICRC, Geneva, 1999, pp.291–3.
34. Daryl A. Mundis, 'New Mechanisms for the Enforcement of International Humanitarian Law', *American Journal of International Law*, Vol.95, No.4, Oct. 2001, pp.934–52.
35. The Headquarters Agreements concluded between the ICRC and some 69 states provide varying degrees of protection against the requirement to give evidence. See ICRC, *Annual Report 2001*, p.35
36. 'Guidelines in the Event of Breaches of International Humanitarian Law', *International Review of the Red Cross*, No.221, April 1981, pp.81–3.
37. Arts 126 GC III and 143 GC IV. See also ICRC press release 02/03, 18 Jan. 2002.
38. Prosecutor v. Simic et al., IT-95-9, ICTY Trial Chamber III, Decision of 27 July 1999, para.73.
39. Ibid., paras.73 and 74.
40. *Rome Statute for the International Criminal Court*, Rules of Procedure and Evidence, Privileged Communications and Information, sub-rules 73.4-73.6, adopted by consensus by the PrepCom on 30 June 2000. See Stéphane Jeannet, 'Testimony of ICRC Delegates Before the International Criminal Court', *International Review of the Red Cross*, No.840, Dec. 2000, pp.993–1000.
41. ICTY (n.38 above) para.76.
42. Pictet (n.10 above) p.59.
43. While the US considers them as 'unlawful combatants' (for failing to respect international humanitarian law, or to wear identifying insignia or to carry arms openly), the ICRC considers these detainees as prisoners of war and therefore entitled to the protection under the Third Geneva Convention (see ICRC press release 9 Feb. 2002). See also the Organization of American States' Inter-American Commission on Human Rights decision of 12 Mar. 2002 adopting precautionary measures, according to which it asks the US government 'to take the urgent measures necessary to have the legal status of the detainees at Guantánamo Bay determined by a competent tribunal'. See www.humanrights.org.
44. ICRC press release (n.37 above).
45. See Meinrad Stauder, 'The ICRC and Civil–Military Relations in Armed Conflict', *International Review of the Red Cross*, No.842, June 2001, pp.378–84.
46. Resolutions 46/182 (1991), 47/168 (1992), 48/57 (1993), 49/139 (1995) and 50/57 (1996).
47. Code of Conduct for the Red Cross Movement and NGOs in Disaster Relief (1994), the Humanitarian Charter and Minimum Standards in Disaster Response developed by the Sphere Project (1997), the Humanitarian Accountability Project (HAP) (2000) and the International Federation of the Red Cross's International Disaster Response Law Project (2001).
48. Ted A. van Baarda, 'A Legal Perspective of Cooperation Between Military and Humanitarian Organizations in Peace Support Operations', *International Peacekeeping*,

Vol.8, No.1, Spring 2001, pp.99–116.
49. 'Statutes' (n.1 above), Art.5.2(c).
50. Arts 5.2(g), 5.4(a) and 10.2, ibid., and 6 AP I.
51. 'Statutes' (n.1 above), Arts 5.3, 5.2.(c)–(d) and 5.4. See also Arts 9, 23 GC I, 9 GC II, 9, 73, 123, 125–126 GC III, 10, 14, 59, 61, 140, 142–143, 146 GC IV and 33 AP I, 10/10/10/11 GC, Common Art.3.
52. *Inter alia*, ICRC press releases 00/42 (21 Nov. 2000), 01/58 (23 Nov. 2001).
53. 'Action by the International Committee of the Red Cross in the Event of Breaches of IHL', *International Review of the Red Cross*, No.221, April 1981, pp.76–80.
54. Marie-Claude Roberge, 'The New International Criminal Court: A Preliminary Assessment', *International Review of the Red Cross*, No.325, Dec. 1998, pp.671–91; Special Issue: 'International Criminal Jurisdiction and International Humanitarian Law: The Tribunals for the Former Yugoslavia and for Rwanda', *International Review of the Red Cross*, No.321, 1997.
55. ICTY (n.38 above) para.79.
56. Alain Destexhe, *Rwanda: essai sur le génocide*, Brussels: Editions Complexe, 1994. This criticism is not new, in fact it goes back to Second World War. See Jean-Claude Favez, *The Red Cross and the Holocaust*, Cambridge: Cambridge University Press, 1999.
57. Amir Pasic and Thomas G. Weiss, 'The Politics of Rescue: Yugoslavia's Wars and the Humanitarian Impulse', *Ethics & International Affairs*, Vol.11, 1997, p.113. See also Thomas G. Weiss, 'Principles, Politics and Humanitarian Action', *Ethics & International Affairs*, Vol.13, 1999.
58. Larry Minear, 'The Theory and Practice of Neutrality: Some Thoughts on the Tensions', *International Review of the Red Cross*, No.833, Mar. 1999, pp.68, 70.
59. 'Diary of a Mad Place', *TIME*, 22 Jan. 2001, pp.36–9; 'The Man Who Knew Too Much', *Newsweek*, 22 Jan. 2001, p.60.
60. ICTY (n.38 above) para.71.
61. See Chandler (n.20 above) pp.678–700.
62. Peter Macalister-Smith, *International Humanitarian Assistance: Disaster Relief Actions in International Law and Organization*, Dordrecht: Martinus Nijhoff, 1985, p.88. See also David P. Forsythe, 'Human Rights and the International Committee of the Red Cross', *Human Rights Quarterly*, Vol.12, May 1990, pp.265–89.

Human Rights NGOs in
UN Peace Operations

FELICE D. GAER

How to protect human rights in the places where abuses occur has long been a concern of those seeking to advance human rights. In the UN context, an initial period of human rights standard setting began in 1945 and was followed by an era beginning in the 1970s instigating efforts to implement those norms. UN investigators – 'special rapporteurs' – were appointed to examine charges of human rights violations, case by case. Early human rights work at the UN was largely theoretical, legal and inexpensive. Human rights protection was advanced in conference rooms in New York and Geneva, and was then buttressed by short-term visits by 'special rapporteurs' to certain hot spots where violations were most pronounced.

During the past decade, however, personnel have begun to be dispatched beyond UN headquarters in Geneva or New York on a long-term basis to on-site operations in countries where individuals suffer human rights problems or seek human rights assistance and protection. Such deployments of human rights experts –'field presences' – have varied in size, duration, mandate and the UN agency responsible for managing them. These human rights field-based programmes are often complicated and can be very expensive.

There are now more than 25 UN human rights 'field presences' with hundreds of on-site staff.[1] Many have been dispatched in the context of peace operations, while some were also originally emergency deployments.

In response to these developments, human rights nongovernmental organizations (NGOs) have tried to inject human rights concerns into the decision-making process of establishing and running those peace programmes. Accordingly, they have argued that human rights issues are central to peace agreements and to peacekeeping, and that human rights components should be part of every such peace and other complex field operation that is launched.[2] To accomplish this international human rights NGOs have used a number of advocacy methods with which such groups have typically excelled: to expose

facts and report on them publicly; to demand new machinery tailored
to meet the needs revealed by the reporting; and to engage directly
with government representatives formulating mandates to establish
field presences and new machinery, mainly through the United
Nations.

Early on, several major non-governmental human rights
organizations reported on the performance of a series of human rights
monitoring operations established as part of the earlier peace processes
in El Salvador or the complex peace operations established in former
Yugoslavia and Rwanda, or the joint UN/OAS Civilian Verification
Mission in Haiti (MICIVIH).[3]

Peace processes of the 1990s opened the door to on-site UN
peacekeeping operations containing human rights components, most
commonly engaged in monitoring and reporting. With these efforts,
often dubbed 'verification' of peace agreements rather than 'human
rights monitoring', there emerged a new human rights product and
approach, consisting of more than human rights reports written by
outside investigators. Training and institution building became a focus
of some of these programmes.

Individuals, from governments and international institutions on the
one hand, and from non-governmental organizations, on the other,
were involved directly or indirectly in these monitoring and training
programmes. Freed from the conference rooms of Geneva and New
York, the new human rights field presence programmes have provided:

- monitoring, investigations, and reporting about human rights
  compliance;
- technical assistance, capacity building and training of local activists;
- protection and security for civilians under threat; and/or
- coordination and facilitation of human rights activities by other
  international actors outside of the bureaucratic responsibility of the
  Office of the UN High Commissioner for Human Rights, including
  the Department of Peacekeeping and the Department of Political
  Affairs.

NGOs and Field Operations

The inclusion of human rights activities in peace operations began at a
time when the human rights movement and its NGO advocates had
still been focused on refining advocacy techniques that would improve
the treatment of individuals affected by repression. The predominant
paradigm of human rights repression was characterized by an

authoritarian leader who caused political repression of dissidents and who, when pressured enough, freed people simply by issuing an order. Change took place one prisoner at a time. The tactics used were 'the mobilization of shame' (that is, monitoring followed by public reporting), along with demands for the release of those unjustly detained. Press releases and public reports were key to this activism. Non-governmental groups developed advocacy and reporting techniques grounded in solid facts.

A second, closely related avenue of NGO activism focused on communicating with decision-makers, both nationally and internationally. Armed with precise information, communicated persuasively, human rights NGOs often mobilized decision makers to take action; they also often set the agendas of governments, especially in the UN's human rights programmes, to address the matters they presented so meticulously.

A third approach had developed primarily in situations in which human rights NGOs were able to be present in a country. This involved delivering services such as legal aid, training in public advocacy, and providing education so individuals and groups will 'know their rights' and how to act upon them. Advocates often developed a new perspective: some moved from the vantage point of being 'outsider' human rights critics to becoming 'insiders' concerned with prevention of abuses, protection of civilians, and institution-building which extended beyond political and legal civil society organizations to development programmes as well.[4]

In the 1980s and 1990s, the NGO movement's information and reporting approach was transferred into the United Nations Commission on Human Rights, the preeminent international human rights deliberative body. Special rapporteurs or working groups of experts were being created within the United Nations human rights machinery and authorized to examine information, including on cases affecting individual victims of human rights abuses, cases of torture, disappearances, political killings and free speech. Human rights treaty bodies were established to monitor and review country reports on their compliance with norms.

In the 1990s, and especially following the end of the cold war, human rights matters moved from the margins to the centre of foreign affairs policy. The emergence of ethnic and religious struggles, genocide in Rwanda and Bosnia, and massive refugee outflows, all brought a search for new solutions through preventive diplomacy and humanitarian intervention. Human rights solutions have been a focus of much of this search, particularly when examining ways to address 'root causes' of conflicts. In those years, new human rights institutions, from 'truth commissions' to war crimes tribunals to national human rights commissions were set up to identify those responsible and hold perpetrators to account for their actions. These were authorized in some instances by the Security Council as part of peace agreements, or, in the case of the International Criminal Tribunal on Former Yugoslavia, as a means of bringing pressure to bear as part of a larger-scale effort aimed at both peacekeeping and negotiating a peace agreement.[5]

The same years saw the expansion of UN peace operations from those that sent lightly armed military personnel to control buffer zones and monitor ceasefires to different field-based programmes engaged in peacebuilding actions, forging peace agreements, preventive deployment, and supervising complex peacekeeping missions. In El Salvador, the UN-brokered San Jose accords of July 1990 provided for human rights monitoring, which went into operation by mid-1991, beginning an important new venture for UN peacekeeping and for the field of human rights. In 1991, the Paris Accords ending Cambodia's civil war included a human rights public education component and broad authority to conduct investigations and 'corrective action', as part of a major UN peacekeeping effort aimed at preventing a return to 'policies and practices of the past' – the genocide and repression of the Khmer Rouge. The latter peace operation saw the first UN appointment, in January 1993, of a Special Prosecutor to bring human rights abuse cases into a judicial setting. That ambitious mandate was not realized in practice.[6]

In January 1992, the first Security Council meeting at the level of heads of state and government asked Secretary-General Boutros Boutros-Ghali to develop a report on settling conflicts and improving peace operations. In *An Agenda for Peace,* Boutros-Ghali affirmed that 'Increasingly, peacekeeping requires that civilian political officers, human rights monitors, electoral officials, refugee and humanitarian aid specialists, and police...play as central a role as the military'.[7]

NGOs Critical of UN Peace Missions

A year later, with peacekeepers in El Salvador and Cambodia buttressed by human rights 'verifiers', the NGO human rights community increasingly expressed disappointment about the way such missions were staffed, operated, and attended to. The reporting by UN missions was also questioned as incomplete and inadequate. The major human rights NGOs advocated a simple goal: more attention needed to be paid to human rights in UN peace operations. Because they had been monitoring human rights violations in the countries concerned, international human rights NGOs had a variety of on-site local activist contacts from which they gathered information and insights. Some groups had on-site staff members based in the countries. Such contacts gave them an independent perspective on the human rights reporting and actions conducted by the UN officials as part of the peace missions.

Often, they were appalled by what they saw. Accustomed to public reporting, the NGOs used their well-honed monitoring and reporting technique to focus on the UN peace missions, looking at them as a group, rather than complaining separately about the UN peace missions in El Salvador and in Cambodia. Amnesty International remarked that these programmes are 'developed in an ad hoc and uncoordinated way and with little or no involvement of the Geneva-based human rights bodies'. Worse, Amnesty complained, 'human rights concerns are still too often marginalized or excessively compartmentalized within the UN system'.[8] With plans in progress for the first UN World Conference on Human Rights since the divisive 1968 Tehran World Conference, these same human rights NGOs began to advocate in favour of actions to ensure that human rights would permeate the work of the UN system, especially its peace operations. In a December 1992 document prepared to help focus attention on the Vienna World Conference on Human Rights (scheduled for June 1993), Amnesty International concluded that the UN 'is increasingly called upon to play a major role in internal conflict situations which present particularly acute human rights crises' and has developed some 'innovative and far-reaching initiatives in the context of recent UN peacekeeping and peacebuilding operations'.

What was needed, the Nobel-prize winning NGO stated, was an early warning and an emergency response capacity in a human rights crisis. And more than that, the UN should begin an expert comparative review of all its experiences with human rights in peace missions and their effectiveness.[9] From an advocacy perspective, these issues could be attended to if the participating governments in the World Conference were to create a high level 'Special Commissioner' for human rights – a different title for the longstanding NGO demand for a UN High Commissioner for Human Rights. The need for that post had been raised by human rights NGOs associated with the UN since shortly after the world organization was founded. Amnesty International, sensitized to what it perceived to be a 'colonialist' tone to the term 'High Commissioner', now proposed a new title for an old

idea. And like other NGO activists focused on the changing shape of
UN human rights operations, Amnesty understood that the
'commissioner' could play a role in influencing New York-based peace
operations, and not merely in conference room diplomacy.

London-based Amnesty International had an office with full-time
representatives at UN headquarters in New York who pressed for
attention to the organization's human rights concerns. As they observed
developments in the Security Council and with peace operations, they
increasingly focused on the need to develop a new form of advocacy,
aimed at the members of that 15-member body. During the same time
period, New York-based Human Rights Watch did not have such an
office or official responsible for UN operations, but was nonetheless
active with Security Council members. Human Rights Watch, which
would later add such a post to its senior staff positions, was deeply
involved in monitoring human rights in Central America, Iraq, and
elsewhere and was acutely aware of the need for a more effective
presence and role of UN field monitors when deployed. The
organization's New York base afforded them an opportunity to bring the
conclusions of their country experts to the attention of the diplomats and
international civil servants engaged in establishing, supervising, and most
importantly, reporting on the new human rights peace operations.

In June 1993, as the World Conference on Human Rights was
convening in Vienna, Human Rights Watch released a 173-page report,
dramatically entitled *The Lost Agenda: Human Rights and UN Field
Operations*. It combined the organization's assessments of five large
UN peace operations – El Salvador, Cambodia, Iraq, Somalia, and
former Yugoslavia. The report argued that human rights concerns had
been 'given a low priority by the officials who oversee UN field
operations', and that despite the rhetoric being quite good,
'enforcement is...weak'. Moreover, the organization insisted, human
rights should be seen as 'a central element in the success of UN
peacekeeping'. But, instead, upholding human rights had become a
marginal item in peace operations, which generally prioritized getting
a final peace agreement over enforcing or verifying human rights
guarantees which were included in preliminary agreements.[10] The
result of this 'downgrading human rights' in the field, HRW explained,
is 'damaged credibility, operational missteps, and impaired
effectiveness' of peace operations themselves.[11] These failings resulted
from certain structural problems associated with the UN's approach to
peace and conflict: misguided neutrality, diplomatic caution,
operational blackmail, and the cost and complexity of field operations
in human rights.[12]

The UN was put on notice: Amnesty's complaint that mandates and programming by human rights units of peace operations were being reinvented by those outside the human rights programme would now be heard. When would the international community face up to the latest failures about which the organization had written? Human Rights Watch, with its media focus, and armed with detailed country-specific assessments also highlighted the issue as a failure of the UN. A certain indignation was added to the sweeping assessment of failure: why support all those UN human rights programmes meticulously drafting norms, all those special rapporteurs and treaty bodies, and large meetings in Geneva, if a few planners at New York headquarters and field mission personnel could redefine both what constituted core human rights and how to measure those rights? And, what was worse, how could this be done without any consultation with Geneva-based personnel as to their content, meaning, and reach? Human Rights Watch called for a High Commissioner for Human Rights to be appointed and based in New York, as a part of an effort 'to raise the profile of human rights within the UN bureaucracy and to facilitate the flow of human rights information to the Secretariat and Security Council'.[13]

Boutros-Ghali publicly opposed the idea of a senior-level High Commissioner, explaining on the eve of the conference that 'striking new departures on behalf of human rights have occurred just in the past year' including integrating human rights into peacekeeping and peacemaking.[14] He concluded pointedly that 'proposals for new bureaucracies, [and] high level positions...may only arouse discontent and resistance...This is a time for dialogue'. Human rights activists disagreed publicly. And so did the United States delegation, led by Under Secretary of State Timothy Wirth, which pressed not only vigorously but effectively for the creation of the post of High Commissioner. Together, the assembled 171 states at the Vienna World Conference on Human Rights also recommended that the UN (1) 'assume a more active role in ... human rights ... in ensuring full respect for international humanitarian law in armed conflicts' and (2) 'take into account the reporting, experience and capabilities of the Centre for Human Rights and human rights mechanisms' in peacekeeping operations, particularly regarding human rights components of peace operations.[15] The doctrinal authority to integrate human rights more fully in peacekeeping was now a priority concern not only of NGOs, but the entire human rights movement, including governments. The post of High Commissioner, encouraged in the Vienna document, was established by the General Assembly that autumn.

Establishment of High Commissioner

Much has happened to expand field presences in human rights since the creation of the post of UN High Commissioner for Human Rights (UNHCHR) in December 1993. The first High Commissioner, Jose Ayala Lasso of Ecuador, took office a day before the Rwandan president's plane was shot down, triggering genocide in the country. Lasso soon called for an emergency session of the Commission on Human Rights, where a special rapporteur was appointed, to be aided by a number of officers posted in the field. Two officers were sent to the field; but it took time before many more followed. Although the Geneva-based Centre for Human Rights had no track record of field involvement, it would dispatch over a hundred monitors to the field over the following year. The mandate included investigating the past, monitoring the present, providing technical cooperation, and promoting local-level conflict resolution.[16]

The UNHCHR then responded to these charges in a confidential document sent to donor missions, rebutting, point by point, alleged inconsistencies and inaccuracies in the Africa Rights report. Amnesty International also visited and criticized the managerial problems stemming from Geneva's operational inexperience, substandard recruitment, and inadequate briefing and guidelines. A lack of regular and public reporting by the Rwanda human rights field mission contributed to the controversy about its effectiveness. So, too, its unclear relationship to the UN's regular peace mission in the country. Although the early missions could be criticized for acting outside the Geneva framework, the Rwanda mission revealed quite starkly the incapacity of Geneva to recruit, launch, and manage an emergency mission on its own. The need for better methodologies and better 'lessons learned' exercises could not be more clear. NGOs have been writing about the mission ever since, critiquing its operations, design, staffing, supervision, financing, and implementation.

UN Secretary-General Kofi Annan, who took office in 1997 and who had previously served as head of UN peacekeeping operations, and as a temporary head of the field mission in Bosnia, seemed to accept NGO arguments about the importance of 'mainstreaming' human rights, but also the need to do it well if human rights monitors were sent to the field. Early in his first term, he publicly identified human rights as a 'cross-cutting issue and vital component of all aspects of the UN's work' including humanitarian and peacekeeping efforts. More significantly, he has made additional resources available for the expansion of human rights activities in New York, and assigned the

UNHCHR, who is based in Geneva, to serve on each of the four Executive Committees he has established to set policy on UN affairs. His actions show an unprecedented understanding of the importance of the subject of human rights, but even more significantly, an acceptance of the NGO demand that human rights programming could not be conducted in splendid isolation from the very heart of UN operations on human rights based in Geneva. Calling the next century 'the age of prevention', Kofi Annan has helped inject human rights issues into all aspects of the world body's activities, notably those conducted by the UN Security Council and the development bodies. The second High Commissioner, Mary Robinson, did so as well, buoyed by the new level of support for human rights stemming from the UN's front office.

The mandate establishing the post of High Commissioner had called for an 'active role' in meeting challenges to full realization of human rights and in preventing violations, and for measures aimed at securing respect for all human rights. The concept of an 'active role' in the High Commissioner's mandate reflected the hopes of non-governmental activists who advanced and supported the position's creation for decades before it was established. The establishment of field missions had helped ensure the United Nations could carry out such measures 'at ground level'. NGOs had helped advocate for, and shape, the mandate for the war crimes tribunals on former Yugoslavia and Rwanda, as they had done for the post of High Commissioner. While the major human rights NGOs recognized there were many areas in which they could be engaged with field presences, they turned their considerable energies largely to the shaping of the mandates of specific field presences. It was in many ways the issue on which human rights NGOs could have the maximal multiplier effect.

NGOs Focus on Mandates of Peace Operations

Since the early 1990s, human rights NGOs have paid considerable attention to the formulation of mandates for promoting and protecting human rights that are set out in the resolutions and Memoranda of Understanding which authorize peace operations, and particularly their human rights functions. This is quite consistent with the norm-setting function conducted over a period of decades by human rights NGOs. With such a focus, human rights NGOs can strive for the best authorizing language on permissible human rights protection for field missions in a conflict or post-conflict situation. The intensity with which they have fought for precise language in the numerous human rights instruments adopted by the UN can be and was easily transferred to their advocacy with the 15-member Security Council.

The importance that human rights NGOs attached to the mandate of each peace operation can be explained by several factors. First, there has been longstanding resistance by some governments, most notably China, and before 1991, the Soviet Union, to admitting *any* reference to human rights into the work of the Security Council. Humanitarian law standards or humanitarian emergencies would, from time to time, merit mention as they pertained to war; but human rights was quite another matter. If the human rights function is not explicitly and firmly spelled out in the mandate of a peace mission, it is more likely that governments will later reject human rights activities or personnel being deployed in the field. Second, most major international human rights NGOs lack operational and in-country experiences in peacekeeping or peacebuilding missions, making it easier for them to focus on a headquarters issue like defining a strong mandate. Third, those NGOs that do have direct operational on-site experience can work behind the scenes with UN bureaucrats in considering the approaches and mandates needed; some have even served as consultants to the UN to train or otherwise help improve performance in the field. Finally, NGOs and others commonly encounter resistance, both at headquarters and in the field, from on-site mission leaders and central office specialists alike who insist that various desirable actions cannot be done because it was not explicitly authorized in the mandate. In short, mandates matter.

William O'Neill, a former human rights NGO leader, and top manager and consultant to UN human rights field missions, notes that mandates and terms of reference are often a key to effectiveness. For example, he describes the shortcomings of the joint UN-Organization of American States mission to Haiti (MICIVIH): 'The terms of reference did not mention the importance of working with Haitian groups, especially local human rights and civic organizations. Some Haitian human rights activists believed that '[we] had come to replace them. There were serious misunderstandings and lack of trust' between the UN mission and 'what should have been its most natural and crucial local partners'.[17] Such misunderstanding can easily be avoided if mandates clearly articulate human rights responsibilities.

There is great diversity – by function, managerial responsibility, size and duration – in the mandates authorizing different field presences. Such mandates can be limiting or empowering regarding the promotion and protection of human rights. Among the most useful analyses of the UN field presences have been book-length studies of human rights and post-conflict institution building convened by the Aspen Institute's Justice and Society Program. Two conferences produced volumes assessing UN human rights field operations, large and small. In each case, personnel who served in UN field missions in human rights were principal authors, but it was an NGO that convened the group, and brought other NGO experts to argue with and critique their findings.

In a May 1998 speech, Mary Robinson paid specific tribute to the work of the NGO think tank, the Aspen Institute, and stated that she endorsed the conclusions of their two books. In referring to the recommendations by the NGO think tank's consultants, she pointed to their emphasis on the need for 'clear methodologies ... careful planning, training, the identification of stable funding sources, recruitment of [experienced] persons' as well as balancing monitoring and advisory functions in such field missions.[18] Robinson further emphasized that 'we must integrate human rights work into peacekeeping', which remains the most consistent human rights NGO goal regarding the Security Council and peace operations.[19] Significantly, the first Aspen volume urged that UN field presences 'should guarantee the independence of human rights reporting from ongoing political negotiations'.[20] While sensitive to this issue, the High Commissioner differed slightly, noting that the issue of whether or not to make public the information gathered may vary, but 'the integrity of monitoring and reporting processes must always be protected'.[21]

The Brahimi Report and Human Rights

After Secretary-General Kofi Annan appointed a Panel on UN Peacekeeping Operations, headed by Lakhdar Brahimi, former foreign minister of Algeria, a report on this complex issue was produced quite speedily.[22] This was followed quickly by another study, by the Secretary General, on the implementation of the panel's report.[23]

Both were breakthroughs in the UN because of their recognition of the value of human rights personnel and approaches as part of peace operations. Particularly important in this regard was the affirmation that Office of the HCHR needs to be more closely involved in the planning and design of human rights components of peace operations, including the definition of effective human rights strategies and the integration of human rights perspectives and methodologies into other components of peace operations. Serious attention must be paid to these recommendations, including, in particular (1) creating a standardized system for information management (which would presumably include the issue of standardized reporting of human rights information) and its consistent application in peace operations, (2) the need for a new system of vetting candidates to serve as human rights personnel in such missions, and (3) creating partnerships with non-governmental organizations and national institutes to advance these ends. Before this report was written, all of these issues have been raised directly by NGOs, with reference to the various human rights field presences.

The Brahimi Report can be seen as a natural outgrowth of the earlier work and recommendations on a regular and timely basis by human rights NGOs who have closely watched the expansion of field-based human rights missions so closely. The Brahimi report itself appears aimed at finding ways to utilize human rights expertise. It particularly emphasizes the need to better coordinate human rights missions, and to involve personnel at early stages of planning for integrated mission task forces in New York.

The Brahimi Report's emphasis on human rights and conflict prevention, identification of applicable law in a conflict, or how to conduct lessons-learned exercises are potentially of major significance. These issues draw their inspiration from the writing of NGOs as well as former participants in UN field operations who publish memoirs and participate in lessons-learned exercises. They do not, however, represent a path on which human rights NGO experience has ready-made solutions to offer.

The Brahimi Report recommends, for example, that there be efforts to 'develop cooperative arrangements and partnerships with non-governmental organizations...with a view to establishing standby arrangements for the staffing of human rights components of peace operations'.[24] It is worth noting that many of the staff of UN human rights field missions come from human rights non-governmental organizations; indeed, so have many of the heads of the missions.

Today, peace operations in most of the recently created UN programmes have human rights components. Kosovo, East Timor and Sierra Leone, among others, contain important on-site human rights components; only the longstanding older missions do not. From the beginning the new peace operations have been heavily dependent upon human rights NGOs – both international groups and those located in and near the country in which the UN programmes are located. Personnel from NGOs have played a leading role in advocating for and designing human rights operations for these projects, and have helped staff many of these programmes. They have been engaged in all aspects – from the development and refinement of relevant norms, to the promotion of legal systems that implement them, to staffing, operationalizing and critiquing them. The movement to develop human rights mainstreaming in UN peace operations has been heavily promoted by human rights NGOs.

One of the most significant endorsements of the Brahimi Report was Kofi Annan's statement that:

> I fully agree with the Panel's conclusions on the centrality of human rights to United Nations peace activities and on the need to integrate human rights more effectively into prevention, peacekeeping, and peace-building strategies. To this end, it is necessary to strengthen the Organization's capacity both to plan, conceptualize and deploy human rights elements of peace operations.[25]

In this way the highest UN official has taken up and reaffirmed the main goal sought by Amnesty International, Human Rights Watch and other human rights NGOs: the affirmation of the centrality of human rights to all UN programmes.

It is of course, one thing to affirm that human rights are central to the UN's work across the board, and another to work to make it so. Many different functions are conducted by the field presences run by the High Commissioner's office. Such mandates encompass monitoring and reporting of human rights developments; assisting in human rights capacity building; coordinating technical assistance projects, electoral assistance, facilitating truth and reconciliation processes including addressing impunity, supporting human rights components of peace operations, and assistance to UN partner organizations, country teams, regional organizations. Great emphasis is increasingly placed on the protection components in human rights field presences, with acknowledgement of the ways in which presence itself, combined with facts, reports, public advocacy and support of the role of other non-governmental actors can all advance practical protection in the field.[26]

Such positive affirmation of the central, indeed vital role of human rights NGOs in UN peace operations, and the articulation of new functions that can be accomplished by such NGOs, is not without its critics. Some observers argue that NGOs can have a 'disruptive' effect on peace negotiations and related conflict resolution efforts. Others complain that human rights NGOs bring values opposed to the use of force and prioritizing the prevention of violence in world affairs, thereby prolonging conflicts. As was argued regarding the Dayton peace talks on Bosnia, people were dying there and NGOs who sought a perfect outcome should accept some responsibility for this.[27] Some say that by monitoring human rights of one or another group, NGOs try to empower them in the conflict. Or that too much attention on building civil society in transitional society prohibits the strengthening of the state and its own concentration of power and legal control.[28]

Human rights NGOs have emphasized the importance of 'mainstreaming' the relevance of human rights into other fields of endeavour, among them peace operations, humanitarian assistance, and development programmes. One critic of mixing rights-based strategic ends with the humanitarian ideal has gone so far as to argue that the mix has justified 'the denial of humanitarian principles'. UNHCR, it is claimed, is taking on 'a new, more invasive role as a human rights actor' by dealing with 'root causes' of refugee problems. Those who would link respect for human rights with the provision of aid, the argument goes, have distorted the humanitarian project. 'Through the human rights discourse, humanitarian action has become transformed from relying on empathy with suffering victims and providing emergency aid to mobilizing misanthropy and legitimising the politics of international condemnation, sanctions, and bombings'.[29]

But other observers have argued that 'a comprehensive, well designed human rights strategy can buttress a conflict resolution strategy, and…the integrated application of both approaches is required for sustainable peace'.[30] Indeed, those who would criticize the role of human rights NGOs with regard to UN peace operations may not be familiar with the very humanity of the norms which are being upheld by these groups or the range of activity undertaken, the impact these groups have had on the mandates adopted, personnel involved, and assistance to civil society groups and partners for UN programmes and projects on the ground. Where humanitarian groups concentrate on relieving the suffering of individuals after or while abuses are occurring, the human rights organizations, and particularly those focused on field-based presence and protection, are focused on the protection of civilians from attack or persecution in the first place.

Observations

Advocacy at the UN Security Council in the 1990s transformed a conviction by human rights NGOs that the subject of human rights had to be central to UN peace operations from the margins to the mainstream. This required not only advocacy but a receptive environment, headed by officials who value the role of human rights in securing long-term peace and security.

Attention is needed on ways to sustain such programmes including establishing closer partnerships with other UN agencies, national governments and/or civil society institutions. An enthusiasm for in-country field presences can lead to a heightened awareness of resource constraints and what is possible and sustainable in such programming. Human rights NGOs emphasize the need for 'sustainable human rights' – in which local capacity and institutions are developed.

The difficulties inherent in sustaining such a large array of programmes should lead human rights NGOs and others to a discussion of resources, capacities and exit strategies, but it is rare that NGOs consider such matters. The usual NGO concern is to question why governments do not provide added resources and enable international programmes to be made more perfect, as recommended in their reports and critiques. More often than not, comparative opportunity costs are cited as a reason for putting more money into preventive human rights monitoring and less into armed conflict.

All of the human rights field presences run by the Office of the High Commissioner (except Cambodia) are financed from voluntary contributions. And there are very serious limits on what can be sustained.

Mainstreaming human rights calls for the appointment of human rights officers in every UN agency or programme, as well as the presence of regional officers focused on national capacity building. There is clearly a need for more serious strategies for entry and exit – and some realism – about UN human rights field presences, monitoring and peace operations. Mainstreaming human rights does not merely add to the list of things to be done by UN peacekeeping missions, it adds value to the things already being done by them and other UN agencies. Some field presences have been created as alternatives to 'ordinary' human rights scrutiny by a special rapporteur – the Colombia programme being the most prominent example of this. Indeed, it was a far more effective programme than appointing a special rapporteur would have achieved; but only because the office of the High Commissioner had a clear interest in it. Such a programme was not, however, a peace operation of the Security Council or related body.

Partnerships help sustain a field presence and render it more effective. Non-governmental organizations are a key factor, but much depends on whether UN agencies are willing to engage in true partnerships or not. The need for realistic explanation of the mandate and the meaning of human rights terms to governmental and intergovernmental agencies is worth attention – when these terms are used casually, they may not be advanced but merely devalued.

Human rights field presences have been a genuine breakthrough in the UN by moving human rights issues out of the conference room and directly to the individuals, institutions and societies where these issues are being explored, developed, and implemented in often difficult circumstances, pre- and post-conflict. These programmes are only at the beginning of their development. Much work remains for human rights NGOs to do as a part of this process.

NOTES

1. OHCHR website, www.unhchr.ch/html/menu2/5/field.htm.
2. See Amnesty International, 'Peace-Keeping and human rights', IOR 40/01/94, Jan. 1994, esp. pp.35 ff.; Human Rights Watch, *The Lost Agenda: Human Rights and UN Field Operations*, New York, 1993, see esp. pp.8–11.
3. Ibid.; see also, Lawyers Committee for Human Rights, *Improvising History: A Critical Evaluation of the UN Observer Mission in El Salvador*, 1995; and *Learning the Hard Way: The UN/OAS Human Rights Monitoring Operation in Haiti, 1993–94*, 1995.
4. Felice D. Gaer, 'Reality Check: Human Rights NGOs Confront Governments at the UN', in Thomas G. Weiss and Leon Gordenker (eds.), *NGOs, the UN and Global Governance*, Boulder, CO: Lynn Rienner, 1996, pp.57–8.
5. See the exchange between: Anonymous, 'Human Rights in Peace Negotiations', *Human Rights Quarterly*, Vol.18, No.2, 1996, pp.249–58 and Felice Gaer, 'UN–Anonymous: Reflections on Human Rights in Peace Negotiations', *Human Rights Quarterly*, Vol.19, No.1, 1997, pp.1–8.
6. See articles by Diego Garcia Sayan, Denis McNamara, and Ian Martin in Aspen Institute (Justice and Society Program), *Honoring Human Rights and Keeping the Peace: Lessons from El Salvador, Cambodia, and Haiti*, Washington DC, 1995; Human Rights Watch, *The Lost Agenda*, 1993, pp.37–74 on Cambodia; Lawyers Committee for Human Rights, *Improvising History: A Critical Evaluation of the UN Observer Mission in El Salvador*, 1995. Also see Michael Doyle, *UN Peacekeeping in Cambodia: UNTAC's Civil Mandate*, Boulder: Lynn Rienner. On the Bosnian peace agreements, see Christine Bell, *Peace Agreements and Human Rights*, Oxford: Oxford University Press, 2000.
7. UN Doc. A/47/277-S/24111, 17 June 1992.
8. Amnesty International, *Facing up to the Failures: Proposals for Improving the Protection of Human Rights by the United Nations*, IOR 41/16/92, pp.4–5.
9. Ibid., p.19.
10. Human Rights Watch, *The Lost Agenda*, p.1.
11. Ibid.
12. Ibid., pp.5–7. Human Rights Watch made similar arguments in the reports that followed in subsequent years. For example, see 'Angola: Between War and Peace', Feb. 1996; 'Bosnia-Hercegovina: A Failure in the Making', June 1996.
13. Ibid., p.8.
14. *Washington Post*, 9 June 1993.
15. Vienna Declaration and Programme of Action, UN Doc. A/CONF.157/23, paras 96, 97.
16. Martin (see n.6 above), pp.100–101. London-based Africa Rights first studied and reported on the deployment: it questioned the mission's intentions, management, standards, investigations, and recruitment. See also Aspen Institute (Justice and Society Program), *Honoring Human Rights: From Peace to Justice*, 1998. T. Howland, 'Mirage, Magic, or Mixed Bag? The UN High Commissioner for Human Rights' Field Operation in Rwanda', *Human Rights Quarterly*, 1999, Vol.21, pp.1–55.

17. William F. O'Neill, 'Gaining Compliance without Force: Human Rights Field Operations', in S. Chesterman, *Civilians in War*, Boulder, CO: Lynn Rienner, 2001, p.102.
18. Address by Mary Robinson, International Symposium 'Strengthening Human Rights Field Operations', Bonn, 26–27 May 1998, p.1.
19. Ibid., p.2. See also, 'Human Rights: An Integrated Approach', Amnesty International Report 1998, pp.53–65.
20. Aspen (n. 6 above), p.19.
21. Robinson speech (n.18 above), p.4. For another perspective on the deliberate failure to publicize human rights reporting conducted within a field mission, see K. Cain, 'The Rape of Dinah: Human Rights, Civil War in Liberia and Evil Triumphant,' *Human Rights Quarterly*, 1999, Vol.21, pp.1–55.
22. UN doc. A/55/305-S/2000/809, known as the Brahimi Report. Its principal drafter had worked with the Henry Stimson Center, a security-oriented NGO in Washington, but not with a human rights NGO.
23. Report of the Secretary General on the implementation of the Panel on UN Peace Operations', UN doc. A/55/502, 20 Oct. 2000.
24. Ibid., para.245.
25. Ibid., para.144.
26. See, for example, Diane Paul, 'Protection in Practice: Field-Level Strategies for Protecting Civilians from Deliberate Harm', Relief and Rehabilitation Network, Paper No.30, July 1999.
27. See Anonymous (n.5 above).
28. Norbert Ropers, 'Eight critical statements on the contribution of NGOs to Conflict Prevention and Transformation', which while noting the high esteem of NGOs in preventing and transforming violent conflicts, cites some of these critical views.
29. David Chandler, 'The Road to Military Humanitarianism: How the Human Rights NGOs Shaped a New Humanitarian Agenda', *Human Rights Quarterly*, Vol.23, No.3, 2001, pp.678–700.
30. James Kunder, 'How Can Human Rights Be Better Integrated into Peace Processes? A Conference Report', Fund for Peace, Washington DC, 1998, p.3.

Sexual Violence:
NGOs and the Evolution of
International Humanitarian Law

FRANCES T. PILCH

Some argue that 'the logics of peace and justice are contradictory'. Whereas peace is forward looking, seeking reconciliation between former enemies, justice is seen by some as backward looking, seeking punishment for those who have committed past crimes.[1] However, the argument can be made that 'until such time as those guilty of crimes against humanity are brought to book as we move from a culture of impunity to a culture of international accountability, the local populace will feel neither secure nor at peace'.[2]

The prosecution of crimes of sexual violence that have occurred during internal or international conflict is both alike and different from prosecution of other egregious violations of human rights and international humanitarian law. It is alike in that most crimes involving sexual violence are as serious as grave breaches of the Geneva Conventions. They are also crimes against humanity, despite the fact that this was not accorded full recognition until 1998 – the year when J-P Akayesu was convicted by the International Criminal Tribunal for Rwanda (ICTR) in Arusha for rape crimes against humanity and when the ICC statute specified rape as a crime against humanity. It is different because crimes involving sexual violence pose difficult questions concerning issues of witness protection, command responsibility, and rules of evidence. Victims and their families may be reluctant to come forward when questions of 'honour' are involved. However, there is an important distinction between individual incidences of rape and sexual violence, and a pattern of crimes of this type in which particular minorities or groups are targeted. In the latter case, rape becomes part of a strategy of war and terror. When this occurs, sexual violence can be an assault not only on the individual victim, but also on communities, religious values, and even entire national, religious, racial or ethnic groups. In the famous Akayesu judgment, the ICTR found that rape had taken place in the context of genocide, and may itself constitute genocide.[3]

While peace may be defined as simply the absence of conflict, sustained peace requires respect for the rule of law. While some may see the prosecution of crimes of sexual violence as a quest for retribution, others, including this author, see it as an indispensable part of norm recognition and institution building for the protection of human rights. In some cases national criminal justice prosecutions may be utilized, in others truth commissions may be the best vehicle to use. In the most egregious cases, the new International Criminal Court may serve as the most effective venue for justice; in other cases, ad hoc tribunals may still be constructed. Generalization concerning the mechanisms for dealing with crimes of sexual violence may not be possible. A recognition of their importance, however, is critical for the construction of norms and institutions that cement peace.

NGO Responses to Sexual Violence

The relationship between justice and the deterrence of crimes, or of conflict itself, is widely debated. Some advocate amnesty for perpetrators of crimes during conflict or prefer the kind of truth commission approach utilized in South Africa. Others believe that justice is an indispensable ingredient of peace. The UN Secretary-General, Kofi Annan, in his introductory message concerning the Rwandan tribunal, noted that 'there can be no healing without peace; there can be no peace without justice; and there can be no justice without respect for human rights and rule of law'.[4]

In February 2001, the International Criminal Tribunal for Yugoslavia (ICTY) handed down a landmark decision in the march towards justice for the victims of sexual violence during war. Three former Bosnian Serb commanders received sentences ranging from 12 to 28 years for raping, enslaving and torturing Muslim women and girls in 1992.[5] Although the Ad Hoc Tribunals had dealt before with questions concerning rape and genocide, this case, commonly referred to as the Foca case, was the first in which the tribunals had dealt solely with rape and sexual enslavement, treating them as crimes against humanity. Presiding Judge Florence Mumba noted that: 'Rape was used by members of the Bosnian Serb armed forces as an instrument of terror. The three accused are not ordinary soldiers whose morals were merely loosened by the hardships of war... they thrived in the dark atmosphere of the dehumanisation of those believed to be enemies'.[6]

Students of international relations have frequently noted the explosion of non-governmental organizations and their increasing impact within the international system. Women's groups and other non-governmental organizations with a human rights focus have made significant progress in bringing instances of sexual violence to the attention of the international community. They have researched and documented abuses, urged international aid agencies to pay attention to victims of sexual violence and to formulate plans for dealing with widespread rapes and pregnancies, and have pressed tirelessly for justice for victims. In the cases before the Ad Hoc Tribunals on the former Yugoslavia and Rwanda, they have pushed for indictments to include crimes of sexual violence and have provided *amicus curiae* (friends of the court) briefs. In the debates concerning the Statute of the International Criminal Court and its rules and procedures, NGOs have lobbied for important provisions on the legal treatment of sexual violence, forcible pregnancies and sexual slavery.

The Vienna Conference on Human Rights and the Beijing Conference on Women provided the impetus for the growth and intercommunication of many women's advocacy groups. Modern technology has facilitated communication between activists and groups interested in human rights. Most of the important groups and coalitions of groups are closely intertwined – often sharing expertise and databases. Many of them have well-developed websites and sophisticated e-mail lists. Most work in concert with grass roots organizations, often worldwide. Their conscientious advocacy, collective expertise, and information and education campaigns have greatly contributed to a genuine revolution in the international law dealing with sexual violence. Because so many hundreds of groups are active, only the actions and achievements of a few can be documented here. However, they are representative of a pattern of interest articulation that is truly altering the face of the international system and its conduct of international legal affairs concerning sexual violence.[7] This essay explores the involvement of non-state actors in the evolution of international law on sexual violence in terms of (1) documentation of human rights abuses; (2) contribution to legal indictments, judgments and interpretations; and (3) inclusion of a gender-sensitive perspective into the Statute of the International Criminal Court.

NGOs have often been in the vanguard of reporting on sexual violence in areas of conflict. Their reports have documented incidences of rape, placed the incidents in the context of the conflicts, and suggested legal interpretations of those crimes. Documentation of crimes of sexual violence has not only raised public consciousness but also provided invaluable information for criminal investigations. These reports have encouraged the international community, through the

UN, to name Special Rapporteurs in many areas of concern. Investigative reports by NGOs are valued as independent assessments of human rights crises. Because organizations such as Human Rights Watch, Médecins Sans Frontières, and Amnesty International have excellent working relationships with grassroots organizations, they are often able to investigate where others fear to, or are unable to, tread. Examination of the testimony before the Commission on Security and Cooperation in Europe in 1993, indicates the importance of NGOs in providing documentation of systematic rape in the former Yugoslavia.[8] The work of Amnesty International, Helsinki Watch, and the US Committee for Refugees in substantiating claims of widespread rape of women during the conflict in Bosnia and Herzegovina was critical to an understanding of the systematic nature of these crimes.[9] Their contributions were noted in several of the Helsinki Commission hearings. In another example of the documentation efforts of NGOs, Physicians for Human Rights, a non-governmental organization, assembled an international team of female physicians under the auspices of the UN Commissioner on Human Rights to investigate reports of widespread rape and other forms of sexual abuse. In addition to documenting instances of rape, the reporting team instituted standard questionnaires for rape victims and argued that the collection of information about rape in war 'must be handled by professionals trained to gather legal testimony and to recognize the psychological vulnerability of victims of rape'.[10]

Equality Now is an NGO devoted to the rights of women. Its activist branch, the Women's Action Network, consists of almost 20,000 members in more than one hundred countries around the world.[11] The Vice-Chairman of the Board of Directors of Equality Now testified before the Commission that she had just returned from Bosnia and Herzegovina, where she had spoken to 'hundreds of survivors of rape camps and concentration camps'. She noted that 'women are being raped and killed systematically just because they are Muslim.'[12] Equality Now was also active in assisting with the Final Report of the UN Commission of Experts, under the direction of Cherif Bassiouni, which preceded the establishment of the ICTY by the UN Security Council.[13]

The investigations into sexual violence in the former Yugoslavia conducted by the European Community noted the use of 'a wide variety of interlocutors', including refugee centres and governmental and non-governmental organizations.[14] Refugee organizations were often critical sources of information. The Women's Commission for Refugee Women and Children, which also led a team to Croatia and

Bosnia, issued a report entitled 'Balkan Trail of Tears – On the Edge of Catastrophe', that chronicled crimes of violence against women. Frequently, investigation teams would visit refugee centres and interview aid workers and refugees themselves. In the Kosovo crisis, this pattern was repeated. A report on internal displacement in Kosovo and its impact on women and children noted that volunteer physicians working with the displaced were seeing signs of sexual abuse among the refugees, although the women themselves were often reluctant to speak of rape.[15]

As issues affecting women gained attention, several of the human rights NGOs incorporated special 'women's rights' units into their organizations. These units have employed very able personnel who have produced some insightful documentation and legal commentary on issues of sexual violence. For example, Human Rights Watch, in cooperation with several other NGOs, corroborated many accounts of rape. The conclusions of their report included classifying rapes into three categories – rapes in women's homes, rapes during flight, and rapes in detention.[16] The report asserted that Serbian and Yugoslav authorities knew that rape was going on, yet no precautions were taken to further prevent such war crimes. The report noted that the ICTY has jurisdiction over the crimes committed in Kosovo, but that so far, no indictments had listed charges relating to the use of rape and other forms of sexual violence. An important contribution of reports such as these has been the clarification of international law concerning sexual violence through a review of recent judgments of the tribunals and other courts on sexual violence.[17]

Human Rights Watch was also responsible for a groundbreaking report on sexual violence that accompanied the genocide in Rwanda in 1994. This report, *Shattered Lives: Sexual Violence during the Rwandan Genocide and its Aftermath*, documented rape, sexual mutilation, forced pregnancy and sexual slavery that had taken place. It noted that rape was directed primarily against Tutsi women because of both their gender and their ethnicity. It argued that 'The extremist propaganda which exhorted Hutus to commit the genocide specifically identified the sexuality of Tutsi women as a means through which the Tutsi community sought to infiltrate and control the Hutu community. This propaganda fuelled the sexual violence perpetrated against Tutsi women'.[18] This report had direct implications for the activities of the Ad Hoc Tribunal on Rwanda, including the landmark case of Jean-Paul Akayesu, which linked the crime of rape with genocide.

In another international crisis, that pertaining to East Timor, sexual violence has also been a tool of war. In the violence and destruction that followed East Timor's vote for independence from Indonesia in 1999, scores of women were raped, tortured and humiliated by the Indonesian military and by members of local militias, opponents of independence. A report by East Timor's leading women's aid association, Fokupers, carefully documented these abuses.[19] A newly created tribunal in East Timor will hear charges of rape in one of its first cases.

Rape has also been widespread during the recent crises in Sierra Leone. In its report 'Sexual Violence within the Sierra Leone Conflict', Human Rights Watch not only documented the perpetration of sexual violence but also placed these acts in the context of the development of international law. The report states that the Human Rights Watch had conducted extensive research on sexual violence and had taken hundreds of testimonies throughout the war and from all areas of the country.[20] It also noted collaborative efforts among organizations such as Médecins Sans Frontières, Forum for African Women Educationalists, Cooperazione Internazionale, UNICEF, and the International Rescue Committee in response to the crisis. A task force representing these and other actors had been set up to deal specifically with sexual violence; several counselling centres and a network of medical practitioners, to treat victims were also instituted.[21]

In addition to providing indispensable documentation of sexual abuse during armed conflict, NGOs have been exceptionally active in providing expert legal interpretation and advice. UN Security Council Resolutions 798 and 820 condemned the reports of 'massive, organized and systematic detention and rape of women' in Bosnia.[22] These resolutions and media reports of the 'rape camps' played a large role in ensuring that rape was included within the jurisdiction of the Statutes of the Ad Hoc Tribunals. The first prosecutor of the Tribunals, Justice Richard Goldstone, who was extraordinarily sensitive to issues of sexual violence, noted that:

> Nongovernmental organizations also played a significant role in supporting the work of both the Yugoslavia and Rwanda tribunals. Soon after I arrived in The Hague, I was besieged by thousands of letters and petitions signed by people, mostly women, from many countries, urging me to give adequate attention to gender-related war crimes.[23]

The *Akayesu* case of September 1998 proved to be a watershed case in the development of international law dealing with sexual violence.[24] When Jean-Paul Akayesu, the mayor of the Taba commune in Rwanda, was first charged in 1996, the 12 counts in the indictment did not include sexual violence. During early testimony in the Akayesu case, one of the three tribunal judges questioned a witness who had described witnessing the rape of her daughter (the prosecution had failed to do so). Based on this record and subsequent testimony, several NGOs, including Equality Now, wrote to the Chief Prosecutor, then Louise Arbour, urging her to amend the indictment to include charges of rape in this case. An *amicus curiae* brief was filed by the Coalition on Women's Human Rights in Conflict Situations in May 1997.[25]

This brief, incorporating the input of many legal scholars, provided a convincing legal argument for the inclusion of the sexual violence charges in an amended indictment. The brief was signed, among others, by representatives from the International Centre for Human Rights and Democratic Development (Montreal and Kigali), the International Women's Human Rights Law Clinic of the City University of New York, the Working Group on Engendering the Rwandan Criminal Tribunal (Toronto), and the Center for Constitutional Rights (New York) on behalf of the NGO Coalition on Women's Human Rights in Conflict Situations.

The brief attempted to show that the Trial Chamber had the authority and responsibility to ensure that rape and other forms of sexual violence be properly charged and also that a factual and legal basis existed to warrant its intervention in this regard. Section 5 of the Introduction indicated that 'this intervention is precipitated by concern that the Prosecutor has not charged rape and sexual violence, despite testimony in the record, and other documentation indicating the availability of other probative evidence, that sexual violence was part of a campaign of violence constituting genocide, crimes against humanity, and war crimes under Articles 2,3, and 4 of the Statute.'[26]

Finally, the brief established a convincing argument for Jean-Paul Akayesu's criminal responsibility for the rape of Tutsi Women in Taba. Under V (2) it stated that Akayesu could be held criminally liable for the sexual violence against Tutsi women if it could be proven that he 'knew or had reason to know that the subordinate was about to commit such acts or had done so and [as] the superior [he] failed to take the necessary and reasonable measures to prevent such acts or to punish the perpetrators thereof'.

Their cooperative effort was rewarded by one of the most important decisions ever rendered in the field of international law. The indictment was amended to include Counts 13-15, Crimes Against Humanity (rape), Crimes Against Humanity (other inhumane acts), and Violations of Article 3 Common to the Geneva Conventions and of Article 4(2)(e) of Additional Protocol 2, as incorporated by Article

4 (e) (outrages upon personal dignity, in particular rape, degrading and humiliating treatment and indecent assault).[27]

In September 1998, Jean-Paul Akayesu was found guilty of genocide and crimes against humanity by Trial Chamber I of the International Criminal tribunal for Rwanda. In addition to the fact that this was the first conviction of the crime of genocide under international law, the case was remarkable in its explicit inclusion of rape as an instrument of genocide. The *Akayesu* judgment included a definition of rape and a clarification of sexual violence. 'The Chamber defines rape as a physical invasion of a sexual nature, committed on a person under circumstances which are coercive. Sexual violence, which includes rape, is considered to be any act of a sexual nature which is committed on a person under circumstances which are coercive'.[28] This broad and gender-neutral definition of sexual violence provided the framework for discourse on rape in the subsequent work of the tribunals.

Another issue concerning which the NGO Coalition on Women's Human Rights in Conflict Situations has been very active is that of witness protection. The issue has continually evoked controversy, as the rights of defendants are balanced against the needs of witnesses to be protected against retaliation and humiliation.[29] Women's advocacy groups have worked to ensure the protection of those who have testified before the tribunals on matters involving sexual violence. For example, in a letter to Louise Arbour, Chief Prosecutor of the ICTY and ICTR in 1997, the Coalition asserted that the danger to past and future witnesses who testify before the ICTR is clear, and that protection of 'all people who cooperate with the Tribunal at any stage' could be facilitated by more cooperation with Rwandan women's groups, the use of trauma counsellors, advisors on the trial process, and the provision of follow-up counselling.[30] Other initiatives have included efforts to preserve anonymity of witnesses, sometimes even from defence counsel, through darkened glass and voice-altering devices. In addition, a 24-hour hotline was instituted in conjunction with the Tribunals for witnesses to use if their safety was threatened in any way.

The provision of expert analysis and information on this issue by NGOs is further exemplified by the extensive report by the Coalition on Witness Protection, Gender and the ICTR, that fully explored several reprisal killings and intimidation of witnesses and others who had cooperated with the ICTR. The report noted that the Rwandan women's community was comprised of survivors of sexual violence who were often the only ones who could provide information and testimony. It urged that several steps be taken to improve communication with potential witnesses and to better ensure their protection in general. The report was especially critical of the relationship between the ICTR and Rwandan women's associations. It noted the lack of communication between the ICTR and the women's groups, which it felt could be a valuable bridge between the work of the tribunal and the community at large.[31]

The work of NGOs on witness protection has borne unanticipated fruit. It has led to a new endeavour on 'restitutive justice', or assistance to victims. This concept has been pioneered to complement the retributive justice against perpetrators of crimes such as genocide, crimes against humanity and war crimes. In a recent press briefing, an ICTR spokesman noted that 'in the context of the proposed permanent International Criminal Court, several non-governmental organizations and some Governments, in response to and in agreement with the Registrar's [of the ICTR] advocacy, [have] pushed for the inclusion of such a framework in the Rome Statute of the International Criminal Court (ICC), leading to the provision for a Trust Fund for victims in the Statute of that Court'.[32]

Women experts and women's organizations have been critical actors in formulating the provisions of the Statute on the International Criminal Court. They have been active in the negotiations on the proposed court from the beginning. Pre-eminent among these has been the Women's Caucus for Gender Justice. Avril McDonald, a leading expert on the relationship between international law and women's issues, notes that 'clearly the NGOs, especially the Women's Caucus for Gender Justice, hugely influenced the provisions concerning sexual violence, substantive and procedural, and were especially effective in countering the Arab states and the Vatican's opposition to broadening the definition of sex crimes, and especially to the criminalization in the Statute of forced pregnancy'.[33]

An ever-broadening international delegation of feminist attorneys and advocates brought a gender perspective into the United Nations negotiations on the ICC. 'Engendering' has come to mean not only the critical attention paid to crimes of sexual violence against women, but also the fair representation of women in these institutions. Since Justice Goldstone, all of the Chief Prosecutors of the ICTY/ICTR have been women, and women have also been appointed as tribunal judges. Women's groups also lobby for the use of female investigators in the gathering of evidence on rape and other crimes involving sexual violence, arguing that women may be more comfortable sharing their histories with other women rather than with men. Yet, the importance of gender balance on the bench of the Tribunals is still not recognized. In March 2001, the General Assembly elected the 14 judges who will serve on the ICTY from November 2001 to 2005. Only one, Florence Ndepele Mwachande Mumba (Zambia) is a woman. In fact, she was the only female among the 25 nominees.

Reports from the ICC Preparatory Commissions (PrepComs) describe the early lobbying of groups such as the Women's Caucus on issues ranging from gender balance on the court to the inclusion of crimes of sexual violence, such as forcible impregnation, as crimes against humanity in the Statute. These issues required great skill in negotiation. For example, the question of gender representation needs to be balanced with considerations concerning geographic balance and the criminal trial experience and expertise of prosecutors and judges.[34] After a hard-fought debate, the Statute was written to include 'a fair representation of female and male judges' and states parties were directed to 'take into account the need to include judges with legal expertise on specific issues, including, but not limited to, violence against women or children'.[35]

The above examples have shown that NGOs have been influential in documentation of cases of sexual violence, in providing legal interpretations and expertise, and in lobbying for gender-sensitive perspectives in the Tribunals and the ICC. One of the principal characteristics of the organization and behaviour of NGOs today is the cooperation between various actors – state and non-state, NGOs themselves, and groups of experts and individual experts with state and non-state actors. The advent of the Internet and the vast possibilities for communication have augmented this revolution in cooperation. For example, the Rights and Democracy Program, based in Montreal, promotes cooperation between quasi-governmental institutions and non-governmental organizations to create a formidable force in the human rights arena. Created in 1988 by Canada's Parliament, this programmme is a non-partisan organization with an international mandate to encourage and support the universal values of human rights and the promotion of democratic institutions and practices around the world.

NGOs that have been involved in the development of international law on sexual violence come in all shapes and sizes, and function both independently and collaboratively, formally and informally. Their 'most salient feature is diversity'.[36] Each group – from the grassroots women's organizations in Latin America and Africa to the new breed of caucuses and coalitions that sometimes draw on hundreds of groups and individual members – has made important contributions, enhanced by the new paradigm of global, instantaneous communications.

Conclusion

NGOs have played critical roles in the developing system of international criminal justice. Their roles are evolving daily, and certainly few anticipated the coalition formations between NGOs and the proliferation of NGOs themselves that has occurred. The interrelationship between peace, prevention of conflict, and justice is still widely debated. However, it is clear that NGOs will continue to play major and unexpected roles in the journey towardsjustice for victims of breaches of international humanitarian and human rights law. It is clear that NGOs have contributed extensively to the profound revolution taking place concerning issues of sexual violence in international law. Not only have they collected information and participated in the education of the public, they have also utilized the technological revolution to communicate their information and their message, and to forge ties with each other. They have mobilized expert legal assistance and sought gender balance on the tribunals and as a goal in the Statute of the International Criminal Court. They have pursued an agenda to ensure that the tribunals have paid attention to sexual violence and have treated it with the gravity it deserves. They have fought for the treatment of sexual violence as crimes of the most serious nature in the Statutes of the Ad Hoc Tribunals on the former Yugoslavia and Rwanda and the International Criminal Court, and have achieved major victories along the way. NGOs are changing the way in which international law is evolving – and bringing the world a little closer to the goal of universal justice.

ACKNOWLEDGEMENT

This article is solely the work of the author and should not be attributed in any way to the US Department of Defense or the US Air Force Academy.

NOTES

1. Ramesh Thakur, 'Cambodia, East Timor, and the Brahimi Report', *International Peacekeeping*, Vol.8, No.3, Autumn 2001, p.123.
2. Ibid.
3. Prosecutor v. Jean-Paul Akayesu, Judgment, No.ICTR-96-4-T, 2 Sept. 1998, reported in *The New York Times*, 3 Sept. 1998, p.A14.
4. Kofi Annan, Introductory Message, International Criminal Tribunal for Rwanda Brochure, United Nations, 4th edn., available from Press and Public Affairs Unit, ICTR, Arusha, Tanzania.
5. *The New York Times*, 23 Feb. 2001, pp.A1 and A10.
6. Cited in www.news.findlaw.com/news/s/20010222/warcrimesrapedc.html.

7. Scholarly literature on gender issues in international law and human rights has greatly expanded knowledge in these areas. See for example, Kelly Dawn Askin and Dorean M. Koenig, *Women and International Human Rights Law*, Ardsley, NY: Transnational Publishers, 2000; Vesna Nikolic-Ristanovic, *Women Violence and War*, Budapest: CEU Press, 2000; Lois Ann Lorentzen and Jennifer Turpin, *Women and War Reader*, New York: New York University Press, 1998.

8. The Organization for Security and Cooperation in Europe (OSCE) monitors human rights in Europe.

9. Reported in Alexandra Stiglmayer, 'The Rapes in Bosnia-Herzegovina', in Alexandra Stiglmayer (ed.), *Mass Rape: The War Against Women in Bosnia-Herzegovina*, Lincoln, NB: University of Nebraska Press, 1994.

10. OSCE, 'War Crimes and the Humanitarian Crisis in former Yugoslavia', 25 Jan. 1993, p.74.

11. E-mail to the author from Jessica Neuwirth, President of the Board of Equality Now, 18 Mar. 2001. Equality Now's website address is www.equalitynow.org.

12. OSCE (n.10 above), 25 Feb. 1993, p.7.

13. *Final Report of the United Nations Commission of Experts Established Pursuant to Security Council Resolution 780 (1992)*, UN Doc. S/1994/674/Add.2 (Vol.V), 28 Dec. 1994. Annex IX of this report dealt specifically with 'Rape and Sexual Assault'.

14. OSCE (n.10 above), appendix.

15. Julie Mertus, *Internal Displacement in Kosovo: The Impact on Women and Children*, June 1998, available at www.law.onu.edu/organizations/international/displaced.htm.

16. Martina E Vandenberg and Joanne Mariner, 'Kosovo: Rape as a Weapon of "Ethnic Cleansing"', *Human Rights Watch Report*, Vol.12, No.3 (D), Mar. 2000.

17. Human Rights Watch, *Shattered Lives: Sexual Violence during the Rwandan Genocide and its Aftermath*, New York, 1996. See, for example, Section V, 'International and National Legal Protections against Rape and Other Forms of Sexual Violence', pp.30–34, accessed at www.hrw.org/hrw/summaries/s.rwanda969.htm.

18. Ibid.

19. *The New York Times*, 3 Mar. 2001, pp.A1 and A10.

20. See www.hrw.org/backgrounder/africa/sl-bck0226.htm.

21. Ibid.

22. UN Doc. S/RES/798 (1992), 18 Dec. 1992, see esp. p.1, UN Doc.t S/RES/820, 1993, 17 Apr. 1993, esp. para.6.

23. Richard J. Goldstone, *For Humanity*, New Haven: Yale University Press, 2000, p.85.

24. *Prosecutor v. Jean-Paul Akayesu*, Judgment, No.ICTR-96-4T, 2 Sept.1998, accessed at www.un.org/ictr/english/judgements/akayesu.html. Also *The New York Times*, 3 Sept 1998, p.A14.

25. The *Amicus*, accessed at www.ichrdd.ca/111/english/commdoc/publications/womtrirw.htm.

26. Ibid., p.2.

27. *Amended Indictment, Prosecutor of the Tribunal Against Jean-Paul Akayesu*, Case No.ICTR-96-4-I, accessed at www.ictr.org/ENGLISH/cases/Akayesu/indictment/actamond.htm.

28. *Akayesu*, sec.6, para.4.

29. See, for example, Monroe Leigh, 'Editorial Comment: The Yugoslav Tribunal: Use of Unnamed Witnesses Against Accused', *American Journal of International Law*, Vol.90, 1996, p.235.

30. *Letter to Justice Louise Arbour, Chief Prosecutor of the ICTY and ICTR*, 17 Oct. 1997, from the NGO Coalition on Women's Human Rights in Conflict Situations, accessed at www.ichrdd.ca/111/english/commdoc/publications/womtrirw.htm.

31. Connie Walsh, *Witness Protection, Gender and the ICTR: A Report Prepared as a Result of Investigations in Rwanda in June and July 1997*, for the Centre for Constitutional Rights, International Centre for Human Rights, and Democratic Development, International Women's Law Clinic, and MADRE, accessed at www.ichrdd.ca/111/english/commdoc/publications/womtrirw.htm.

32. *Press Briefing by the Spokesman for the ICTR,* 19 Oct. 2000, accessed at www.ictr.org/English/pressbrief/brief191000.htm.
33. E-mail communication from Avril McDonald to author, 22 Feb. 2001.
34. *TerraViva,* No.13, 1 July 1998, p.4. *TerraViva* was the NGO newsletter at the Rome Conference.
35. Rome Statute for the International Criminal Court, UN Doc.A/Conf.183/9, 17 July 1998, at Annex II, reprinted in 37 *International Legal Materials* 999, 1998, accessed at www.un.org/low/icc/statute/romefra.htm. See Sec.8:a:iii and 8:b.
36. Helen Durham, 'Women and Civil Society: NGOs and International Criminal Law', in Askin and Koenig (note 7).

Peace beyond the State?
NGOs in Bosnia and Herzegovina

BRONWYN EVANS-KENT and
ROLAND BLEIKER

We float leaf-words to the ground
and gaze in each other.
Who got left out of the song?[1]

NGOs played an important role during the Cold War. But the significance of this contribution has often been limited by a political climate dominated by states and international security organizations. Once the bipolar structures of Cold War politics had collapsed the international community became increasingly aware of the benefits of non-state organizations. In recent years NGOs have become a popular vehicle for the delivery and implementation of services that states are unable or reluctant to provide.

This essay scrutinizes the potential and limits of NGO contributions to peacebuilding and long-term stability. We examine the work of several organizations in the context of post-conflict reconstruction in Bosnia and Herzegovina (hereafter referred to as Bosnia). NGOs have been active in Bosnia for a decade, and hundreds of organizations have developed and implemented various projects, from victim advocacy to income generation and agricultural drainage. The sheer number and diversity of these activities has created a situation that reveals much about NGO participation in the process of post-conflict reconstruction. Mary Kaldor stresses that the global attention which the Bosnian conflict has received makes it 'a paradigm case, from which different lessons are drawn'.[2]

Some lessons can, indeed, be drawn from the Bosnian case, and they are of relevance to the general debate about the advantages and disadvantages of NGOs.[3] Those who stress the benefits of the nongovernmental sector focus primarily on the ability of NGOs to act outside the formal structures of national and international politics. NGOs are flexible, it is argued. They can provide technical expertise and specialized knowledge on particular topics.[4] They tend to enjoy a high level of credibility in populations, for they often have access to low and medium level leaders in the conflicting communities.[5] These grassroots contacts, and the ensuing intimate knowledge of local circumstances, can be used either to foster awareness of disputes or even to attempt to solve them. NGOs are thus seen as effective vehicles to engage parties in formal, low-key, non-threatening dialogue. This flexibility allows them to deliver services where states experience far more constraints. In the context of a humanitarian crisis, for instance, states need to navigate the political and legal problems of interfering with the domestic affairs of another state, which can pose difficulties and tensions even if the latter welcomes humanitarian assistance. Some commentators thus stress that the increasing centrality of NGOs has actually altered the very relationship between the state and the public sphere.[6]

While their ability to operate at the grassroots level and to provide specialized services is of great practical significance, the contribution of NGOs to the reconstruction of war-torn societies is often idealized. Various commentators see the strength of NGOs in their autonomy from the constraints of international or state-based politics. The official document of the Rio Earth Summit, for instance, stresses that 'independence is a major attribute of nongovernmental organizations and is the precondition of real participation'[7] The reality of post-conflict politics is, however, far more complex. Many NGOs remain limited by ad hoc or narrowly directed funding sources and by the overall policy environment in which they operate. As a result, their ability to promote and implement truly autonomous policies is often compromised. This is, of course, particularly the case of NGOs that take on the role of implementing post-conflict policies of states or their agencies. And such contracting functions have sharply increased since the 1980s, when it became clear that states alone could not provide all the services necessary to deal with humanitarian crises.[8] Many states have thus begun to encourage NGOs to take over a range of tasks that governments could no longer meet alone, from humanitarian relief to the provision of welfare.[9] According to Stephen Biggs and Arthur Neame this devolution of responsibility has evolved to the point that NGOs are now seen as the most 'cost effective instruments for the delivery of inputs and achievement of outputs'.[10]

Limits to autonomy exist even for those NGOs that are openly critical of states and their policies. Consider Amnesty International or Human Rights Watch, who speak for those who have no voice. But such a representational practice is not unproblematic, as Gayatri Spivak and other postcolonial critics have shown. The subaltern, they argue, cannot be represented easily. Indeed, the very process of doing so says more about the values and interests of the representer than the situation of the represented.[11] It is thus not surprising that many NGO activities are dominated by Western values and agendas. Diana Francis and Norbert Ropers, for instance, detect a clear preference for projects that have Western initiators and project leaders. In many contexts, the urban is privileged over the rural and English-speaking trainers are given preference, often to the detriment of very competent indigenous experts.[12]

The shadow of the state or of state-sponsored discourses remains omnipresent. Unless this relational dependency is understood and addressed, NGOs will ultimately be little more than an extension of prevalent multilateral and state-based approaches to post-conflict reconstruction. By identifying some of the ensuing problems in the context of Bosnia, we hope to provide a modest contribution towards an alternative vision for NGOs – one that would allow them to take on a more independent role in peacebuilding processes.

NGOs and the Challenge to Reconstruct

The challenge of reconstructing Bosnia, and the role of NGOs in particular, is intrinsically linked to the process of coming to terms with the traumatic memory of ethnic war and the resulting post-war identities. Significant here is the fact that the Bosnian conflict was not, as it is stereotypically perceived, a natural and inevitable product of historical animosities. Michael Ignatieff correctly stresses, 'that it would be false to the history of this part of the world to maintain that ethnic antagonisms were simply waiting, like the magma beneath a volcano, for a template to shift, a fissure to split open'.[13] Violence emerged from a very deliberate and manipulative strategy to use identity in the pursuit of specific political goals. The conflict was, as David Campbell points out, 'a question of history violently deployed in the present for contemporary political goals'.[14] Until the outbreak of hostilities, Bosnians possessed a variety of parallel identities: man or woman, old or young, mechanic or office worker, mother, uncle or son. Differences in religion and ethnicity did exist, but they were, as Ignatieff stresses, of a minor nature.[15] The political manipulation of the Bosnian situation created a conflict zone in which a person's ethnicity was often literally a matter of life and death.

The Dayton agreement, which brought an end to open hostilities in 1995, has resolved only some aspects of the legacy imposed by years of war and ethnic cleansing. At first sight Dayton seems an attempt to retain a multiethnic Bosnia. Arranged by Richard Holbrooke, the key US negotiator to the Balkans, Dayton was a basic agreement reached by the parties to the conflict – Serbs, Croats and Muslims – that consisted of retaining Bosnia as a country, rather than splitting it up into three distinct ethnic states. The elections of 1996 produced a parliament and a presidency that was to rotate between the three ethnic groups. A 60,000 strong NATO peacekeeping mission, drawn from 34 different countries, was stationed in Bosnia to make certain that all parties involved in the conflict were upholding the terms of the Dayton agreement. The Office of the High Representative (OHR) was established to oversee the implementation of the agreement.

A closer look at the Dayton agreement does, however, reveal far less commitment to multicultural principles. While it ended outright violence, Dayton also legitimized the ethnic divisions that had been created by the war. The three ethnic communities now control their own territories. The Bosnian Serbs received 49 per cent of the land in the form of the Republika Srpska. The rest went to a Muslim–Croat federation. In addition, the District of Brcko was created to resolve border issues. It is administered at the federal level.

The problematic legacy of Dayton has added layers of difficulties to the already gargantuan task of reconstruction. Ethnic tensions and extreme nationalist discourses continue to drive not only politics but also society. Consider, among many examples, the fact that children learn in separate education systems, absorbing only their own history, religion and language. Add to these entrenched sources of tension raising factors such as inequality, widespread domestic violence, an unemployment figure as high as 40–50 per cent in some regions, and the strong presence of organized crime such as the drug trade or the trafficking of women and children.[16]

It is in this problematic and blurred transitional context that hundreds of international and domestic NGOs have been working on various aspects of post-conflict reconstruction. Respective activities not only focus on shelter and food relief, which is still a problem in many parts of Bosnia, but also cover issues as diverse as agriculture, health, psycho-social work, children and youth, human rights, the elderly, women, the media, education and training, de-mining and mine awareness, micro-credit and income generation.[17] We now proceed to discuss some of the key dilemmas that NGOs face in this reconstruction process. We identify three main challenges. The first revolves around the often problematic relationship between donors and NGOs.

The Problematic Donor–NGO Relationship

Donors are essential to post-conflict reconstruction. To assess their role is, however, no easy task, for aid reaches its destination through varied and complex routes. The donors themselves can be states, as is often the case, but they can also be individuals, charitable trusts, nongovernmental organizations, corporations or multilateral institutions.

The donor community responded quickly and generously to the need to rebuild Bosnia. In late 1995 the Peace Implementation Council in London set the stage for implementing the Dayton Accords. Eight other multilateral pledging conferences followed.[18] Most donor activity has focused on reviving the economy but other funding has sought to support an independent mass media, democratization and human rights, as well as the training and modernization of the military, the promotion of police reform or the supervision of elections.[19] The international community has spent an estimated US$5.1 billion on the medium-term Priority Reconstruction and Recovery Programme. Pledges from donors in the most recent major donor conference in 1999 reached US$1,052 million. These pledges were received from representatives of 45 countries and 30 international organizations.[20]

The extraordinary amount of aid pledged to Bosnia, however, cannot hide the problematic aspects of the relationship between donors and NGOs. Indeed, this relationship creates at least some of the problems for which NGOs have been criticized. Several key issues can be identified. One of these is the often conditional nature of aid. Donors may require economic or political conditions to be fulfilled before the delivery of aid can be implemented. The agendas of multilateral organizations and pledging states display a strong preference for projects that promote democratization and reforms aimed at establishing a market economy.[21] Assistance from the US, for instance, was conditional on holding democratic elections. Elections, therefore, proceeded at a time (1996) when, at least according to observers from the Organisation for Security and Cooperation in Europe (OSCE), the electoral process could not be free and fair.[22] This policy preference has continued ever since. Consider how the US Agency for International Development (USAID) gives priority to NGOs focusing on democracy-building.[23] As a result, NGOs that focus on different but equally urgent forms of reconstruction or peacebuilding face difficulties in securing adequate funding. The very principle of conditionality tends to favour projects that operate according to the priorities of the donors rather than the needs of communities. Local capacities for peace maintenance are generally underfunded or underexplored. And local organizations continue to struggle in their attempt to fit into the funding structures of international organizations and multilateral institutions.[24]

Another key issue affecting the NGO–donor relationship is the scarcity of funds and the resulting intense competition for them.[25] During the initial phases of reconstruction funding was relatively abundant.[26] Half a dozen years later, however, the situation had changed dramatically. Organizations now need to work much harder to secure funding.[27] In an environment of scarce funding the art of writing project proposals has taken on an increasingly central role. The Canadian International Development Agency (CIDA) is a case in point. It stresses that success for funding is largely dependent on high quality proposal writing.[28] But this transparency, desirable as it seems, has not made the distribution of funds more fair or equal. Take the very example of CIDA, which has been very active in Bosnia. Its policies are directed towards providing training, technical assistance and equipment in local capacity projects.[29] Given the often highly technical nature of this endeavour, experienced international NGOs stand a much greater chance of being funded than local grassroots organizations. To be successful a local NGO must not only submit a proposal in English, but also be familiar with the structure, expectations and even the jargon of the respective donor organizations. Such information and skills cannot always be acquired locally. This is why an increasingly competitive funding environment tends to discriminate against local NGOs or those that are unfamiliar with the requirements of donors or lack the support of an international organization.

One of the most problematic aspects of donor–NGO interactions in Bosnia is located in the often ad hoc nature of their relationship. Donor priorities and expectations frequently change, as a result of either new policy trends or a high turnover of senior staff (who tend to impose their own strategic choices).[30] Added to this level of uncertainty is the fact that relief and development activities are designed by a multitude of departments and agencies which all have different – and at times competing – interests. The result is, as Stewart Patrick stresses, an 'often dissatisfactory amalgamation of interests, mandates and capacities'.[31] The problem is that trends in funding change and, as a representative of a local NGO puts it, donors 'can be interested in mushroom farming one day and reconstruction the next'.[32] Likewise, a Bosnian woman involved with several local NGOs stresses that they had to alter their projects regularly to suit the changing priorities of donors. Often effective projects could not be repeated, as they were no longer of central concern to a new donor.[33] It is, indeed, not uncommon that NGOs are prevented from extending successful projects. Mission goals have to be rewritten frequently in order to adjust to changes in donor priorities. A move from one type of project (old trend) to another (new trend) may thus be more successful in gaining funding than the continuation of a project that has worked well and would continue to benefit the population.

In stark contrast to the long-term nature of the peacebuilding process the specific missions are often dictated by pragmatic and short-term imperatives.[34] In many situations NGOs can only secure funding for as little as three months at a time.[35] Since renewal of funding is contingent on meeting the requirements of donors, it is virtually impossible for NGOs to develop a vision that can be implemented in the long run. The pressure to behave according to the expectations of donors is simply too strong. Indeed, funding may disappear altogether if the priorities of the international community – and the resulting media attention – shift to another 'hotspot'. Support for Bosnia was, as mentioned, very strong in the early stages of reconstruction, but then the focus of international rescue efforts moved to Kosovo, just to be replaced by East Timor and, most recently, Afghanistan.

The clash between the long-term needs and the short-term realities of the reconstruction process creates serious difficulties. NGOs tend to deal with this tension by stressing the importance and urgency of the immediate challenge. Representative of such an approach is a member of a local NGO, who argued that there is little point in defining peacebuilding, but rather that 'We do it'.[36] There is, of course, a clear need for immediate, contextual and commonsensical action. But such an engagement should not be to the detriment of long-term planning and coordination. The latter is far too often lacking in Bosnia. Those NGOs that seek to develop and coordinate a vision tend to have difficulties finding the funding necessary to implement their programmes. The international community has a responsibility to provide local NGOs with the freedom and the ability to bring promising projects to a successful conclusion. This would entail moving away from a deeply entrenched practice of seeing development aid as a business that deals 'in money, not in social processes'.[37] A social engagement, in turn, may require a commitment over an extended period of time. While a school can be rebuilt in three months, for example, it takes several years to implement a curriculum that breaks down the stereotypes entrenched by the war. Without a vision for such long-term projects, and the funding to back it up, the peacebuilding process in Bosnia is unlikely to be successful.

Tensions between Local and International Organizations

The second major issue facing post-conflict reconstruction in Bosnia is the divide that has emerged between local and international organizations. Bosnian groups or individuals engaged in peacebuilding activities often resent being dominated by the funding power of international NGOs. The latter, by contrast, tend to perceive local organizations as lacking sufficient skills or competence.

Resentment and suspicion towards international NGOs and international governmental organizations is rooted, at least in part, in their reluctance to engage the local population actively.[38] The Office of the High Representative (OHR), for instance, is perceived as a massive structure imposed upon Bosnia it drafts most of the legislation and does so with the help of foreign (mostly US) lawyers who often lack sufficient understanding of the societal dynamics in a former Socialist economy.[39] As a result, international organizations are perceived as outsider institutions that ignore potentially valuable local forms of peacemaking or problem solving.[40] Consider how a representative of a local organization lamented the way in which rape victims were treated. The initial response of many international organizations, he argued, was to treat the rape as an incident in isolation, rather than a tragedy that is part of a larger issue, which includes the potential loss of security, identity, home, family and support.[41]

The process of distributing aid adds to the already problematic relationship between local and international representatives. External consultants at OHR, for example, were paid out of pledged aid. This reduced the numbers of local staff that could be employed, even though local capacity was actually greater and stronger than portrayed by donors.[42]

Resentment and problems can emerge even in domains where no harm is intended. Consider the widespread willingness of the international community to support Bosnia in its attempt to reconstruct a war-torn society. The ample funding that emerged in the initial phase created a situation in which many individuals or groups formed themselves into NGOs simply because this was one of the most promising ways of gaining employment. But the rapid influx of funds has created what some call a 'false economy'.[43] In Sarajevo, the presence of the international aid community has engendered an entire industry, sustaining not only direct NGO employees, but also translators, drivers, hotel and restaurant employees, fuel providers and many more. The international community tends to pay salaries or rent at rates that are highly inflated in the local context.[44] In the short run such a stark division between the local economy and the presence of the international aid community further fuels an already lingering sense of resentment. In the long run, an economy inflated by the artificial presence of a development industry is simply not sustainable, especially since much of the aid is of a short-term nature and likely to further decrease as world attention shifts to geographical areas with a more dramatic need for assistance.

The divide between domestic and international organizations is perhaps at its most problematic when it comes to valuing local approaches and knowledges. John Paul Lederach convincingly argues that peacebuilding must come from within a culture. Although his approach oversimplifies many issues, Lederach is correct in drawing attention to the crucial need for building upon knowledge and experience that has come directly out of specific social conflict contexts.[45] He is accurate too in expressing suspicion towards an approach to conflict transformation that revolves around (international) experts training (local) participants. The foundation of this model, which prevails in much of Bosnia,[46] is the principle of transferability and universality.[47] According to this model there is a predefined agenda for a predefined need. The expert thus controls the agenda, and the task of local participants is to learn and execute an already existing model.

Resentment of such outside impositions is widespread in Bosnia. By contrast, those few organizations that seek to draw upon local knowledges and expertise are often seen as doing a highly valuable job. Representatives of several local organizations have expressed the importance of creating better partnerships between domestic and international projects. The latter should shift more responsibility to local organizations, so that achievements can be sustained even once aid funds dry up and the development community leaves permanently.[48]

The Lack of Regulation and Coordination of NGO Activities

In the early stages of reconstruction the international community strongly encouraged the growth of a local NGO community.[49] Funding was, as mentioned, relatively ample. As a result, the number of NGOs grew from a handful in the mid-1990s to around 1,500 half a decade later.[50] The lack of adequate regulation and coordination, however, seriously undermines the functioning of this new and relatively large NGO 'industry'.

There are two coordinating NGO bodies in Bosnia: The

International Council of Voluntary Agencies (ICVA) and the Centre for Information and Support to NGOs.[51] The OHR, in cooperation with the OSCE, has created the Civil Society Coordination Group, which consists of several intergovernmental and donor organizations that address human rights and democratization. While these efforts are aimed at coordinating the projects of individual organizations, there is little nation-wide legislation that governs NGOs or charitable funds.[52] The OHR has initiated a campaign to develop respective legislation. The ensuing debates and procedures are well underway, but a high degree of tension between the different parties has slowed down the process.[53]

In the absence of adequate regulation, quality control of NGOs is very difficult. NGOs are defined formally as including anything from sporting organizations to theatre troupes, and many have organized themselves as NGOs simply for the sake of receiving funding.[54] The commitment to peacebuilding efforts thus varies greatly. And so does the sustainability of the respective organizations.[55] To address this and similar problems, USAID introduced an NGO Sustainability Index in 1998.[56] This so-called Democracy Network, or Dem-Net Project, forms a core group of strong, sophisticated local organizations that have already proved themselves. USAID pays their operational costs and provides training and support. The participating organizations are run on four principles: adherence to the rule of law, democracy building, economic development and social safety. The programme began with 28 NGOs that were given institutional support but had to conform to particular standards of administration. The latter included a board, rather than a management structure dominated by one person. The respective NGOs were also encouraged to cooperate with local governments, businesses and communities. These and other attempts at regulating the NGO industry can play an important role in improving the quality of services. In many situations well-funded training is necessary to translate motivation and willingness into concrete projects that yield measurable benefits. Regulation may also help to avoid the duplication of projects or lack of communication between the people associated with them.

There are highly revealing examples of NGOs that were successful in coordinating their activities, even in the competitive and under-regulated context of post-war Bosnia. Consider briefly the case of the Centre for Drama in Education in Mostar and an organization called Corridor, in Sarajevo. Both are local and collaborate with local communities on peacebuilding projects. Each was aware of its limitations and thus learned how to operate successfully by engaging in two strategies: (1) exploring a particular niche and developing a reputation in this domain; and (2) embarking on extensive cooperation with larger organizations. This strategy was successful even though the funding policies of donors did not necessarily encourage specialization. But both organizations managed to develop a strong reputation in their field, gained the trust of donors and were thus able to sustain themselves in the long run.[57]

The Centre for Drama in Education or Centar za Dramski Odgoj (CDO)[58] based in Mostar is an NGO that has sought to use drama and theatre tools to work on peacebuilding, conflict resolution and youth trauma. While the organization has contact and cooperates with other organizations in the former Yugoslavia and Albania, CDO's greatest value is in its development of school curricula in drama, which are aimed at breaking down some of the stereotypes created by the war and its aftermath. Each year the organization runs an international festival of drama, publishes a journal and organizes an international conference. Its representatives recognize that once the needs of food, shelter and security are secured people need to regain a sense of place. Such recognition is now widely accepted:

> In crisis and post-crisis situations, humanitarian aid naturally focuses upon essential emergency relief. Because these situations have the character of emergencies, matters of the body and material infrastructure tend to predominate. But it is well known that the citizens of Sarajevo during the siege…braved bullets and mortars not only to fetch water and firewood, but to attend plays and concerts. Children and young people wrote poems and stories, and so on. In the most dehumanising conditions human beings still demanded meaning and sustenance of the spirit.[59]

CDO aims to build 'metaphorical bridges'. Rather than forging ambitious plans for reconciliation they acknowledge that 'in a country steeped in blood plans must be modest'.[60] As part of their collaborative strategy, CDO has established a partnership with CARE International. They created the Pax Project, which has operated throughout Bosnia. Its objectives are two-fold: The 'promotion of multi-ethnic peacebuilding work with youth theatre groups' and the 'development of a participatory learning approach for classroom peacebuilding work'.[61] The themes addressed by theatre groups included drugs, displaced persons and refugees, violence, women's rights, children's rights and the struggle for freedom.[62] The project operates in 175 schools with 400 primary teachers, reaching some 11,000 students.[63] CDO believes it has been successful because it tried to adapt to changing circumstances and collaborated with other organizations while, at the same time, retaining its key mission, for which it has gained a good reputation.[64]

The second example of a successful organization is Corridor, based in Sarajevo. It too believes its success stems from having developed and retained a strong mission.[65] During the war Corridor ran counselling centres, magazines, radio and TV programmes aimed at keeping people informed and connected. Corridor's post-war activities take place in the general area of psychosocial work, covering issues such as alcoholism, the demobilization of the military, and the return of minorities. For instance, Corridor organized a trip back to Srebrenica for both Serb and Muslim women. It also developed a pilot project for a Children's Parliament in Dobrinje, on the edge of Republica Srpska. Other engagements include a series of lectures for demobilized soldiers about the effects of alcoholism.[66] Corridor too seeks collaborative relationships with other organizations, especially in the Republica Srpska, where it is often difficult to establish ties.

Corridor and CDO demonstrate that NGOs can be successful, even in difficult circumstances. Rather than working in isolation and adjusting their programmes to the ever-changing priorities of donors, Corridor and CDO chose to develop specialized expertise. They have gained the trust of donors as a result of a sustained engagement in their respective fields of activity.

Both of these NGOs also demonstrate that sustainable peace requires more than a mere physical reconstruction of the damaged infrastructure. At least as important is the task of dealing with the antagonistic identity constructs that continue to cause various tensions. By fostering education, tolerance and cross-ethnic interactions, Corridor and CDO make an important contribution to dismantling the artificially constructed threat images that had given rise to the conflict in the first place. Such an engagement does, of course, take time. Respect for difference cannot emerge overnight in a society that had been devastated by years of war. This is why the contribution of NGOs to post-conflict reconstruction must be seen (and supported) as a medium- to long-term challenge.

Conclusion

> ...If we fall
> it's someone else's dark. How, after that, can we
> be an upright pole, or grow bark
> like a tree?[67]

NGOs have taken up a unique place in various humanitarian challenges of the last decade. They have become useful instruments to deliver humanitarian services, especially in highly politicized conflict environments, such as Bosnia. But NGOs are not as independent as they are often taken to be.

The first major challenge to NGO work in Bosnia is their relationship to donors. While outside aid is crucial, and was readily available in the initial phases of reconstruction, the competition for funding has become more difficult in recent years. Valuable time is spent developing detailed proposals, often for projects that may receive funding only for short-periods of time. Long-term planning and commitment has become very difficult. This is all the more the case since donors – states, state institutions or individuals – often possess interests that either change frequently or are not necessarily of benefit to the community. Local NGOs thus have no alternative but to adjust to new funding trends, even if it means giving up projects that have worked well and would continuously benefit the population.

A second challenge for NGOs is located in the divide between international and local organizations. Differences in power, resources and priorities have created a great deal of resentment on both sides. International organizations tend to see local NGOs as lacking the necessary expertise for particular projects. Local organizations, by contrast, believe that their unique knowledge of the conflict and local circumstances is ignored in favour of often inappropriate outside expertise. The resulting tension has produced resentments and structural difficulties that hamper the reconstruction process.

The third problem is rooted in the relatively unregulated nature of the new but substantial NGO 'industry'. Quality control has become an important task, for projects are often duplicated or developed by organizations that possess no adequate training. Relief agencies, for instance, began to do psychosocial work or micro-credit business despite the lack of respective qualifications. Absent as well are bureaucratic, tax and other concessions that NGOs enjoy in most other states. Initiatives are underway to rectify these and other problems through the introduction of respective legislation. But at this stage the largely unregulated nature of NGO activities has created employment patterns that are not sustainable in the long run. It is, of course, not easy to promote the critical capacity and autonomy of NGOs while, at the same time, trying to establish mechanisms that would improve the quality of their work. Such regulatory attempts can easily end up in more state-control over the activities of the NGO sector. The purpose cannot be to impose a uniform standard or to prescribe what kind of vision civil organizations ought to pursue. Indeed, the greatest potential contribution of NGOs perhaps lies in their very ability – incomplete as it is – to defy prevailing norms and structures. Various visions need to co-exist, and NGOs that are successful should be given the means to pursue their project for the duration that is required to bring it to successful completion.

While these and other challenges pose serious obstacles to the prospects of achieving lasting peace, they are not insurmountable. One can, at the same time, find instances of projects that have worked successfully. We have drawn brief attention to the work of CDO in Mostar and Corridor in Sarajevo – two organizations that demonstrate how collaboration between different local and international institutions can produce sustainable long-term peacebuilding projects. The responsibility to extend such successful models to the overall peacebuilding process lies with all parties involved. Donors and international organizations need to abandon preconceived universal models and rely more actively on local knowledge and expertise. Domestic organizations, by contrast, must find ways to collaborate more effectively by developing common visions while, at the same time, accommodating the differences and tensions that inevitably remain in a society traumatized by the memory of war.

NOTES

1. Hadze Hajdarević, 'The Voices are Coming', in Chris Agee (ed.), *Scar on the Stone: Contemporary Poetry from Bosnia*, Newcastle: Bloodaxe Books, 1998, p.126.
2. Mary Kaldor, *New and Old Wars: Organized Violence in a Global Era*, Stanford, CA: Stanford University Press, 1999, p.6.
3. NGOs are affected by a common set of dynamics and constraints, although they differ greatly in size, skills, scope and level of independence. They can be international, international with local staff, local but funded by a separate international organization. NGOs can also exist simply for the express purpose of implementing the policies of government agencies. See Steve Charnovitz, 'Two Centuries of Participation: NGOs and International Governance', *Michigan Journal of International Law*, Vol.18, No.2, 1997, pp.185–286. On the comparative advantage of NGOs and intergovernmental organizations in former Yugoslavia, see: Paul Stubbs, 'NGO Work with Forced Migrants in Croatia: Lineages of a Global Middle Class?', *International Peacekeeping*, Vol.4, No.4, winter 1997, pp.50–60; Philip Peirce and Paul Stubbs, 'Peacebuilding, Hegemony and Integrated Social Development: The UNDP in Travnik', in Michael Pugh (ed.), *Regeneration of War-torn Societies*, Basingstoke: Macmillan, 2000, pp.157–76.
4. Charnovitz (note 3), pp.274–75.
5. Anja Weiss and Aleksej Nazarenko, 'Strategies and Needs of NGOs Dealing with Ethnopolitical Conflicts in the New Eastern Democracies', *Berghof Occasional Paper No.7*, 1997, www.b.shuttle.de/berghof/eng/ind_pub.htm, p.3. For accounts of the benefits of NGOs see David Korten, *Getting to the 21st Century: Voluntary Action and the Global Agenda*, West Hartford, CT: Kumarion Press, 1990; and Laura Macdonald,

Supporting Civil Society: The Political Role of Non-Governmental Organizations in Central America, Basingstoke: Macmillan, 1997.

6. Yasemin Topçu, *Humanitarian NGO-Networks: Identifying Powerful Political Actors in an International Policy field*, Berlin: Social Science Research Center, 1999, p.23.

7. Rio Earth Summit, 1992, Agenda 21, Ch. 27, www.un.org/esa/sustdev/agenda21chapter27.htm. For various accounts of NGO autonomy, implied or explicitly argued, see *Annual Report of the Global Policy Forum*, 2000, www.globalpolicy.org/visitctr/annreprt/ar2000-5.htm; M. Edwards and D. Hulme (eds.). *Beyond the Magic Bullet: NGO Performance and Accountability in the Post-Cold War World.* West Hartford, CT: Kumerian Press, 1996, p.44; Susan Finch, 'NGO/Military Cooperation in Complex Emergencies: The Need for Improved Coordination', *Canadian Centre for Foreign Policy Development, 2000,* www.cfp-pec.gc.ca/OtherAnnualEvents/Susan_Finch.htm.

8. Korten (note 5), p.6.

9. Tadashi Yamamoto and Susan Hubbard, 'Summary Report on the Osaka Symposium on Philanthropic Development and Cooperation in Asia Pacific', in T. Yamamoto (ed.), *Emerging Civil Society in the Asia Pacific Community – Nongovernmental Underpinnings of the Emerging Asia Pacific Regional Community*, Tokyo: Japan Center for International Exchange, 1995, p.50.

10. Stephen D. Biggs and Arthur D. Neame, 'Negotiating Room to Maneuver: Reflections Concerning NGO Autonomy and Accountability within the New Policy Agenda', in Edwards and Hulme (note 7), p.41. See also Thomas G. Weiss and Leon Gordenker (eds.), *NGOs, the UN and Global Governance*, Boulder, CO: Lynne Rienner, 1996, pp.17–47.

11. Gayatri Chakravorty Spivak, 'Can the Subaltern Speak?', in C. Nelson and L. Grossberg (eds.), *Marxism and the Interpretation of Culture*, Chicago: University of Illinois Press, 1988.

12. Diana Francis and Norbert Ropers, 'Peace Work by Civil Actors in Post-Communist Societies', *Berghof Occasional Paper No.7*, www.b.shuttle.de/berghof/eng/ind_pub.htm, 1997, pp.7–8.

13. Michael Ignatieff, *The Warrior's Honor: Ethnic War and the Modern Conscience*, London: Random House, 1998, p.38.

14. David Campbell, *National Deconstruction: Violence, Identity and Justice in Bosnia*, Minneapolis: University of Minnesota Press, 1998, p.86.

15. Michael Ignatieff (note 13), p.38.

16. Interview with an employee of the UN High Commission for Human Rights. Sarajevo, 17 Aug. 2000.

17. ICVA, *The ICVA Directory of humanitarian and development agencies in Bosnia and Herzegovina*, Sarajevo, 2000. International NGOs in Bosnia are from: Canada, the US, Italy, France, Germany, Switzerland, Denmark, the Netherlands, Turkey, Austria, the UK, Belgium, Spain, Sweden, Finland, United Arab Emirates, Japan, the Sudan, British Virgin Islands, Norway, Qatar, Ireland, and Croatia.

18. Zlatko Hertić et al., 'Bosnia and Herzegovina', in S. Forman and S. Patrick (eds.), *Good Intentions: Pledges of Aid for Postconflict Recovery*, Boulder, CO: Lynne Rienner, 2000, p.319.

19. Ibid., p.326.

20. World Bank, *Chairmen's Statement – Fifth Donors' Pledging Conference for Bosnia and Herzegovina: May 20–21, 1999*, Brussels, www.worldbank.org/html/extdr/extme/pr052099b.htm; European Union External Relations, *International donors ask government to accelerate privatization in Bosnia and Herzegovina.* http://europa.eu.int/comm/external_relations/news/02_00/doc_00_4.htm DOC/00/4, Sarajevo, 3 Feb. 2000.

21. For articles regarding the agendas of donors at the 5th Pledging Conference in Brussels see World Bank 1999 *Chairmen's Statement – Fifth Donors' Pledging Conference for Bosnia and Herzegovina: May 20–21, 1999, Brussels,* www.worldbank.rg/html/extdr/extme/pr052099b.htm; Centre for Peace in the Balkans 2000 *Donors community sets*

conditions for future financial aid to Bosnia, Sarajevo, May 26, www.balkanpeace.org/hed/archive/may00/hed154.shtml.

22. Jane M. O. Sharp, 'Dayton Report Card', *International Security*, Vol.22, No.3, 1997, pp.101–37, p.114. The Coordinator for International Monitoring expressed strong reservations, arguing that 'the general climate in which the elections took place was in some cases below the minimum standards of the OSCE Copenhagen Commitments... Until the problems affecting the integrity of the elections have been addressed and solved, these elections [municipal] should not be held.' Preliminary Statement of The Coordinator For International Monitoring (CIM) 14 Sept. 1996 – OSCE, www.osce.org/odihr/documents/reports/election_reports/ba/bih1-1.pdf.
23. Interview with an employee of USAID. Sarajevo, 8 Sept. 2000.
24. Information regarding project proposals from interviews with employees of local NGOs, CIDA and USAID.
25. Shepard Forman and Stewart Patrick, 'Introduction', in Forman and Patrick (n.18 above), p.1; Hertić et al. (note 18), p.343.
26. An employee of OHR stressed that in the immediate post-war period the international community would provide funding to virtually any organization that advertised itself as an NGO. Interview with employees of OHR, Sarajevo, 1 Sept. 2000.
27. Interview with employees of USAID, Sarajevo, 8 Sept. 2000.
28. Interview with an employee of CIDA, Sarajevo, 30 August 2000.
29. Ibid.
30. Local organization, Sarajevo, Sept. 2000.
31. Stewart Patrick, 'The Donor Community and the Challenge of Postconflict Recovery', in Forman and Patrick (n.18 above), pp.36, 39.
32. Local organization, Sarajevo, Sept. 2000.
33. Local organization, Sarajevo, Aug. 2000.
34. Patrice McMahon argues that the development of a Bosnian civil society has been severely limited due to high levels of NGO dependence on the donor community. Patrice C. McMahon, 'What Have We Wrought? Assessing International Involvement in Bosnia', *Problems of Post-Communism*, Vol.49, No.1, 2002, pp.18–29.
35. Interviews with staff of international organizations, Sarajevo, Aug.–Sept. 2000.
36. Interview with local peacebuilding organization, Mostar, Sept. 2000.
37. Korten (note 5), p.xii.
38. Interview with an employee of UNHCHR, Sarajevo, 17 Aug. 2000.
39. Ibid.
40. Several local organizations interviewed.
41. Interview with local organization, Sarajevo, Sept. 2000. For a detailed discussion of the issue see Lene Hansen, 'Gender, Nation, Rape: Bosnia and the Construction of Security', *International Feminist Journal of Politics*, Vol.3, No.2, 2001, pp.56–75
42. Hertić et al. (note 18), pp.344–5.
43. Interview with an employee of an international organization. Sarajevo, Sept. 2000.
44. Discussions with local people and local NGOs.
45. John Paul Lederach, *Preparing for Peace: Conflict Transformation Across Cultures*, Syracuse, NY: Syracuse University Press, 1995, p.27.
46. Local youth, psycho-social and democratization organizations, Sarajevo, Brcko and Srpsko Sarajevo, Aug. 2000.
47. Lederach (note 45), pp.48–53.
48. Interviews with local organizations, Sarajevo, Aug.–Sept. 2000.
49. Interview with employees of OHR, Sarajevo, 1 Sept. 2000.
50. This number includes anything from human rights organizations to sporting associations as they all fall under the same general legislation.
51. Centre for Information and Support to NGOs (CIP), www.geocities.com/cip_sarajevo/index-eng.html, accessed Nov. 2001.
52. Interview with employees of OHR, Sarajevo, 1 Sept. 2000; See also OHR Press Release, *Launching of Campaign to Change NGO Legislation*, www.ohr.int/ohr-dept/presso, 1998; and Global IDP Network, *International community supports the*

capacity of the civil society to address human rights issues, www.db.idpproject.org, 2000.

53. See Global IDP Network, *International community supports the capacity of the civil society to address human rights issues,* www.db.idpproject.org/Sites/IdpProjectDb/ idpSurvey.nsf/1c963eb504904cde41256782007493b8/752c6733308d2d46c12569a7 0050dd55?OpenDocument, 2000.

54. This is the case even though NGOs are fully taxed in Bosnia – a fact that most donor agencies do not take into account.

55. Interview with employees of OHR, Sarajevo, 1 Sept. 2000.

56. Interview with employees of USAID, Sarajevo, 8 Sept. 2000.

57. Interviews with CDO and Corridor and international organizations with whom they had links.

58. Interview with CDO, Mostar, 7 Sept. 2000.

59. Geoff Gillham, *Pax Project: A Multi-layered Approach to Peacebuilding and Social Reconstruction in Bosnia and Hercegovina (An Evaluation Report),* CARE International, 2000, p.33.

60. Interview with employees of CDO, 7 Sept. 2000.

61. Gillham (note 59), p.4.

62. Ibid, p.13.

63. Ibid, pp.15–16.

64. Interview with local organization, Sarajevo, Sept. 2000.

65. Interview with employees of Corridor, 8 Sept. 2000.

66. Ibid.

67. Hajdarevic (note 1), p.127.

Humanitarian International NGOs and African Conflicts

WAFULA OKUMU

As the number of collapsing African states increases, humanitarian international NGOs (HINGOs), alongside UN agencies and sub-regional organizations, are increasingly being called upon to play more and significant roles in complex emergencies. Besides mitigating the social and economic consequences of collapsing states, HINGOs are also implementing peace accords, promoting democratic and economic reforms, protecting human rights, and encouraging the settlement of conflicts.[1] Although scrutiny of humanitarian assistance was mainly focused on criticism of its delivery, analysis of its guiding principles and the evaluation of its position in the humanitarian–development continuum, there is now increasing concern over its adverse effects on its beneficiaries and on its role in prolonging or solving the conflicts that produced them. There are now widespread indications that humanitarian assistance that is being delivered through HINGOs may actually be prolonging conflicts.[2] Thus, the premise of this article is that aid may be important in assisting people in complex emergencies but it might also prolong conflicts by diverting attention from the real causes of the conflicts and by inadvertently assisting warring parties.

What is a HINGO?

A humanitarian international NGO is a private, not-for-profit organization that engages in transnational activities to relieve human suffering wrought by human activities such as wars, and by natural disasters, such as floods and earthquakes. The present number of HINGOs in existence is difficult to ascertain,[3] although the 2000 *Yearbook of International Organizations* reported that there were more than 26,000 international NGOs with an annual budget of over US$6 billion.[4] One reason why it is difficult to know the number of operational HINGOs is that many of them, known as 'come 'n' gos', mushroom during complex emergencies and scale down with the mitigation of the crises. HINGOs range from the 'first generation' organizations, such as CARE and Save the Children, to newer ones like MERLIN and Emergency Medical Corps. But eight HINGOs control about 75 per cent of all emergency funds.[5] Most of the first-generation HINGOs have in the recent past integrated psycho-social care, conflict resolution and peacebuilding into their portfolios.[6]

Humanitarian aid is aimed at saving lives and helping people to enjoy the most basic rights which are threatened in conflicts. Conflicts destroy necessities for survival like shelter, water and food.[7] Warring parties in contemporary conflicts have adopted nearly similar military strategies of disrupting life and forcing people to leave their places of abode – essentially depopulating the conflicted regions and using civilians as pawns. It is at this point that HINGOs respond to complex emergencies – by helping uphold both international humanitarian law and human rights, particularly related to the right to aid for all in emergencies.[8]

Mandates of HINGOs to Act in Conflict Situations

Although international humanitarian law recognizes the rights of non-combatants in intra- and inter-state conflict zones not to suffer as a result of lack of food and medical care, one of the challenges facing the providers of relief aid is how to immunize that aid from political manipulation by warring parties. This partly explains why there is a strong preference for humanitarian assistance to be channelled through NGOs. Humanitarian NGOs for their part have, since the end of the Cold War, become more aggressive in exercising their claimed *right to assist the victims* of conflicts. But in order to gain access to these victims the NGOs, while operating under the 'neutrality' principle, have dabbled in diplomacy as they negotiate with warring parties to guarantee the safe passage of relief food, medicine and equipment. To gain access to the needy, they have been forced to negotiate with the perpetrators of violence – both military dictators and the rebels fighting them. In the process, and in most cases, HINGOs have ended up making concessions, ranging from political recognition in the case of southern Sudanese rebels, to provision of artillery and vehicles to armed intermediaries who deliver food in Somalia.[9]

The aid agencies know that they are caught in a quandary: to be allowed to feed the civilians who are virtually held hostage by the warring parties they have to make provisions for the fighters too; and to gain access to the weak and powerless civilians under the control of the rebel and government forces, they have to strike deals with some of the most notorious warlords in the world. In the end, HINGOs have unwittingly been used to enhance the war objectives of the combatants and prolong the conflicts – raising the question: Are the 'right to assist the victims of conflicts' and the principle of neutrality being subverted? And furthermore, have HINGOs also compromised diplomatic efforts towards resolving conflicts and in fact contributed to the protraction of these conflicts? In the end we are stuck with an irony that aid may prolong war, even as it saves lives.[10]

In an analysis of the ways in which humanitarian aid prolongs conflict in Africa, John Prendergast notes that 'warring parties are becoming increasingly sophisticated' in using humanitarian aid as a weapon.[11] HINGOs' relief supplies have enabled the armies and rebel groups to keep fighting by presenting opportunities to make money that is used to buy weapons. At the local level, this offers a disincentive for political action to end the conflicts; and at the international level, once the problem has been defined as 'humanitarian', the underlying causes of the conflict are usually left untouched, leaving humanitarian assistance as a band-aid that only alleviates suffering for a short period of time.

African Contexts for Humanitarian Intervention

The wars that result in complex emergencies in Africa have changed considerably since the end of the Cold War. These wars are usually intra-state, fought with no clear battlefields and use civilian populations as targets. In all of the African conflicts, civilians have paid the heaviest prices – as 'pawns, hostages, and objects of conflict, if not the deliberate targets of violence'.[12] These conflicts have been attributed mainly to greedy leaders who use war not as a means of restoring justice but of enriching themselves. Huge numbers of refugees and internally displaced people have been forced to flee from their homes. It is in this context that humanitarian assistance is provided to feed the hungry and treat the sick. But this assistance has been given under very complicated conditions in which wars are not fought according to international codes of war, particularly those related to civilian populations; attention must be given to questions of sovereignty and conditions for intervention, since the conflicts are internal; and decisions must be made on the moral questions of making pacts with devils, and of whether or not to exclude them from the benefits of the operations.

African conflicts have violated civilian rights under international humanitarian law. Obviously targeting civilians is a grave breach applicable to internal wars under the four 1949 Geneva Conventions.

The two Additional Protocols of 1977 to the 1949 Geneva Conventions govern civilian infrastructure and humanitarian relief in internal armed conflict. The Protocols are not technically binding because of insufficient state-party ratifications, but they have considerable influence and many argue they are binding under customary international law. Articles 4, 13 and 14 of the Second Protocol would prohibit starvation or destruction of civilian infrastructure essential to survival, including food, agricultural land, crops, domestic animals and water supplies. Article 69 imposes on occupying powers the obligation to provide relief supplies to the population of its adversary 'without any adverse distinction'. Article 70 holds that offers of aid should not be seen not as interference in domestic affairs so long as it is 'humanitarian and impartial in character'. Though consent from host states is required for HINGOS to gain access, most legal authorities and HINGOS argue that HINGO access is binding under customary international law. The strongest argument is that the binding Fourth Geneva Convention of 1949 imposes on all parties to allow 'free passage of all consignments of medical and hospital stores', though many believe this requirement only applies to international, not internal laws. As a practical matter, victims of war such as in Southern Sudan must be given access by the Khartoum government, even if legally it cannot be refused. However, since the need arose to protect the Kurds in northern Iraq in 1991, this loophole has now been sealed by a series of UN Security Council resolutions that allow HINGOs, in conjunction with the UN and other international agencies, to directly provide assistance to victims of state terror. Now HINGOs can work on both sides of the conflict by 'crossing the border' into rebel territory or crossing the line in and out of government areas. But this has subjected HINGOs 'to a host of new problems, ranging from negotiating access for staff and relief commodities with warlords and on occasion hiring armed protection, to working alongside the military'.[13]

HINGOs have now found themselves in a 'balancing act between the operational impartiality of the "political eunuch" ("we are here to save lives, politics is not our business") and the shrewd manoeuvring of the "humanitarian prostitute" ("we are ready to compromise so that we can get through")'.[14] Mary Anderson has argued that a HINGO 'often becomes intertwined with the forces that drive the conflicts that prompted the aid in the first place'.[15] This view was also supported by UN Secretary-General Kofi Annan in his 1998 report on Africa when he acknowledged that humanitarian organizations help foster conflicts when they are manipulated by both sides trying to turn aid into a means to reach their own political ends, to gain economic advantages or retain means to go on with fighting.[16] This abuse of aid to prolong conflicts in Africa is not a recent phenomenon.

HINGOs made their debut in Africa in the 1968 civil war over Biafra in Nigeria. Since then, HINGOs have paid a keen interest in Africa because of the increased numbers of intractable conflicts that target civilians and cause more deaths among them. 'One of the most comprehensive humanitarian operations on the entire continent' has been the response to the civil war that has ravaged Southern Sudan for nearly four decades.[17] Since 1989, Operation *Lifeline Sudan* (OLS) has subjected Southern Sudan to 'a humanitarian transfusion' that, in terms of its degree and amplitude, is 'one of the most widespread undertakings of its kind, with the obvious exception of European interventions in the Balkans, which enjoy a much larger budget'.[18] OLS, one of the world's longest-running relief operations run by UNICEF and World Food Programme in close conjunction with 35 NGOs, at its height fed 1.3 million people 10,000 tons a month. Serving both sides in the war, OLS has become the most costly relief operation in history and turned out to be 'one of the great human endeavours of the post-war years, comparable logistically with the Berlin airlift'.[19]

Despite the presence of a myriad of UN agencies and HINGOs, the conflict in Southern Sudan still causes persistent starvation. In fact, as we shall see below, the material goods they bring in have exacerbated the conflict. Humanitarian aid, when 'siphoned off by combatants for military and strategic ends', can have a political dimension that has far-reaching implications for the resolution of the conflict.[20] Besides prolonging the Sudanese conflict, humanitarian assistance has also been criticized for heightening ethnic antagonisms, ruining local agricultural production, perpetuating famine, reducing indigenous people to the status of international beggars, and for creating a state of dependence that has undermined the people's *amour propre*.[21]

Similarly, blunders of HINGOs in Rwanda have 'challenged the very concept of humanitarianism' and the 'moral principles and operational tenets that govern, or should govern, humanitarian action'.[22] After the Rwanda Patriotic Front (RPF) took over power in Rwanda in July 1994 millions of Hutus left the country and sought refuge in eastern Zaire, where aid agencies found themselves feeding not only innocent refugee women and children, but also the Hutu militias and former government soldiers and officials who had participated in the 1994 genocide. Those who committed the genocide used the UN safe havens to survive, regroup and launch guerrilla attacks into Rwanda. Although some HINGOs, such as Médecins sans Frontières (MSF) and the International Rescue Committee, withdrew in early 1995 when they came to this realization, other HINGOs such as (the American) Doctors Without Borders immediately replaced them. This only reinforced the emerging perception that humanitarian aid had become a business and media stunt. It is ironic, as will be pointed in a later section, that while war has attracted mercy, it has also been transformed by mercy.

How HINGOS Can Prolong Conflicts in Africa

While it is generally accepted that HINGOs are doing good work, there are many instances where their relief efforts have produced unintended and even counter-productive consequences.[23] In this section, I identify a number of ways in which HINGOs have prolonged conflicts in Africa.

Manipulation

HINGOs have been manipulated not only to provide resources used to fuel wars but also to gain access to the civilian population in need of humanitarian assistance, and to give de facto recognition and legitimacy to warlords and their rebel movements. In countries where states have collapsed, such as the Democratic Republic of the Congo (DRC), rebel leaders[24] heavily rely on HINGOs and international agencies to provide for the welfare of the people under their control while using the money levied from mining companies operating in the territory to buy weapons which they use to fight the government forces and other rebel groups. The mere facilitation of medical and food provisions, as well as other forms of assistance, have earned warlords legitimacy from the local population and the will to prolong the conflicts.

Using People as Shields

By locating their military and training bases near food centres or positioning themselves near civilians and airstrips, governments and rebel groups have used the starving population as shields against attacks. Besides being used for protection, relief centres have become reservoirs for 'fresh recruits for military missions' by both the rebels and the governments.[25] The case of the Rwandan refugee camps in Eastern Zaire were probably the best example of how humanitarian aid was used to control the population by former Hutu militias and government officials. For instance, the Hutu militants set up a military camp at Bilongue so as to access the nearby Chimanga civilian camp that was close to the border with Rwanda and was one of the main staging locations for the cross-border military incursions into Rwanda.[26]

The Sudan People's Liberation Army (SPLA) has also been 'constantly assured of a food supply line from aid agencies in strategic locations' by moving large civilian populations along the Sudan–Kenya border. Also adept in manipulating HINGOs in his war plans is Riek Machar's South Sudan Independence Army (SSIA) that uses relief centres as buffer zones for its military bases. For instance, in January 1993, Machar moved thousands of civilians and his forward garrison to Yuai, which came under heavy attack from SPLA forces in April. The press reported this attack as one on civilians rather than on a military garrison – just as Machar had planned.[27]

Creating Theatres of Operation

The governments have also exploited humanitarian assistance in the execution of their military strategies. By moving the civilian population into 'safe areas', HINGOs and international agencies can also inadvertently promote one of the warring party's military objectives of depopulating the theatre of operations.[28] One such government was Mozambique's, which in the late 1980s encamped large populations that were fed by HINGOs under the protection of FRELIMO forces. This not only bolstered the government's legitimacy but also allowed its forces to mop up RENAMO rebels in the areas that had been depopulated. In Southern Sudan, facilities such water wells, schools and health centres provided by HINGOs have become easy military targets of the Sudanese government, which adroitly manipulates humanitarian assistance in insidious ways.[29] For instance, in the mid-1990s it bombed and raided the Nuba mountains to push the people from their land into rebel-controlled areas. When these areas were hit by drought in 1998, the government, in conjunction with the UN World Food Programme and HINGOs, established 'peace camps' that were used as magnets to drain the rebels of their fighters who were lured by food. This was a deliberate government strategy to weaken the rebels and strengthen the government's position in the then on-going peace process.[30]

Looting and Bartering Relief

Humanitarian assistance – particularly food, medicine, equipment and vehicles – has also been used to fuel war when it is looted and bartered or sold to obtain weapons. The food is looted while being transported in convoys or on rails and barges, and at warehouses and distribution centres. The rebels have also subjected relief supplies to 'taxation' or inflated the number of recipients when receiving food to distribute to the people under their control. For instance, the SPLA has been known to falsify the number of refugees in areas under its control and to divert food intended for refugee camps and sell it in Uganda. Similar practices of looting humanitarian inputs and selling them to buy weapons have been reported in Somalia, Liberia, Sierra Leone and the DRC.

Extortion

Humanitarian assistance can also exacerbate conflict when militias, rebel groups and governments demand from HINGOs bribes, 'access fees' at checkpoints and roadblocks, and 'protection fees' for convoys and warehouses. HINGOs have also underwritten war economies by being charged outrageous currency exchanges, some as high as four times above the normal rates. The most extreme example was in the 1980s when the Sudanese government restricted the foreign exchange rates charged to HINGOs at 4.4 Sudanese pounds to $1 US instead of the market rate of 17 Sudanese pounds to a dollar.[31] The profits made from these transactions were then used to buy war matériel. In Somalia, HINGOs paid salaries for 'technicals', rents to warlords, and entered into transport and storage contracts with businessmen who were also financiers of the clan lords. The warlords also earned large amounts of money by imposing import duties, license and visa fees, and port or airport charges on HINGOs' relief supplies and personnel. Warring parties have also demanded to be included in the needs assessment exercises, where they use inaccurate and incorrect data that is obtained through manipulation of sources. The aim of influencing needs assessment is to control and manipulate the scarcity and supply of food so as to later reap huge profits.

Fungibility

Relief aid has indirectly increased the resources of conflict through fungibility. By providing aid HINGOs have relieved governments of the responsibilities of providing for the welfare of their populations, 'thus freeing resources for combat and often leading local populations to shift from productive activity to pursuing aid and in the process become more dependent and politically compliant'.[32]

Recognition and Legitimacy

HINGOs have also given recognition and legitimacy to the war efforts of governments and warlords by being forced to enter into 'prior agreements' and arrangements for 'security services', such as those with the Khartoum government and the Sudan Relief and Rehabilitation Association (SRRA) in order to guarantee that at least part of the aid will reach the desperate people. By making agreements with warring parties, HINGOs have given de facto recognition, which is used to entrench and expand their activities, to the warring parties despite their lack of legitimacy. Such arrangements were also made with Charles Taylor's National Patriotic Front of Liberia (NPFL) in early 1990s, with SPLA since the 1980s, with Somali warlords after the demise of the Barre regime in 1991, and with the Eritrean People's Liberation Front (EPLF) and the Tigray People's Liberation Front (TPLF) in the 1990s during the Ethiopian civil war against the Mengistu government.

Furthermore, combatants have also specifically targeted humanitarian aid for political and economic goals – particularly those of solidifying legitimacy over the population under their control and providing employment opportunities, which are only offered by the relief operations. This was quite common in the days preceding the downfall of the Mohamed Siade Barre government in Somalia in 1991 when war was fought among clan lords over the control of resources such as land, animals, and sources of employment for 'technicals'. However, particularly in the period 1991–92, humanitarian aid became 'the predominant liquid asset and a major resource' that the warlords fought to control.[33] This was indirectly aggravated by the well-meaning approach of dispensing aid through local organizations and using local staff; but which instead gave warlords opportunities to establish fronts staffed with their 'technicals'. In providing aid through rebel-controlled organizations, such as SPLA's SRRA, HINGOs have played a role in legitimizing the main rebel organizations and their leaders.

Dual Use of Infrastructure

There have also been numerous cases in which warring parties have promoted their military objectives, using 'humanitarian infrastructure and assets' such as reconstructed roads and bridges, and personnel and agreements to facilitate delivery of relief supplies. This frequently happen in Southern Sudan where reconstructed roads have enabled combatants to move farther and faster, and human assets, particularly health workers, have been conscripted into military service after being trained. In Liberia and Eastern Zaire, HINGOs' physical assets such as vehicles and communication equipment were 'borrowed' by rebels and never returned.

Creating Perceptions of Power Imbalance

HINGOs have prolonged conflicts by creating perceptions of power imbalance among warring parties. In Southern Sudan, 'perceptions by Jikany Nuer leaders of the disproportionate aid benefits accrued by Lau Nuer has helped fuel Jikany cattle raiding…into Dinka areas' since 1991.[34] In Somaliland, aid imbalances have been cited as contributing to the Garhajis' opposition to the government, whom it accuses of benefiting from aid disbursement and controlling their access to it.[35]

Criticisms of HINGOs in Africa

Despite the laudable work of HINGOs in saving lives in complex emergencies, their increased involvement in the management and transformation of violent conflicts is now being widely criticized. But what is the motivation for HINGOs prolonging conflicts? Alex de Waal argues that aid agencies are motivated by two interests: a 'soft' or altruistic interest aimed at helping those who are suffering, and a 'hard' interest which is based on the HINGO's need to justify its existence.[36] Two of the most vocal critics of HINGOs have been Clare Short, British Secretary for International Development, and Raakiya Omar of Africa Rights. They both argue that the zeal of HINGOs to reach the victims is driven by market forces that have made them operate more or less like businesses – competing for scarce resources, jockeying for attention, and selling themselves to potential donors. In June 1998 Clare Short caused a storm when she criticized the methods used by aid agencies to raise famine relief funds. She pointed out that the use of 'unbearable' images of starving African children not only made 'people flinch and turn away' but also led to 'compassion fatigue' in the long run.[37] Rakiya Omaar has referred to this tactic of promoting their profiles to raise funds as 'disaster pornography'.[38] Omaar asserts that these NGOs cross the line of common decency when they use 'ghastly photographs'.

Almost all African conflicts have attracted hundreds of HINGOs that are too small, amateurish and confused in their aims. In order to survive they have to compete with each other in raising money and winning accolades for their noble missions of saving the most unfortunate of the human race.[39] Some agencies, with MSF being the most accomplished, have become masters of spinning the story of an event to influence public opinion of the donors.[40] Since they have to depend on the media to publicize their activities and fund-raising, HINGOs require resources, both money and time, to market themselves. A review of their operational budgets shows that they are spending between 15 and 25 per cent of their funds on marketing and fundraising.

Despite such criticisms that have been levelled at HINGOs, David Bryer, the Director of Oxfam GB, strongly defends humanitarian assistance by contending that 'tens of thousands of lives are saved every year, and an enormous amount of further human suffering is avoided'.[41] David Shearer, in his defence of HINGOs, argues that relief aid from 'a more macro perspective...appears to have had little impact on the course of civil wars'. And that most conflicts such as Sudan's have proved extraordinarily resilient to peace and have 'continued unrelentingly'. In view of the elusive quest for peace, 'the assertion that aid is fuelling war in Sudan ignores the historical realities'. In Somalia, Shearer points out, there has also been 'little observable correlation between amounts of aid and levels of violence'.[42] Furthermore, it is 'impossible', on the micro-level, to quantify the economic and organizational benefits brought to warlords by relief aid.[43] Despite some individuals benefiting from the war, it is difficult to pinpoint exactly how much earnings warlords have pocketed from the war.

To be fair, aid can be less pernicious than scarce commodities.[44] In Angola, UNITA was earning around US$500 million from diamonds per year before sanctions were imposed on 'blood diamonds' that were being used to finance its war against the Angolan government. Shearer argues that UNITA did not start the war in 1966 to make profits from it and that Charles Taylor also financed his guerrilla war mainly by exporting hardwoods from the areas under his control.[45] Humanitarian aid also 'played virtually no part in Sierra Leone's brutal and ugly war' in which the RUF armed and equipped its fighters through diamonds that were found in the territory under its control.

Shearer's spirited defence of humanitarian assistance overlooks the fact that HINGOs have seriously taken into consideration manipulation of food aid and regard it as normal practice. It is a fact that some HINGOs regularly include a 30 per cent loss in their budgets, and others have made payments to militias to guard relief supplies or local army units to transport food safely; or in other words, paid the people who would otherwise attack their lorries.

Recommendations

After describing three ways, the 'mandate blinders',[46] 'aid on our terms only',[47] and 'do no harm',[48] in which NGOs have responded to the political effects of their work, Mary Anderson recommends that

HINGOs should give up their apolitical stance by first denouncing war itself.[49] Their assistance should then be directed towards supporting and protecting local opposition to war, and to promoting people's efforts to disengage from the conflicts. But this will require developing alternative methods of distributing assistance that are not easily misdirected into the war effort such as supporting local capacities for peace and capacities for community self-reliance.[50] When aid is given in ways that 'provide or enlarge the safe space where people act and speak in non-war ways' it gives the people incentive and motivation 'to disengage from conflict'.[51] HINGOs have a responsibility to promote 'these positive side effects and mitigate the negative ones'.[52] Fostering economic cooperation and interdependence between non-combatant members of warring groups can make positive contributions to peacebuilding efforts.

According to Ben Hoffman, those NGOs without political or partisan positions can 'gain access and entry, build relationships, and offer conflict resolution, mediation, and negotiation services in situations where more formal diplomacy has not been immediately welcomed'. By providing humanitarian assistance, NGOs can 'lay the groundwork for more in-depth conflict resolution initiatives'.[53] But this is only feasible if HINGOs' agenda is designed, and humanitarian action is undertaken, to complement the peace agenda, as pointed out below, as part of a comprehensive peacebuilding strategy that also includes recovery and development of society.

HINGO workers, who have no training in conflict resolution and diplomacy, can complicate the resolution of conflicts when they dabble in peace-making activities with the aim of facilitating their relief efforts. Nevertheless, HINGOs can build trust in areas of conflict, thereby creating an opening for peacebuilders to come in. As the peacebuilding efforts get under way, HINGOs can continue working more closely with peacebuilders to coordinate the transition to post-conflict reconstruction. Regardless of how long it takes for peace negotiators to come in, humanitarian workers should never assume the burden of ending the conflict.

According to Nobert Ropers, there are four ways HINGOs can contribute to conflict resolution.[54] The first way is by 'empower(ing) single or all parties to deal with the conflict constructively and/or to support them to avoid a violent outbreak'. This can be done through measures such as monitoring and lobbying for human rights and the protection of minorities, building the capacity and protective measurements for disadvantaged or endangered groups, and training peace activists in conflict transformation skills. Second, HINGOs can 'create channels and forums to balance out the influence of power-differences, power-political positions and negotiation strategies in favour of an orientation towards basic interests, the clarifying of relationships and the enabling of common problem-solutions'. In other words, HINGOs can serve as a bridge between warring parties and peace negotiators/makers. Third, HINGOs can 'help the victims of violent conflicts regardless of interests of power and sovereignty'. But this 'well-meaning approach' is now under review as a result of the on-going debate that humanitarian assistance has negative sides. And fourth, HINGOs can civilize 'conflicts by promoting skills and capabilities for a constructive conflict-management to as many individual persons as possible'. But regardless of the role they are called upon to play besides the primary one of helping those suffering due to conflict, HINGOs should guard against being sucked into being players in the conflicts. The danger of HINGOs becoming players in the conflicts increases when their workers engage in conflict resolution; but instead they should create 'the stimulus for the continuation of the conflict – albeit involuntarily'.[55] To help them avoid overreaching their mandate and capabilities, HINGOs should always bear in mind the words of Oxfam's Bryer that 'relief is, after all, exactly what it says. It is not the solution to violence.'

To summarize, HINGOs should take into careful consideration the following:

- *Avoid being pawns*: HINGOs should not allow themselves to be used as 'humanitarian alibi' by Western governments who want to misuse the humanitarian idea and humanitarian workers by doing little or nothing at all in economically dreary regions like sub-Saharan Africa.

- *Set clear goals and operate with realistic objectives*: HINGOs should not exceed their limit. Besides lacking 'sufficient legitimacy' to end conflicts, HINGOs also lack internal structures that can support their primary functions and engage in highly specialized roles of conflict prevention, management and resolution.[56] In particular, HINGOs lack finances to pursue activities beyond feeding the hungry and treating the sick victims of complex emergencies. HINGOs need not only take a more cautious approach but also realistically reassess what they can and cannot accomplish. Having the moral courage to pull out once the relief has been compromised through the manipulation of the aid is a higher moral principle than that of helping the victims of conflict and in the process supporting those who are victimizing them.[57]

- *Adopt strict moral standards*: HINGOs should be directed by moral standards in their fundraising activities and eschew 'disaster pornography', obsession with publicity and violation of the universal humanitarian code of conduct that is based on serving humanity.

- *Use proper evaluation criteria*: HINGOs' performance of providing the minimum requirements of relief assistance – shelter, food, water and health care, as well as educational and social support – should be judged not only by how many lives they save but also by how they avoid being part of the conflict.

- *Train humanitarian workers*: The aid workers, before and during the relief operation, must 'understand the cultural, political, social, and religious tensions that lead to war' and its victims whom they are assisting.[58] This also means that HINGOs should ensure that their contributions to peacebuilding are not pulverized by the rather macho mentality of their workers who – despite their poor, or lack of, conflict analysis and diplomatic skills – undertake messianic adventures. It is in a climate of ignorance and arrogance that grievous mistakes are made.

- *Engage in greater coordination*: And lastly, since 'experience shows that aid is highly likely to do more harm when the number of aid organizations and aid resources is large and when coordination efforts are minimal',[59] it logically follows that HINGOs must work in greater coordination under the principles laid out in the Sphere Project's *Humanitarian Charter and Minimum Standards in Disaster Response*. HINGOs must also differentiate between those 'who support war and have a vested interest in its continuation' and those 'who represent either existing or incipient capacities for peace' so as to be 'able to identify situations where their aid might support or undermine existing and latent local capacities for peace'.[60] HINGOs must 'carefully plan their delivery strategies so that the substance, timing, and modalities of delivery support local capacities for peace and not the forces of war'.[61] This is similar to the 'Norwegian model', which is based on close, but informal and flexible, cooperation between the authorities and NGOs that allows humanitarian assistance to develop local knowledge and contacts which are later used in peace and reconciliation processes.[62]

HINGOs can continue providing relief without fuelling or prolonging conflicts by working within a comprehensive framework of a peace support partnership with development, democratization and human rights agencies, the military, and civilian police operations. But this would only be possible if the mandates given by the UN Security Council or regional organizations for humanitarian intervention in internal conflicts should contain all the key components of peace support operations – humanitarian aid, restoration of rule of law, diplomacy, promotion of human rights, and development assistance – and stipulate the structures which reflect this comprehensive approach.

Beyond the central dilemma of sticking to the humanitarian assistance principles or withdrawing aid when it is abused, there are a number of other dilemmas which HINGOs must confront: whether to aim at reaching those who are in most need, or only those victims allowed access to by the combatants; whether to provide the type of aid most needed (such as water pipes, fertilizer, seeds and educational material), or only that which the combatants allow; and whether or not to use the military or local militias (or 'technicals', as they are called in Somalia) to provide security for their workers and food warehouses.

Some HINGOs have taken a positive step in reaction to the criticism of their massive involvement in civil wars and 'complex emergencies' by adopting the Hippocratic Oath policy of 'Do No Harm'. The following two examples illustrate choices that can be made by HINGOs to avoid being used to harm victims of conflicts. The first case took place in 1995 in Liberia after the warlords looted more than 400 aid vehicles and millions of dollars of equipment and relief goods from the HINGOs to directly support the war.[63] The vehicles and radio equipment were then used for military purposes and also to transport diamond and gold to buying centres and return with weapons. When the 13 humanitarian agencies, including the International Committee of the Red Cross (ICRC),[64] came to the realization that they had unwittingly fuelled the war in Liberia, they decided not to renew major operations in June 1996.[65] The 13 HINGOs resorted to using 'locally-available equipment' and stopped bringing new resources into Liberia that could fuel the 'war economy'. They also limited their relief work to distributions of food to those directly threatened with starvation. Oxfam made a bold move of cutting off relief efforts, such as improvement of the water supply in south-east Liberia, to prevent their vehicles and equipment from being seized to fight the war. It was Oxfam's conviction that more lives would 'be saved by preventing such looting than by providing humanitarian aid'.[66]

Another significant and relevant example was the decision taken by some of the largest HINGOs operating in southern Sudan not to sign a memorandum of understanding to operate joint relief operations with the humanitarian wing of the main rebel faction, the Sudan

People's Liberation Movement (SPLM), whose military wing is the SPLA. These HINGOs have rejected SPLM's arrangement on the ground it would undermine their neutrality and have opted to withdraw from OLS operations despite the fear that such an action would adversely affect civilian populations benefiting from their relief efforts.[67] This is in line with Pamela Aall's admonishment that HINGOs 'must identify and ally themselves with forces seeking to resolve political differences, not with groups trying to fuel the conflict'.[68]

ACKNOWLEDGEMENTS

The author is deeply grateful to Samuel Makinda and Caroline King for their editorial comments.

NOTES

1. See Refugee Policy Group, *Hope Restored? Humanitarian Aid in Somalia, 1990–1994*, Washington DC: Refugee Policy Group, 1994, pp.94–6.
2. See African Rights, *Food and Power in Sudan – A Critique of Humanitarianism*, London: African Rights, 1997; Alex de Waal, 'Dangerous Precedents? Famine Relief in Somalia 1991–93', in Joanna Macrae and Anthony Zwi (eds.), *War and Hunger: Rethinking International Responses to Complex Emergencies*, London: Zed Books, 1994; Mary B. Anderson, 'Humanitarian NGOs in Conflict Intervention', in Chester Crocker, Fen Hampson and Pamela Aall (eds.), *Managing Global Chaos*, Washington DC: United States Institute of Peace Press, 1996.
3. United Nations Office for the Coordination of Humanitarian Affairs (OCHA) has listed over 260 NGOs on its website, www.reliefweb.int/contacts/dirhomepage.html #ngo.
4. See Union of International Associations, *Yearbook of International Organizations*, Munich: K.G. Saur Verlag, 2001.
5. See Hugo Slim, 'To the Rescue: Radicals or Poodles?', *The World Today*, Vol.53, No.8–9, Aug./Sept. 1997.
6. Ibid.
7. David Bryer, 'Providing Humanitarian Assistance During Internal Conflicts', address to International Peace Academy Annual Conference, Vienna, 23 July 1996, www.oxfam.org.uk/atwork/emerg/vienna.htm).
8. Ibid. See also Monika Sandvik-Nylund, *Caught in Conflicts: Civilian Victims, Humanitarian Assistance and International Law*, Turku: Institute for Human Rights, Abo Akademi University, 1998, pp.75–80.
9. Mary B. Anderson, *Do No Harm: How Aid Can Support Peace – or War*, Boulder, CO: Lynne Rienner, 1999, pp.37–53.
10. See Peter Beaumont 'Starving and shot', *The Observer* (London), 10 May 1998.
11. John Prendergast, *Crisis Response: Humanitarian BandAids in Sudan and Somalia*, London: Pluto Press, 1997, p.18.
12. See Antonio Donini, 'Asserting Humanitarianism in Peace-Maintenance', in Jarat Chopra (ed.), *Politics of Peace Maintenance*. Boulder, CO: Lynne Rienner, 1998, p.82.
13. Ibid., p.88.
14. Ibid.
15. See Anderson (n.9 above), p.344.
16. See Report of the Secretary-General to the United Nations Security Council, *The Causes of Conflict and the Promotion of Durable Peace and Sustainable Development*

in Africa, New York: United Nations, 1998.
17. See Marc-Antoine Perouse de Montclos; 'A crisis of humanitarianism', *Forum for Applied Research and Public Policy*; Vol.16, No.2; Summer 2001.
18. Ibid.
19. See W.F. Deedes and Victoria Combe, 'Feed me and I will live: the plea that shines from a child's eyes', *The Daily Telegraph* (London), 22 June 1998.
20. See de Montclos (n.17 above).
21. Ibid.
22. See Donini (n.12 above), p.82. See also Jos Havermans, 'Great Lakes Traumas Puzzle NGOs: 'Many people feel burned out', *Conflict Prevention Newsletter*, Vol.1, No.1, Mar. 1998, p.2.
23. See Anderson (n.2 above), p.345.
24. Such as Jean-Pierre Bemba of the Mouvement de Libération du Congo (MLC).
25. Prendergast (n.11 above), p.21.
26. Ibid., p.20. For details on how HINGOs assisted the perpetrators of genocide in Rwanda, see John Erikson, *The International Response to Conflict and Genocide: Lessons from the Rwandan Experience*, Copenhagen: Steering Committee of the Joint Evaluation of Emergency Assistance to Rwanda, Mar. 1996.
27. See Prendergast (n.11 above), p.21.
28. Ibid., p.29.
29. See Ian Fisher, 'Can International Relief Do More Good than Harm?', *New York Times Magazine*, 21 Feb. 2001.
30. Ibid.
31. See Mark Duffield, 'The Political Economy of Internal War: Asset Transfer, Complex Emergencies and International Aid', in Macrae and Zwi (n.2 above), pp.60–61.
32. See Prendergast (n.11), p.25.
33. Ibid., p.30.
34. Ibid., p.28.
35. Ibid.
36. See Alex de Waal, 'Dangerous Precedents? Famine Relief in Somalia 1991–1993', in Macrae and Zwi (n.2 above), pp.139–58.
37. See Raymond Whitaker, 'Well said, Clare Short', *The Independent* (London), 7 June 1998.
38. Quoted in ibid.
39. See Michael Maren, *The Road to Hell: The Ravaging Effects of Foreign Aid and International Charity*, New York: Free Press, 1997.
40. Ibid.
41. See Bryer (n.7 above).
42. David Shearer, 'Aiding or Abetting? Humanitarian Aid and Its Economic Role in Civil War', in Mats Berdal and David Malone (eds.), *Greed and Grievance: Economic Agendas in Civil Wars*, Boulder, CO: Lynne Rienner, 2000, p.194.
43. Ibid.
44. Ibid., p.195.
45. Ibid.
46. This is the approach in which HINGOs feel that the primary purpose of their work sufficiently justifies ignoring secondary effects of their actions. See Anderson (n.9 above), p.349.
47. This approach is used by HINGOs to monitor the negative consequences of their relief effort and, if the negative impact begins to outweigh the positive, withdraw it and offer to return when conditions become more conducive for effective humanitarian assistance.
48. HINGOs who use this approach, modelled on the 'Hippocratic Oath' of physicians, seek to do whatever they can to aid their targeted populations while taking responsibility for the unintended consequences of their actions and actively seeking to better understand the consequences of their activities.
49. Anderson (n.9 above), pp.18–19.

50. Ibid., p.53.
51. Ibid., p.30.
52. Rob DiPrizio, 'Adverse Effects of Humanitarian Aid in Complex Emergencies', in *Small Wars and Insurgencies*, Vol.10, No.1, Spring 1999, p.100.
53. See www.cartercenter.org/hoffmanq&a.html.
54. Norbert Ropers, 'Eight Critical Statements on the Contribution of NGOs to Conflict Prevention and Transformation', *Conflict Prevention Newsletter*, Vol.1, No.2, June 1998, p.10.
55. Ibid.
56. See ibid., p.11.
57. Although the SPHERE Project's 'Humanitarian Charter', once adopted by HINGOs, will serve as 'a tool ... to enhance the effectiveness and quality of their assistance and thus to make a significant difference to the lives of people affected by disaster', it does not establish any conditions under which they can withdraw from a relief operation when the warring parties compromise their objectives.
58. Ibid.
59. DiPrizio (n.52 above), p.100.
60. See Ibid., p.101 and Anderson (n.9 above), p.56.
61. Ibid.
62. See http://odin.dep.no/ud/engelsk/publ/veiledninger/032005-993656/index-dok000-b-n-a.html.
63. Bryer (n.7 above).
64. Although the International Committee of the Red Cross is an intergovernmental organization (IGO), it functions more or less like an NGO. Pamela Aall refers to it as a hybrid of an IGO and NGO. See Pamela Aall et al., *A Guide to IGOs, NGOs and the Military in Peace and Relief Operations*, Washington, DC: United States Institute of Peace, 2000, p.21.
65. This decision subsequently influenced the British and US Governments and the European Union to adopt a similar stance.
66. Bryer (n.7 above).
67. See S.D. Taylor-Robinson, 'Operation Lifeline Sudan', *Journal of Medical Ethics*; Vol.28, No.1, Feb. 2002.
68. Aall (n.64 above), p.105.

NGOs and Peacebuilding in Afghanistan

MAHMOOD MONSHIPOURI

Post-conflict societies face a bewildering array of economic, social and political difficulties. In the absence of international support and commitment, successful recovery from civil war, lawlessness and displacement is virtually impossible. Attempts to simultaneously reconstruct the country and build the capacity of people to provide for their basic needs are crucial. Consequently, confronting the sources of insecurity affecting people and communities on the one hand and promoting nation building on the other are central to building peace in Afghanistan. In fact, these tasks are not entirely unrelated. Without attacking poverty, it is virtually impossible to conduct either a sustained programme against terror or a durable campaign for the country's reconstruction.[1]

It has become increasingly evident that coping with humanitarian crises in post-conflict societies requires a multi-track approach, combining efforts that aim at achieving relief, development and governance. In post-Taliban Afghanistan, the tasks of nation building and refugee repatriation must be juxtaposed. The same is true of the attempt to concurrently promote nation building and establish civil society. Put simply, political rehabilitation and social reconstruction of the country must not be viewed as separate tasks. Similarly, human security must be addressed immediately, in part because it cannot be postponed for the complicated process of political reconstruction. In this basic sense, it is critical to recognize that non-state actors have much to offer in the way of reducing human insecurities and suffering. This reality, however, tells us little about how influential nongovernmental organizations (NGOs) or other non-state actors will actually be in the context of maintaining order and stability.[2] Without cooperation between NGOs, international organizations, civil society and the state, it is virtually impossible to deal effectively with the country's humanitarian crisis.

This study centres particularly on three key themes: (1) order and security are crucial to nation-building in Afghanistan; (2) peacebuilding is inextricably intertwined with the larger context of reconstruction and (3) conflict resolution must be seen as a main goal of development policy. This thematic focus is designed to address several questions: Should efforts at economic reconstruction and humanitarian relief precede political agreements in failed states or war-stricken areas such as Afghanistan? And are NGOs appropriate vehicles for rebuilding Afghanistan, given that their influence on the dynamics of peace and conflict has been limited in the 1990s? While the larger political issues need to be addressed, a commitment to humanitarian development assistance is critical to Afghanis' survival. Consider, for example, Cooperation for Peace and Unity (CPAU), an Afghan network initiated in 1996, which has enhanced the capacity for promoting peace by empowering development workers to handle conflict issues arising in their work. CPAU, which works in cooperation with international NGOs such as Responding to Conflict (UK) and the Norwegian Church Committee, provides an alternative to conflict through rehabilitation and reconstruction at the local level without waiting for a permanent political solution.

This essay will also identify areas in which NGOs have a comparative advantage in their capacity to promote conflict resolution. NGOs – international and local – can address relief, rehabilitation, gender inequality, landmine issues and the longer-term development needs of the Afghanis. Their intervention through capacity-building roles by health professionals, engineers, community development advisers and programme manager advisers will contribute to the peace-building process. The United Nations Fund for Population Activities (UNFPA) must provide for such local and international NGOs working in the area of reproductive health service and gender support.

Background

Afghanistan has been devastated by two decades of civil war, Soviet incursions and several years of drought. The Soviet-Afghan war marked a turning point as a new form of the holy war (*jihad*) became globalized to a degree never seen in the past.[3] The *mujahidin* holy war against the Soviets drew Muslims from many parts of the world, with Afghans and Arabs joining Muslim struggles in other areas, including in Bosnia, Kosovo and Central Asia. Others were trained and recruited in the new *madrasas* and training camps in Pakistan and Afghanistan throughout the 1990s.[4]

The flow of refugees that followed the Soviet invasion created huge demands on aid agencies. The steady increase of refugees in the early

1980s meant that NGOs became basic providers of relief and health care. The UN and the neighbouring countries, such as Iran and Pakistan, lacked the necessary resources and muscle to implement massive relief operations alone. Local NGOs, such as the Society of Afghan Doctors (SAD), Afghan Medical Aid (AMA), and the Afghan Health and Social Assistance Organization (AHSAO), offered basic health care in the refugee camps.[5] NGOs grew in numbers and over the years increased their expenditure and their organizational structure. Specifically, they became important actors in the refugee camps.[6] By the mid-1980s, cross-border operations opened the route to Afghanistan and broadened the space for humanitarian operations by the vast numbers of NGOs. Consequently, NGOs became the dominant humanitarian actors on the Afghan side.[7] As the sole providers of foreign relief aid, humanitarian NGOs in Afghanistan even negotiated deals with the resistance commanders. The UN agencies were not involved, and the International Committee of the Red Cross kept aloof.[8]

The Taliban regime also imposed a strict version of Islamic law (*Shari'a*) on the country, prohibiting almost all public activities. These prohibitions were particularly designed to curtail the freedoms and rights of women and rendered the lives of displaced women far more desperate.[9] Moreover, Taliban rule had debilitating consequences for drawing much-needed external assistance and presence in one of the world's poorest countries. Many public and private international agencies withdrew from Afghanistan during 1998–99, unwilling to operate within the limitations on their freedom of action that the Taliban regime imposed.[10] During the summer of 1998, the Taliban banned 38 international NGOs from the country. At the same time, the European Community Humanitarian Office (ECHO) cut its aid to Afghanistan as a punitive policy against the Taliban.[11]

The humanitarian crisis in Afghanistan, which predates Taliban rule, intensified after the traumatic events of 11 September 2001, when terrorists attacked the World Trade Center and the Pentagon. Initially, the mere threat of military strikes on Afghanistan resulted in massive outflows of refugees and displaced persons, aggravating the country's existing humanitarian calamity. The Afghan crisis took yet another turn for the worse as the first bomb fell on Afghanistan on 7 October 2001. Many Afghanis believed that they cannot rely on the protection of their own government and that any hope of a diplomatic initiative that could save them from poverty and ill health has been dashed. Increasingly, these refugees are at risk of losing their nationality as a result of the dissolution of their home country. The UN High

Commission for Refugees (UNHCR) in Islamabad, Pakistan, has warned that 'security conditions at or near refugee camps are not only fragile but continue to pose a serious obstacle to humanitarian efforts in the region'.[12]

Despite legal protections, such as the right to security, which is fully recognized in international law, many refugees find little comfort in living in the neighbouring countries of Pakistan and Iran. Of particular concern to NGO relief operations are refugee children, who are in danger not only of losing a sense of national identity (by becoming either illegal or legal aliens) but also of being exposed to practices having effects similar to slavery. The exposure of refugee children to physical violence and other violations of their basic rights, such as commercial sexual exploitation and trade, as well as forced recruitment into low-wage labour such as rug-weaving, has raised serious concerns in the international human rights community. In the Hazaratown refugee camp in Pakistan, refugee children from Afghanistan work five to ten hours a day to earn US$5–$7 a month.[13]

Many Afghanis who fled their farmlands, either prior to or after the war, face a very uncertain future. They are unlikely to enjoy the benefits of citizenship in the countries in which they seek refuge. One observer echoes this concern while exploring the roots of Afghan rebellion: 'Few refugees have been integrated into Pakistani society. The government pushes them to the margins, and most say they want to go home when the time comes anyway.'[14] In such circumstances, it is reasonable to argue that only long-term peacebuilding in Afghanistan can bring refugees back to their homeland. To invest in nation building and peacebuilding is the best way to counter the terrorist operations and threats that have plagued the country and the region. Ultimately, addressing the refugee crisis and poverty head-on is the key to sustainable efforts at peacebuilding in Afghanistan.

Reconstruction and Governance

The most pressing question facing both domestic leaders and the international community is how to rebuild Afghanistan. Although it is clear that reconstruction and governance are related, it is unclear how and under what conditions relief and development projects are linked. The issues of reconstruction and sustainable peace in Afghanistan are arguably political questions, in that they relate to investment in the country's long-term development. Some scholars have pointed to the merging of development and security as a novel device to prevent the recurrence of the wars of the 1990s. This convergence has transformed the political discourse in that development is now increasingly seen as security.[15]

Poverty eradication and community empowerment are also vitally significant to the reconstruction of the country and to its security. The UN Development Programme (UNDP) initiated the Poverty Eradication and Community Empowerment (PEACE) project in Afghanistan to solve problems at the grassroots level and to create an environment conducive to reconciliation and lasting peace. This initiative is laying the foundations of such activities by setting up Village Development Committees (VDCs) to identify and supervise the country's reconstruction and rehabilitation. The process involves projects aimed at improving health, shelter, water, sanitation and education facilities. Women, marginalized in much of Afghan society, are specifically targeted in all aspects of the PEACE initiative. As part of a co-funded project by the Japanese UNDP, and in cooperation with UNHCR and UNICEF, as well as a number of NGOs, the PEACE initiative is assisting refugees, primarily living in Pakistan, to return to their home villages in the focus districts of Azro and Sarobi.[16]

Many experts have stressed a shift to more long-term, community-based aid programmes.[17] While there is urgency for short-term humanitarian assistance in certain areas, the larger problem is that many families simply lack the economic means to purchase food and other goods in the markets. Aid agencies must accurately assess and address the real needs of accessible populations. Afghanistan needs tangible and substantive support – in both resources and strategic planning – for the reconstruction of an economic infrastructure.[18] In this context, food-for-education programmes will have adverse impacts. To remain neutral, independent and impartial, aid agencies must keep donor politics at bay while adopting safeguards to prevent the politicization of humanitarian aid.[19]

Integration of the many efforts at relief, reconstruction and development is the most widely recognized challenge of helping Afghanis. An overall strategy of assistance to Afghanistan has been placed under the supervision of the Afghanistan Programming Body. This body includes representation from donors, UN agencies, NGOs and the Red Cross.[20] The main function of this forum, in addition to the field-level coordination, is to bring aid and security agencies together in order to negotiate humanitarian space.[21] In the case of Afghanistan, it is important to recognize that the UN agencies, NGOs and the Afghan government alone have limited access to populations outside Kabul. Particularly alarming is the government's limited capacity. This creates a security concern pertaining not only to the coordination of humanitarian actors but also to its own limited control over large parts of the country, due to the abilities of regional warlords and armed factions.[22]

During the Taliban era, the problem was the collapse of institutions, the rise of personal insecurity, and the deterioration of the means of livelihood for the Afghan population.[23] Most experts agree that without an educated populace, a secure future for Afghanistan cannot be established. NGO projects aimed at addressing the needs of local communities, including health and education, are key to reconstructing Afghanistan. The priority of the international community must shift from ways to combat terrorism in Afghanistan to 'the needs, opinions, and values of the Afghan people, who continue to live in a country in crisis'.[24]

Sceptics have pointed out that given the country's ethnic makeup and the existence of regional warlords, it is extremely difficult to create any unifying political structures. The country's different regions are controlled by a variety of warlords and strongmen, who remain part of Afghanistan's political architecture. The international community has no alternative but to work with them as it has done with other such leaders in the past.[25] International and domestic NGOs must avoid becoming dangerously entangled in local politics.[26] The first step, it is argued, should simply be to re-establish a degree of normal life, even if it is not comparable to life in a modern state.[27]

US foreign policymakers have increasingly viewed nation building as synonymous with stability in Afghanistan. Maintaining political order in Afghanistan has also necessitated a direct UN involvement and force on the ground.[28] In the Bonn agreement, signed on 5 December 2001, the UN brought together Afghan groups opposed to the Taliban and al-Qaeda to take up the central task of re-establishing permanent government institutions. Although the agreement provided a framework for peace building, the implementation of its provisions largely turned on how international donors and the UN system managed the task of reconstruction.[29]

A consensus has emerged that an increase in international presence in the name of state building and nation building was directly linked to re-establishing governance, with the end result of protecting the self-determination and human security of the people of Afghanistan. Today, the international community's own security hinges, to a large degree, on Afghanistan's economic rehabilitation.[30] There has emerged a considerable public space for cooperation between international NGOs (INGOs) and local NGOs on projects for job creation, health, child survival, education, population and agriculture.[31]

The Imperative of Human Security

Although the nexus between human security, basic needs, human rights and peacebuilding is obvious, the dominant discourse in Afghanistan is now associating human security with the maintenance of order. In a society where person and property are in constant jeopardy, the restoration of order can be a defence of human rights. Those analysts and practitioners who advocate integrating human rights and peace work argue that 'sustainable livelihoods' are the precondition for lasting peace: 'The first imperative in preventing conflict and building peace is establishing human security. Without security, human rights are seldom safe.'[32]

In mid-2002 Afghan officials warned that if the United States – or the international community as a whole – did not pay more attention to the war on poverty in Afghanistan, the gains made in the war against terror could soon disappear. 'The country's unchecked poverty', they maintained, was 'feeding the angry tirades of Islamic fundamentalists who charge that the West does not really care about the Afghan people'.[33] Many Western observers, however, argue that it is unfair to accuse the West of a lack of compassion. Security considerations and humanitarian efforts, they insist, are directly linked in Afghanistan. Willy Newman, an Australian Oxfam director in Kandahar, argues that 'many aid agencies are still concerned about the security situation. They are hesitant to start projects in Afghanistan and then see them ripped to shreds by more fighting.'[34]

Following the 11 September attacks in the United States, the world has increasingly come to realize that human insecurities transcend state borders and have serious global consequences. Building institutions of security, order and governance that are accountable and legitimate constitutes the core task of protecting human security in Afghanistan.[35] The human security approach addresses non-traditional threats to people's security related to economic, food, health and environmental factors, as well as issues such as drugs, terrorism, organized crime, landmines and gender-based violence. Human security is about recognizing the importance of the security needs of the people side by side with those of states, minimizing risks and taking preventive measures to reduce human vulnerabilities, and taking remedial action when preventive measures fail.[36]

Refugees and Development

It is generally believed that persecution or the threat of persecution are the main causes of refugee exodus.[37] Today, however, the refugee problem may also be linked to enormous privation, especially for women and children. A report by Physicians for Human Rights suggests that: 'Afghan women who seek refuge outside of Afghanistan should be officially recognized as refugees by the UNHCR and afforded assistance accordingly.'[38]

Estimates of refugees vary, but according to UNHCR, there are 3,695,000 Afghan refugees throughout the world. Since 1978, millions of Afghans have sought refuge in neighbouring countries, with 2 million currently living in Pakistan, and 1.5 million in Iran. An estimated 100,000 live in Russia, 29,000 in the Central Asian Republics, 36,000 in Europe, 17,000 in North America and Australia, and 13,000 in India. At least 900,000 were internally displaced in the country before 11 September.[39] Afghanistan under Taliban rule (1996–2001) never had a functioning government and failed to provide for the human security of its people. For years, experts find, NGOs have been the main actors in several sectors, such as primary education, health care, landmine removal and supplying water to rural communities.[40]

The disjuncture between relief activities and development activities poses yet another formidable challenge for the task of reconstruction in Afghanistan. While relief operations have a long history there, development activities have been spectacularly lacking. Furthermore, while relief activities are of a short-term nature, development policies having to do with building capacity for governance and economic growth are long-term projects. The problem is that the failure to pursue these activities concomitantly is bound to pose a serious threat to the government in place. How can such activities be carried out most effectively in the context of a post-conflict transition?[41]

Health and Human Rights Problems

In recent years the health consequences of civil wars and human rights violations have come under critical scrutiny. Many experts in public health have argued that the promotion of health is inseparable from the protection and promotion of human rights.

Médecins Sans Frontières (MSF), for example, has advocated the fundamental right of ordinary people to humanitarian assistance and protection. In the early phases of the war in Afghanistan, MSF questioned the dual military and humanitarian-aid operation, arguing that it '[was not] in any way a humanitarian-aid operation, but more a military propaganda operation, destined to make international opinion accept the U.S.-led military operation'.[42] MSF's Jean-Hervé Bradol spoke against accepting money from governments in the campaign against Afghanistan.[43] In the aftermath of the Talbian's overthrow, MSF undertook several measles vaccination campaigns in Ghorak and Khakrez in the Kandahar province and mobilized staff and equipment to cope with the earthquakes that hit Nahrin on 25–26 March 2002.

According to the reports collected during a three-month period in the beginning of 1998 by Physicians for Human Rights (PHR), a Boston-based NGO, such human rights violations were 'literally life threatening to women and to their children'.[44] The results of the survey of 160 Afghan women indicated that Taliban rule had serious consequences for women's health and human rights. Seventy-one per cent of participants reported a decline in their physical health under the Taliban. Fifty-three per cent of women described occasions in which they were seriously ill and unable to seek medical care.[45] Ninety-five per cent of women interviewed described a decline in their mental condition over the two years prior to the survey. The overall climate of discrimination, repression and abuse that characterized the Taliban had a profound effect on women's mental health. Additionally, Taliban gender restrictions invariably interfered with the delivery of humanitarian assistance to women.[46] Conditions have deteriorated rather than improved since the Taliban regime was overthrown.

A PHR fact-finding mission to Afghanistan in January 2002 included a visit to Shebarghan Prison, where they observed over 300 prisoners and spoke directly with eight prisoners as well as medical staff in the prison's infirmary. The delegation also conducted several interviews on site with local and international representatives of major NGOs and international organizations, as well as local Afghan officials and community members. Nearly 1,000 of the prisoners were Pakistanis and the rest Afghan Taliban. The investigators reported that conditions at Shebarghan were in grave violation of international standards for those held in detention.[47] The capacity to provide medical care was severely hampered by inadequate supplies and primitive facilities. Dysentery and yellow jaundice, largely due to Hepatitis A, were epidemic. The PHR delegation confirmed that: 'The living conditions are very harsh and expose the prisoners to high risk of illness from gastrointestinal diseases (spread by fecal-oral routes) and respiratory diseases (caused by crowding, poor clothing, and lack of shelter protection from cold weather)'.[48] The report added that medical supports in the infirmary were inadequate, in that there were no signs of intravenous fluid capacities, that necessary medications were depleted, and that four of the eight patients appeared critically ill, with one moribund.[49]

The Landmine Issue

Afghanistan is one of the most severely mine-affected countries in the world. Most of the mines were laid during the Soviet occupation of the country and the subsequent war of resistance (1980–92). Mine operations continued during 1992–96 period, when internal fighting between the Taliban and Northern Alliance intensified.[50] Today, six to eight million mines remain laid in Afghanistan. Human Rights Watch claims that more than 400 cluster bombs were dropped – with each bomb containing 220 bomblets.[51] The contaminated area is estimated at 723 million square metres. There are areas of the country that in mid-2002 were still not accessible. One assessment indicates that if the remaining 344 million square metres of highly impacted mined areas were demined, most Afghans could resume a normal and productive life. This could take seven to ten years if current funding levels for mine operations are maintained.[52]

Eight organizations, according to one study, are currently engaged in clearing mine and unexploded ordnance (UEO) in Afghanistan. Between 1990 and 2000, more than 224 million square meters of mined area and about 320 million square metres of former battle areas were cleared of mines and UEO. During the same period, 21,908 antipersonnel mines, 9,897 antitank mines and 1,305,558 different types of UEO were detected and subsequently destroyed. In 2000 alone, mine clearance organizations cleared more than 24 million square metres of mined area and about 80 million square metres of former battled zones. A total of 13,542 antipersonnel mines, 636 antitank mines and 298,828 UEO were destroyed during these operations.[53]

Afghanistan, however, is not a party to any of the international instruments dealing with landmines. According to *Landmine Monitor*, in the Asia-Pacific region, 16 out of 39 countries are mine-affected. Eleven of these countries have not yet joined the 1997 Mine Ban Treaty.[54] In the three most-affected countries in the Asia-Pacific region – Afghanistan, Cambodia and Laos – several mine action programmes (UN Mine Action Program for Afghanistan – MAPA)[55] are in place and coordinated by civilian structures. Afghanistan has the largest civilian mine clearance programme, coordinating almost 40,000 local deminers and a number of national agencies.[56] Some reports suggest that landmines haunt some regions and that the services in landmine removal are still not within reach of much of the population. Landmine education must be carried out with dispatch to teach people, particularly children, about the perils of new mine types and other unexploded ordinance.[57]

In the past, the two main parties opposed to acceding such instruments were the Taliban and the Northern Alliance. At the NGO Conference in Tokyo, in December 2001, it was recommended that demining be integrated into other reconstruction and development projects. NGOs suggested that new approach to mine action should be investigated and that community-based demining, which was recently introduced in the northern parts of Afghanistan, should be promoted.[58]

Another NGO Conference in Tokyo, in January 2002, also stressed the role of Afghan and international NGOs. These NGOs agreed that a focus on education and training is imperative, particularly for women, to build the capacity of the Afghanis to contribute to reconstruction. It was also stressed that continued dialogue and coordination between NGOs, international organizations, donors and the Afghan Interim Authority (AIA) were essential to ensure efficient use of resources.[59] Hamid Karzai, the Interim President, committed his administration to accede to the Mine Ban Convention. The Conference reported that in 2000, mines and UEO injured or killed two or three people every day.[60]

The clearance of the new explosive devices and other mine action operations may also require integrating mine actions into broader development projects and humanitarian assistance programmes. The NGO Conference in Tokyo recommended that mine actions be integrated into other reconstruction and development projects. A good example of this could be community-based landmine removal applied in the northern parts of Afghanistan.[61] Many NGOs have attempted to increase landmine awareness throughout Afghanistan, especially for refugees returning from Pakistan and Iran. In the year 2000, according to *Landmine Monitor*, 1,076,553 civilians received mine-awareness education in various parts of the country. NGO partners of MAPA provided mine-awareness education to more than 7 million people from 1990 to 2000.[62]

NGOs engaged in mine-awareness education included Afghan Mine Awareness Agency, Afghan Red Crescent Society, Ansar Relief Institute, BBC Afghan Education Project, Handicap International, Organization for Mine Awareness and Afghan Rehabilitation, and Save the Children Fund-US. The latter runs Children in Crisis programmes in Kabul to help children cope with the physical and psychological effects of war. One project is the Landmine Education Project that aims at ensuring that children have basic knowledge of mines and are taking necessary preventive steps to avoid them. Additionally, Save the Children/US supports a Social Reintegration of Disabled Children Project in Kabul. This programme's objective is to help children affected by war to regain a normal childhood experience.[63]

NGOs' joint statement to the Second Review Conference of the Convention on Conventional Weapons (CCW) in December 2001 indicated that unexploded cluster submunitions pose long-term dangers after conflict has ended and that the clean-up of unexploded ordnance is the responsibility of the user. Emphasizing the fact that tackling the humanitarian problems caused by cluster munitions and other explosive remnants of war is an effort that will benefit from collective action by NGOs, international organizations, civil society and states, Richard Lloyd, director of Landmine Action, has pushed for a moratorium to be placed on the use, production and transfer of cluster munitions.[64]

Afghan Women and the Peace Process

Traumatized by years of war and subjugation, as well as by gender apartheid under the Taliban rule, Afghan women have found a glimmer of hope in post-Taliban Afghanistan. Given the centrality of women's work to nation building in Afghanistan, at both community and national levels, the UN Population Fund has stressed the need for women to be involved at the planning stages of Afghanistan's reconstruction.[65] The 2001 *State of the World Population* concluded that enhancing women's opportunities and providing their reproductive health and rights were of paramount significance. 'It is clear that providing full access to reproductive health services,' the report said, 'would be far less costly in the long run than the environmental consequences of the population growth that will result if reproductive health needs are not met'.[66]

During the 1980s and 1990s, NGOs failed to revive conditions conducive to the active participation of local people in the process of rebuilding their village community and economy. Their failure has been attributed to the fact that most NGOs were managed by non-Afghani expatriates whose primary goal was to promote their own political and developmental agenda. Their policies failed to generate sustainable people-oriented development projects, in large part because they often lacked interest in or knowledge of the social, cultural and political conditions in the country and often tried to execute the donor country's development policies.[67] A number of NGOs, therefore, tacitly sided with one or another side of the belligerent parties, causing great local mistrust of their neutrality and broader objectives.[68]

Some experts argue that concern with creating a totally participatory society based on a Western model of development may not be practical and helpful in the immediate post-Taliban era. NGOs should, instead, 'concentrate on how to bring about some change and meaningful involvement of women in the development process in Afghanistan'.[69] The role of NGOs is significant particularly in providing basic social services such as health, education, water and sanitation in the absence of any government agencies to do so. There can be no genuine peace without the restoration of women's rights, including women's security, access to health education and other basic needs.[70]

Many NGOs have worked with and continue to aid Afghani women. These NGOs run target-oriented projects and are comprised of diverse organizations, including the Afghan Women's Resource Center and Afghan Women's Welfare Development, both of which deal with health, education, income generation, skills training and relief distributions.[71] There are also several networks used for advocacy, fund-raising, awareness-raising, and implementing projects. These include the Afghan Women's Network (AWN), the Afghan Women's Council (AWC), and the Revolutionary Association of the Women of Afghanistan (RAWA).[72]

In 1995, after a few Afghan women attended the UN Fourth World Conference on Women, they returned and organized the Afghan Women's Network. The primary goal of this organization has since been to advocate peace.[73] The Defence of Afghanistan Women's Rights (NEGAR), a Paris-based group, organized the 'Conference for Women of Afghanistan', held in June 2000 in Dushanbe, Tajiskistan. The Conference drafted a charter, 'as a basic declaration of rights of Afghan women for all and any governments in power'.[74]

The Afghan delegation to Bonn in December 2001, following UN-sponsored negotiations, included three women. The new interim administration under Hamid Karzai included a new Ministry for Women's Affairs, devoted exclusively to women's issues. It also boasted two female ministers, Dr Sima Samar and Gen. Suhaila Sediqi, who were intent on making the plight of women and girls a priority as well as a key issue in their campaign to involve women in all levels.[75] The commission appointed by Afghan Interim Chairman, Hamid Karzai, set aside 160 seats for women, approximately 11 per cent of the Afghan 1500-member *loya jirga* (Grand Council). The council's commission included three women.[76] The council's meeting in June 2002 ended with mixed results. The Afghans overwhelmingly elected Hamid Karzai as President for the next 18 months and approved his government. The *loya jirga*, however, revealed the country's deep divisions, as regional and tribal rivalries left unanswered the question of whether the Council should serve as an advisory council or a legislative body.[77]

In the meantime, the Feminist Majority Foundation, the American feminist research and action organization, pressured both the US government and UN authorities into taking positive action to improve the lot of the Afghani women. Feminist Majority has been highly critical of the United States and international financial commitments, arguing that the pledges for reconstruction and recovery fell well short of the amount needed to rebuild a peaceful, democratic Afghanistan in which women's rights were fully upheld.[78]

Conclusion

History shows that failure to bring peace to Afghanistan has had profound implications for regional stability. Barnett R. Rubin poignantly makes the case: 'If the international community does not find a way to rebuilding Afghanistan, a floodtide of weapons, cash, and contraband will escape that state's porous boundaries and make the world less secure for all'.[79] The humanitarian community suffered profusely from the limitations under which they worked during the Taliban regime. This essay has explained the reasons why order and peacebuilding in Afghanistan are inseparable from the broader context of reconstruction and nation-building, and why conflict resolution must be seen as a central goal of development policy.

Experts hold that a recovery strategy aimed at security should focus on returning refugees, and should start at the grassroots with loans and grants for community-based small businesses.[80] In many respects, development enhances security. In Afghanistan, NGOs are not just providers of funds and tools for the country's systematic rebuilding but are also the very symbol of change that needs to transpire there if the nation is to chart a new course. By promoting social justice through investing in the social capital of the country as well as strengthening the role of the aid community, the rule of law and civil society organizations, NGOs can initiate and support peace efforts at local and national levels. To be effective, NGOs' strategies should be based on maintaining a position of neutrality in the post-conflict reconstruction era.

The Afghan NGO community must seek equilibrium and coherence between political rehabilitation and economic reconstruction. This requires: (1) that the longer-term goals of economic growth and development override short-term emergency aid and (2) that local leaders, organizations and groups be effectively involved at all levels. These requirements – that is, development and equality – must be achieved to no one's detriment. Particularly alarming are the drawbacks associated with aid and relief operations. Foreign aid and other related relief operations should not limit the development of the local economy. The experience of Afghanistan has shown that the abundance of funds has, in the past, rendered relief projects donor-driven. The result has been that most NGOs have been unable to distance themselves from the aid boom, while proving inept in making long-term decisions.[81]

By all accounts, NGOs' contributions alone need not be exaggerated in such a politically complex and uncertain setting. By cooperating and coordinating their activities with the United Nations and the international financial Institutions, as well as with intergovernmental organizations, NGOs can play a significant part in nudging along the reconstruction of Afghanistan. Because their role in coping with humanitarian crisis is critical, NGOs' involvement should not be made contingent upon any particular political solutions. Beyond that, their legitimacy lies in an ability to provide the most viable ways of meeting Afghanistan's new challenges, especially as they relate to developing human skills and incorporating human rights concerns, particularly those regarding gender, into all developmental programmes.

Without security, nation building and development stand little chance of success. 'Terror cannot be controlled,' Michael Ignatieff writes, 'unless order is built in the anarchic zones where terrorists find shelter. In Afghanistan, this means nation-building, creating a state strong enough to keep al-Qaeda from returning.'[82] Ultimately, investing in nation building and peacebuilding is the best way to combat terrorism. The assets and capabilities of NGOs cannot and should not be underestimated.

NOTES

1. Philip Smucker, 'A Fight to Feed Hungry Afghanistan', *The Christian Science Monitor*, 3 June 2002, pp.1, 9.
2. Some international relations experts have cautioned against romanticizing the role of NGOs, arguing that the cases of Lebanon and Somalia demonstrate the costs and consequences of the negation or end of states. See, for example, Fred Halliday, 'The Romance of Non-State Actors', in Daphne Josselin and William Wallace (eds.), *Non-State Actors in World Politics*, Basingstoke: Palgrave, 2001, pp.21–37.
3. John L. Esposito, *Unholy War: Terror in the Name of Islam*, Oxford: Oxford University Press, 2002, p.157.
4. Ibid.
5. Katarin West, *Agents of Altruism: The Expansion of Humanitarian NGOs in Rwanda and Afghanistan*, Burlington, VT: Ashgate, 2001, p.80.
6. Ibid., p.82.
7. Ibid., p.92.
8. Ibid.

9. Grant Farr, 'Afghanistan: Displaced in a Devastated Country', in Marc Vincent and Birgritte Refslund Sorensen (eds.), *Caught Between Borders: Response Strategies of the Internally Displaced*, London: Pluto, 2001, pp.132–5.
10. Daphne Josselin and William Wallace, 'Non-State Actors in World Politics: A Framework', in Josselin and Wallace (eds.) (n.2 above), p.10.
11. West (n.5 above), p.138.
12. *The Christian Science Monitor*, 11 Oct. 2001, p.6.
13. *The New York Times*, 18 Oct. 2001, p.A3.
14. Ibid.
15. Mark Duffield, *Global Governance and the New Wars: The Merging of Development and Security*, London: New Books, 2001.
16. See 'Integrated Approach to Assist Refugee Repatriation in Afghanistan', accessed at www.undp.org/rbap/Afghanistan.htm.
17. Harvard Program on Humanitarian Policy and Conflict Research, 'A New Era of Humanitarian Assistance', HPCR Central Asia Policy Brief Issue 4, Vol.1, 13 Mar. 2002, available at www.reliefweb.int/w/rwb.nsf.
18. Ibid.
19. Ibid.
20. Koenraad van Brabant, 'Understanding, Promoting and Evaluating Coordination: An Outline Framework', in D.S. Gordon and F.H. Toase (eds.), *Aspects of Peacekeeping*, London and Portland, OR: Frank Cass, 2001, p.149.
21. Ibid., p.150.
22. Harvard Program on Humanitarian Policy and Conflict Resolution.
23. 'Building Peace and Civil Society in Afghanistan: Challenges and Opportunities', a report by Carnegie Council on Ethics and International Affairs and Asian Society, May 2001, pp.1–12, see p.1.
24. Ibid., p.8.
25. Marina Ottaway and Anatol Lieven, 'Rebuilding Afghanistan', *Current History*, Vol.101, No.653, Mar. 2002, p.135.
26. Ibid., p.136.
27. Ibid., p.138.
28. Fareed Zakaria, 'Next: Nation-Building Lite', *Newsweek*, 22 Oct. 2001, p.53.
29. Barnett R. Rubin, 'A Blueprint for Afghanistan', *Current History*, Vol.101, No.654. April 2002, pp.155–6.
30. Ibid., p.157.
31. Peter Gusber, 'The Impact of NGOs on State and Non-State Relations in the Middle East', *Middle East Policy*, Vol.9, No.1, March 2002, p.47.
32. Dayton Maxwell, 'Averting Violations Through Conflict Prevention', *Human Rights Dialogue*, Series 2, No.7, Winter 2002, p.18.
33. Philip Smucker (n.1 above).
34. Quoted in ibid., p.9.
35. Barnett Rubin, 'Afghanistan and Threats to Human Security', accessed at www.ssrc.org/sept11/essays/rubin.htm.
36. Claude Bruderlein, 'The Role of Non-State Actors in Building Human Security: The Case of Armed Groups in Intra-State Wars', Geneva, 20 Mar. 2002, accessed at www.humansecuritynetwork.org/report_may2002_2-e.asp.
37. Bill Frelick, 'Refugee', in James R. Lewis and Carl Skutsch (eds.), *The Human Rights Encyclopedia*, Vol.3, New York: M.E. Sharpe, 2001, p.868.
38. 'Women's Health and Human Rights in Afghanistan: A Population-based Assessment', Physicians for Human Rights, 2001.
39. Margaret Emery and Hiram Ruiz, 'Descent into Disaster? Afghan Refugees', *Middle East Report*, No.221, Winter 2001, accessed at www.merip.org/mer/mer221/221_emery_and_ruiz.html.
40. Arthur C. Helton, 'Rescuing the Refugees', *Foreign Affairs*, Vol.81, No.2, Mar.–Apr. 2002, p.74.
41. Ibid., pp.79–82.

42. *The Columbus Dispatch*, 9 Oct. 2001, p.1A.
43. Ibid.
44. Ibid.
45. Ibid.
46. Ibid.
47. Ibid.
48. Physicians for Human Rights, 'A Report on Conditions at Shebarghan Prison, Northern Afghanistan', 22 Jan. 2002, accessed at www.phrusa.org/research/afghanistan/index.html.
49. Ibid.
50. *Landmine Monitor Report 2001*, accessed at www.icbl.org/lm/2001/afghanistan.
51. Fazel Karim Fazel, 'Briefing of Press Conference', accessed at www.icbl.org/news/2001/136.php.
52. *Landmine Monitor* (n.50 above).
53. Ibid.
54. Convention on the Prohibition of the Use, Stockpiling, Production, and Transfer of Anti-Personnel Mines and On Their Destruction. *Landmine Monitor Report* of the International Campaign to Ban Landmines oversees implementation of and compliance with the Treaty and is the first time NGOs have coordinated in a systematic fashion to monitor a humanitarian law or disarmament treaty. For more on this, see Jody Williams and Stephen D. Goose, 'The International Campaign to Ban Landmine: Toward a Mine-Free World' 7 Sept. 2000, accessed at www.ceip.org/files/events/Landmines.asp?p=7&EventID=208.
55. The Mine Action Program for Afghanistan (MAPA) is coordinated by the Mine Action Center for Afghanistan (MACA). MAPA comprises: the UN Mine Action Center for Afghanistan (MACA), temporarily located in Islamabad, five UN Regional Mine Action Centers (RMAC), all located in Afghanistan, and fifteen implementing partners or NGOs. See *Landmine Monitor Report 2001*.
56. *Landmine Monitor*, 'Humanitarian Mine Action: Landmine Monitor Fact Sheet', p.8.
57. Oxfam America, 'Afghanistan's Humanitarian Crisis is not over yet', 21 Dec. 2001, accessed at www.oxfamamerica.org/humanitarian/afghanistan/updatedec21.html[RTF bookmark start: _Hlt27301889].[RTF bookmark end: _Hlt27301889], pp.1–3; see p.2.
58. 'NGO Conference in Tokyo Focuses on Rebuilding Afghanistan', accessed at www.icbl.org/news/2001/138.php.
59. See 'Co-Chairs' Summary of Conclusions: The International Conference on Reconstruction Assistance to Afghanistan', 21–22 Jan. 2002, accessed at www.icbl.org.
60. International Campaign to Ban Landmines, 31 Dec. 2001, accessed at www.icbl.org/country/afghanistan.
61. See NGO Conference in Tokyo on the Reconstruction and Afghanistan, Sector Working Session D: Landmines, accessed at www.japanplatfor.org/accounting/afghanconference/english/landmine.html.
62. *Landmine Monitor 2001*.
63. American Council for Voluntary International Action, 'Activities of InterAction Members in Afghanistan', No.2, May 1999, accessed at www.interaction.org.
64. See 'NGOs Deliver Joint Statement to CCW', accessed at www.landmineaction.org/news97.asp.
65. Anna McDermott, 'Another Approach', *The Middle East*, No.318, Dec. 2001, pp.42–4.
66. Ibid., p.44.
67. Hafizullah Emadi, 'Rebuilding Afghanistan', *Contemporary Review*, April 2001, Vol.274, No.1623, p.203.
68. Ibid., pp.203–4.
69. Ibid., p.205.
70. Zieba Shorish-Shamley, 'Afghan Women in Peace Processes', accessed at www.wapha.org/peace.html.
71. Sharon Groves, 'Afghan Women Speak Out', *Feminist Studies*, Vol.27, No.3, Fall 2001, p.756.

72. Ibid.
73. Rosemarie Skaine, *The Women of Afghanistan Under the Taliban*, London: McFarland, 2002, pp.138–9.
74. Ibid., pp.134–5.
75. Janelle Brown, 'A Coalition of Hope', *Ms.*, Vol.12, No.2, Spring 2002, p.66.
76. Feminist Majority Foundation, 'Women Will be At Least 11% of Afghan *Loya Jirga*', 1 Apr. 2002, accessed at www.feminist.org/newsbyte/uswirestory.asp?id=6434.
77. *The Economist*, 22 June 2002, p.39. Karzai intended to bypass the Bonn accords, by insisting that it was the president's prerogative to choose his own cabinet members and that the *loya jirga* had no role to play in approving key personnel and the structure of government.
78. Feminist Majority Foundation (n.76 above), p.76.
79. Barnett R. Rubin, *The Fragmentation of Afghanistan: State Formation and Collapse in the International System*, New Haven, CT: Yale University Press, 2002, p.280.
80. For an interesting view on this, see Arthur C. Helton, 'In Afghanistan, Think Small', *The Christian Science Monitor*, 25 June 2002, p.9.
81. West (n.5 above), p.221.
82. Michael Ignatieff, 'Nation-Building Lite', *The New York Times Magazine*, 28 July 2002, pp.26–31, 54, 57, 59; see esp. p.28.

NGO Mediation: The Carter Center

JAMES LARRY TAULBEE and
MARION V. CREEKMORE, JR.

In 1982 former US president Jimmy Carter and his wife, Rosalynn, established The Carter Center to pursue some of the ideas that they had hoped to advance from the White House during a second term.[1] In its early years the Center emphasized three objectives: to promote democratic governance, to help improve health around the world, and to try to resolve conflicts between disputing parties through mediation. The current mission statement identifies five activities as primary areas of concern: monitoring/mediating elections, promoting democracy and economic cooperation in the Western Hemisphere, finding peaceful solutions to civil conflicts, strengthening human rights and economic development in emerging democracies, and preventing human rights violations.[2] With a majority of its funding from private contributions,[3] the Center occupies a unique position among contemporary NGOs in that it has pursued educational, operational and advocacy roles across this broad spectrum of issue areas.[4] This essay focuses on the Carter Center's methods with regard to two very different cases of conflict resolution, the 1990 election mediation in the transitional election in Nicaragua and the North Korean intervention in 1994.

The active participation of the 2002 Nobel Peace Prize winner endows the Center with a set of advantages difficult for other NGOs to match. It deals regularly with the leaders of countries and of insurgency groups rather than with people who have influence on such persons and who are the usual interlocutors of Track II mediators. Carter gives the Center direct access to publicity, heads of state, corporate executives, religious leaders, and top personnel in intergovernmental organizations (IGOs) and foundations. For many projects, the Center has been able to draw upon existing institutional resources and programmes in many different countries without the red tape and political manoeuvring that often accompany requests for assistance. Simply stated: 'When he [Carter] makes phone calls, the other party accepts them. When he needs assistance, academics, political leaders, grass roots leaders and others respond. When he gives a press conference, the media cover it in high-profile ways.'[5]

In conflict resolution initiatives the Carter Center conceives of itself as a useful alternative channel, available when formal restrictions or pragmatic policy considerations preclude actions by IGOs and governments. Many conflicts stand outside the purview of the legal mandate of IGOs, such as the United Nations, or fall into areas where official negotiations by the United States would be contrary to established policy and practice, but not contrary to US interests. Current characterizations of diplomacy speak of Track II and sometimes Track III as ways of distinguishing the initiatives of private individuals and NGOs from Track I diplomacy. Track I generally refers to direct negotiations between responsible government officials who have the authority and power to forge and implement agreements.[6] In Track II diplomacy, neutral mediators, who tend not to be active governmental leaders, work with influential persons on each side to try to frame the structure of a settlement that these persons can sell to their respective leaders. The outcome of a successful Track II negotiation/mediation is usually an agreement by the leaders of the conflicting parties to undertake a Track I negotiation based on the Track II suggestions for a peaceful settlement.

The Carter Center characterizes its own mediation efforts as 'Track I½' because Carter and the Center often deal directly with leaders of disputing governments and/or insurgency groups. The Center's approach, because it relies upon high-level dialogue, depends upon the access and clout provided by an eminent person. The eminent person does not have to participate on an ongoing basis in every project; other personnel may substitute in many cases once the parameters and expectations concerning procedures have been established. The promise of their attention at some point may suffice. We should also note that former President Carter is not the only person capable of generating the access and resources described in this essay. Under this definition, other mediators, such as former Senator George Mitchell in his work in Northern Ireland, or Olof Palme in his Iran–Iraq mediation, have also engaged in Track I½ diplomacy.

Mediation as a Strategy and Technique

The concept of mediation stands at the heart of the two projects we will examine. The Carter Center sees itself as a 'neutral mediator'. Unlike 'principal mediators', such as governments and IGOs, the Center cannot offer tangible resources – economic assistance, trade concessions or military force – to try to achieve a peaceful settlement among conflicting parties.[7] It can only bring to the table intangible resources, such as goodwill, persuasiveness, a passion for peace and an ability to help disputants think beyond their established positions to their fundamental interests. Because neutral mediators do not have constituents that demand success on each involvement, they are less reluctant than principal mediators to become engaged.[8] The Carter Center consciously targets difficult conflicts for its mediation efforts and avoids involvement where others seem ready and able to assume the task.

Mediating Elections: A Special Kind of Conflict Resolution

One of the Carter Center's most successful enterprises over the past 15 years has been its promotion of democracy through mediating elections in countries making the transition from authoritarian to democratic regimes. The Center pioneered the idea of using election mediation as an important instrument for conflict resolution. Election mediation as distinguished from election observation or the more comprehensive election monitoring may be unfamiliar to some. Mediation in the context of elections encompasses a more assertive posture directed towards helping the political leaders of a country negotiate and define the rules of the electoral game and then actively encouraging them to abide by the outcome of the election, as well as monitoring the electoral process.[9] The Center believes that its experience in Nicaragua, Guyana and several other countries demonstrates that elections can be used on occasion to resolve conflicts that do not seem amenable to other solutions.

Election mediation can play a particularly important role in situations where the conditions for successful elections involve a learning experience for all participants. The approach seems particularly appropriate for first elections in emerging democracies to ensure a peaceful transition as well as for first follow-on elections, or as a method of ensuring continued participation and acceptance of the essential rules of the game by the major political players in situations where democratic institutions appear on the verge of collapse.[10] Observers and monitors stand outside of the election process as it unfolds. The ostensible effectiveness of observations and monitoring stems from the idea that the simple presence of an interested, visible and prestigious outside group can induce principals to observe the rules, thus permitting voters to participate with some confidence in the process. Mediation requires an intrusive presence in the form of active, and proactive, problem solving during the process, including assisting in the transition period to help ensure that the voters' wishes are respected.[11]

In mediation, the primary task is to separate the technical problems of election administration from the contest for power which the election should decide. Lest anyone think this an easy task, reflection on the problems and political posturing associated with the November 2000 presidential election in the United States should quickly convince them otherwise. Consider in consequence the problems in weak states with no tradition of electoral success and in which underdeveloped bureaucracies have little or no experience or training in any type of administrative procedures. Add to this extreme distrust where one or another of the electoral contestants sees irregularities as a deliberate manoeuvre to sabotage their chances. Without a process in place, trusted by all participants, that will quickly resolve controversies over procedures or allegations of cheating, simple ignorance or incompetence can have as much impact as deliberate manipulation. In politically charged circumstance, quickly resolving rumours, or accusations of misconduct, in a manner satisfactory to participants forms a crucial part of the process. Finally, effective mediation requires a continuing presence after the election to ensure that opposing parties accept the decision of the voters so that the transition will be peaceful and orderly.[12]

Mediation and the Nicaraguan Election

In early 1989, faced with mounting economic problems from increased military expenditures to counter the Contras, the physical devastation from raids and the effects of US pressure on international financial institutions and governments to deny aid and loans, the Sandinista government sought to reach an accommodation with its opponents.[13] In February, the presidents of Honduras, Nicaragua, Costa Rica, El Salvador and Guatemala met and agreed to take action to demobilize the US-backed rebel army and remove all of the remaining guerrillas from bases in Honduras. In return, the Sandinista government pledged to hold internationally supervised elections by February 1990, nine months earlier than previously promised.[14] The agreement, undercutting any local support for even the minimalist option to keep the Contra effort going (the proposed 'non-lethal' aid option), pushed the new Bush administration to back the effort.[15]

Carter had consulted with Daniel Ortega in Caracas during the February 1989 inauguration of the new Venezuelan president, but the invitation to monitor the elections was issued, not to Jimmy Carter personally, but to the Council of Freely Elected Heads of Governments. As part of the Center's mission, Carter, in collaboration with former President Gerald Ford, had worked to establish an ongoing organization to promote and reinforce democracy in the Western Hemisphere. The Council had come into existence as the result of a conference, chaired by former presidents Ford and Carter, held at the Carter Center in 1986. The Council had designated the Center's Latin American and Caribbean Program to serve as its secretariat. The Council accepted the invitation to monitor the Nicaraguan election based on assurances that it would have unrestricted access to the entire electoral process and the vote count on election day.[16]

Following preparatory trips of Center officials, the Council sent its first mission to Nicaragua in September 1989. Led by Carter and former Argentine president, Raul Alfonsin, Council members met with government and opposition leaders and with the Supreme Electoral Council. The latter confirmed that the Carter Center-led group, along with the observer teams from the Organization of American States (OAS) and the United Nations, would have complete access to the voting and counting and would be given copies of the certified vote tallies so that they could make their own vote tabulation. While the Council was still in Nicaragua, Carter mediated an agreement with the government that would allow the Miskito Indian leaders to return to the country and participate in the election.[17]

The Carter Center established a local office in Managua to facilitate its work. During the next five months Council teams travelled to Nicaragua to observe the voter registration drive, the election campaign, the vote, the counting and the transition. When the Council received complaints about various aspects of the election process it raised these matters with party leaders and election officials.[18] The majority of the disputes involving election administration were resolved prior to the election. One issue, the demobilization of the Contras, remained stalemated. All sides knew that any new government would have to deal with this issue immediately following the election. Failure to reconcile the involved parties would endanger the new Nicaraguan democracy, no matter which party won.

Headed by Carter and former Prime Minister of Belize, George Price, the 34-member Council delegation arrived in Managua two days before the election, met with government and opposition leaders and conferred with the heads of the OAS and UN observer missions. Along with their counterparts from the OAS and UN, the Council delegation publicly pledged to monitor every step of the election process to ensure that the final results would accurately reflect the people's voice.

On 25 February 1990, Nicaragua held its first election in which all major political parties participated and in which both the winners and losers accepted the results and respected them. Eighty-six per cent of those registered cast their ballot. There was a strong expectation among the Sandinistas that they would win the election easily,[19] but early returns suggested that the UNO opposition had a substantial lead. Then, for an extended period no new returns were announced. Indeed, several days would pass before all the returns were officially counted and announced. This delay could have led to efforts to tamper with the results or to charges of manipulation. That it did not reflected the cooperation and commitment of the government and the opposition, and the critical role played by the international observers. At President Ortega's request, President Carter and the OAS and UN leaders met with senior Nicaraguan officials shortly after midnight. The monitors advised that the quick counts of the international organizations showed a 'wide and consistent lead' by the UNO. Fearing that a premature release of the returns or an announcement of victory by the UNO would spark violence among the militant groups on both sides that were already in the streets, Ortega asked for advice.

Here, Carter's personal experience proved to be a valuable asset. He could talk personally and persuasively to the potential losers about how an election loss does not have to shake one's self-image and how life after government can be meaningful. With the consent of Violetta Chamorro, the UNO leader, the following scenario was orchestrated. The election council announced that the returns had been received but indicated that all votes had not yet been tallied. Chamorro publicly acknowledged the results but asked her supporters to remain calm until more complete results were released. At Carter's suggestion, Ortega made a statement before the morning news programmes, taking credit for the democratic election and the accomplishments since the revolution while acknowledging the voting trend and affirming his intention to respect the results of the vote.[20] Both sides also asked the international observers to remain in Nicaragua to help ensure that the transition process would be smooth and orderly. When the final results were tallied, UNO had scored a major victory upset with 54.7 per cent of the vote to the FSLN's 40.8 per cent. The UNO had also won a majority of seats in the legislative assembly and control of more than three-quarters of the municipal councils.

President Carter and Governor Daniel Evans phoned US Secretary of State James Baker to inform him of the UNO victory and urge a 'positive and generous statement' by the US addressed to both sides. Later that day President Bush publicly congratulated Chamorro on her victory, as well as President Ortega on the conduct of the election, and the Carter Center team, the OAS and UN for their role in observing the election. Bush also stated that there was no reason for further military activity. The US announced a few days later that it supported the demobilization of the Contra forces and the repatriation of the resistance forces, to be assisted by the UN-OAS process. On the day after the election, at the request of President Ortega, the leaders of the Carter Center, UN and OAS observers accompanied him to Chamorro's residence to congratulate her on her victory. Subsequently, President Carter met with the officials designated by Chamorro and Ortega to discuss how to handle the main issues involved in the transition. Violeta de Chamorro was inaugurated President of Nicaragua on 25 April 1990. For the first time since 1928, Nicaragua had transferred power peacefully from an incumbent government to its rival as a result of an election judged free and fair; and, for the first time a revolutionary government 'voluntarily gave up the reins of power to its adversary'.

The Case of Korea

Jimmy Carter had closely followed Korean issues since his time in the White House. In addition to media reporting, he had personal contacts in China and Japan who provided him information about developments on the Korean peninsula. He had also met periodically with officials from both Koreas. Carter had first met the foreign minister of the Democratic People's Republic of Korea (DPRK) in the fall of 1991 during the latter's visit to the UN. At that time, Carter had indicated his willingness, if requested by both sides, to try to facilitate discussions between the two Korean governments about possible unification at some future time. Shortly thereafter Carter received a formal invitation to visit North Korea. Following his policy of not undertaking controversial diplomatic initiatives without the agreement or acquiescence of the White House, Carter contacted the Bush administration about his proposed trip. He was told that such a trip would be unhelpful. He advised North Korea that he was unable to come at that time. On two later occasions, in 1992 after he had sent an advance team to both Koreas and again in early 1993, he was strongly urged by Washington not to go to North Korea.

As tensions increased in late 1993 and early 1994 over the nature and extent of the North Korean nuclear programme, Carter and his Center associates followed the issue with growing alarm. In May 1994, US Ambassador to South Korea, James T. Laney, a long-time friend of

Carter, confided his anxiety that the situation could quickly spin out of control. Like Carter, he thought policymakers should take seriously the possibility that North Korea might strike out militarily if UN sanctions were imposed against it. The two men agreed (although Laney was acting without instructions) that Carter should go to North Korea and talk with Kim Il Sung if his earlier invitation was still valid.

The Clinton administration had approached Senators Sam Nunn and Richard Lugar about undertaking a mission to Pyongang in late May, but the North Koreans had turned down their request for visas. Even so, few people showed concern that no president or other senior administration officials had ever talked directly with the top leadership in North Korea. Indeed, many within the administration firmly believed that high-level talks should remain a reward to be granted only when North Korea earned the privilege through 'good behaviour'. In the crisis atmosphere, indications of North Korean willingness to negotiate the issues received little attention. On June 1, Carter called President Clinton to express his deep concern about the North Korean situation. Clinton sent Ambassador Robert Galluci to Plains, Georgia to provide a comprehensive briefing to the former president on the issues surrounding US–North Korean relations. From the briefing, two key problems impressed Carter: the administration had no means of communicating directly with the top leadership in Pyongyang; and top administration officials thought that UN sanctions could be adopted against North Korea with impunity. They also believed that sanctions might have the desired effect of forcing the DPRK to provide the information sought by the International Atomic Energy Authority (IAEA).[21] Carter's own analysis, confirmed by information he had received from some of his private contacts, indicated that UN sanctions would lead to war, and that the only way to prevent war was to try to work out a mutually acceptable arrangement with Kim Il Sung. Considering the gravity and urgency of the situation, Carter made the decision to intercede if the invitation from North Korea was still valid.

Carter informed President Clinton of his intention by letter. Clinton acquiesced to the trip provided that Carter made it publicly clear that he was going as a private citizen representing the Carter Center and not as a representative of the administration. The North Koreans affirmed the validity of the earlier invitation, indicating that Carter would meet with Kim Il Sung if he travelled to Pyongyang. Before departure on 12 June, the Carter-led team received an extensive briefing in Washington by officials from the National Security Council (NSC), State Department, Defense Department and CIA.[22]

By the time he left Washington, Carter had developed his general strategy. Knowing the importance the North Koreans attached to being treated with respect and as equals, Carter was convinced that the US strategy of demanding concessions from North Korea before making any itself would not work. In his view, any viable deal would have to be a package arrangement with both sides taking actions simultaneously. He had learned from his Washington briefers that the Clinton administration would not oppose a package deal and gained information about what the administration would be prepared to consider if the nuclear crisis could be ended. Carter drafted an extensive set of talking points to use with Kim Il Sung and other North Korean officials. In a phone conversation, he went over the points with Ambassador Galluci who expressed no opposition.

Before proceeding to Pyongyang, Carter met with senior American and South Korean officials in Seoul to glean the views of those in the field.[23] Both American and South Korean officials shared Carter's assessment concerning the volatility of the current situation, but some South Korean officials expressed strong concern that the Carter visit would produce a propaganda coup for the DPRK and would undercut international support for sanctions. As evidence of North Korean intentions, the South Koreans pointed out that the DPRK had expelled the remaining IAEA inspectors on the previous day.[24]

On 15 June the small Carter Center delegation crossed the Demilitarized Zone (DMZ).[25] Carter and his team were met by senior North Korean officials and escorted to Pyongyang for an afternoon meeting with Foreign Minister Kim Yong Nam. The foreign minister stressed North Korea's 'peaceful policies', and castigated the policies of the United States and the IAEA as responsible for the current dangerous situation. He condemned the sanctions resolution before the UN Security Council, emphasizing that sanctions would not hurt North Korea but could lead to war. He said that no progress could be made until, and unless, the third round of bilateral talks took place between the United States and North Korea. Drawing heavily upon the talking points he had read to Galluci, Carter responded with tact and firmness. He knew that Kim Il Sung would get a full report (perhaps a full recording) of the meeting in preparation for his Thursday morning session with Carter.

Carter found the meeting with the foreign minister frustrating and disturbing. He knew that if Kim Yong Nam's line prevailed, his own efforts to defuse the crisis would fail.[26] But at the Thursday morning meeting Kim Il Sung's demeanour contrasted markedly with that of the foreign minister the previous afternoon. He responded positively to

Carter's presentation, which reflected respect for Kim Il Sung and North Korea while making clear the seriousness of the current crisis. Kim assured Carter that North Korea did not have nuclear weapons and that it did not intend to develop nuclear weapons. He stated that if trust and respect could be established between the United States and North Korea, he was sure that mutually acceptable arrangements could be found.

Again drawing on his prepared talking points, Carter in turn assured Kim Il Sung that there were no nuclear weapons in South Korea and that the United States did not intend to attack North Korea or use nuclear weapons against it. He then laid out the various provisions of the package approach that had been discussed in Washington. Kim Il Sung responded approvingly to this presentation. He said he was prepared to freeze North Korea's nuclear programme if he obtained assurances from the US that it would not use nuclear weapons against his country and that it would help North Korea find a source and financing to replace its heavy, water-moderated reactors with the safer light water reactors. Kim Il Sung understood that the US would be unable to provide the reactors or financing itself.

After an afternoon meeting with nuclear and military officials, Carter advised the White House on an open telephone line about the deal he had negotiated with Kim Il Sung and of his intention to announce it publicly on CNN a few minutes later. In the CNN interview Carter described his discussions with Kim Il Sung and Kim's decision to freeze North Korea's nuclear programme. He expressed his personal hopes that Washington and Pyongyang would meet soon in a third round of talks to resolve their dispute and that the sanctions move in the UN would stop.

White House officials initially reacted angrily to Carter's interview.[27] Their criticisms ranged from dissatisfaction with Carter going public before returning to Washington to discuss the trip and its ramifications with the administration to pique that Carter appeared to the world to be more in control of US policy towards North Korea than they. As passions tempered, the administration decided to define a North Korean 'freeze' to include an explicit commitment to 'no reprocessing' and 'no refuelling' of the 5-megawatt nuclear reactor. This position was communicated to Carter, again over an open phone line. The former president made clear his displeasure at the additional requirements since neither had been mentioned during his Washington briefing. Nevertheless, Kim Il Sung ultimately accepted the broadened US definition of his 'freeze' promise.

Carter had another long talk with Kim Il Sung on Friday morning. The DPRK leader asked Carter to convey to South Korean President

Kim Young Sam his willingness to hold an early summit meeting with him to seek improved bilateral relations. He also approved Carter's request for a collaborative US–North Korean effort to recover the remains of US troops killed in North Korea during the Korean War. When Carter advised Kim Young Sam of the North Korean president's willingness to meet at the summit, he quickly announced his own approval, and the two governments began planning for such a meeting towards the end of July.[28]

In a conversation with Kim Il Sung, Carter stated that he was sure the US would cease its efforts to get the UN Security Council to adopt sanctions against North Korea if the DPRK carried out the commitments made to him. A CNN microphone recorded this comment. In his earlier conversations, Carter had carefully drawn the distinction between his own personal hope that the sanctions move would be held in abeyance and the fact that Washington alone would decide what US policy towards sanctions would be. Administration spokesmen quickly went public to reaffirm that the sanctions campaign was continuing, coupling this announcement with strongly implied criticism of the Carter statement. When Carter saw the CNN report, he immediately and publicly declared that only US government officials could state national policy – both at a press conference before he left Seoul on Saturday and again in Washington on Sunday.

This presumptuous statement, reinforced by Carter's CNN interview Thursday evening announcing his deal with Kim Il Sung, led administration officials to downplay the Carter achievement. Many distrusted his report of what Kim Il Sung had agreed to do. Carter put these concerns to rest shortly after he returned to the United States. He wrote to Kim Il Sung spelling out his understanding of their agreement. Kim Il Sung confirmed Carter's complete understanding in a return letter to him and through an exchange of diplomatic notes with officials in the administration. For several weeks afterwards, press articles quoting unnamed administration officials belittled the Carter effort and asserted that the pressure of UN sanctions was responsible for the North Korean decision to 'freeze' its nuclear programme and return to the negotiating table. President Clinton, however, praised Carter publicly in a worldwide CNN interview on Wednesday, 22 June, when he announced that early bilateral talks would be held and that the sanctions move had been terminated.

Four months later the United States and North Korea signed a Framework Agreement in Geneva that provided for the continued freeze of the North Korean nuclear programme, the replacement of its old reactors with new light water reactors supplied by South Korea (and paid for largely by South Korea and Japan), annual supplies of approximately $50 million worth of heavy fuel oil by the United States, gradual improvement in US–North Korean relations, and the complete clarification of the amount of plutonium possessed by North Korea before the core elements of the new reactors were put in place.

Conclusions

The two Carter Center initiatives illustrate the possibilities for, and constraints upon, NGOs that seek to provide mediation services for ongoing or potential conflicts. NGOs can often act when governments and IGOs cannot or will not. While they lack the ability to promise or mete out physical inducements, NGOs may be attractive to participants exactly because they lack the means of coercing the principals into a settlement that one or the other side would find unacceptable. The Carter approach exploits 'normative leverage'.[29] In the Nicaragua case, government actions developed the context in which the elections took place and other IGOs (the UN and OAS) had sent large delegations to monitor the conduct of the election. Within the political environment established by these other agencies, the Carter mediation effort was able to focus media attention, defuse potential trust-breaking issues, convince Ortega to concede defeat, and induce the US government to support the outcome because the Center clearly had no stake in the outcome beyond certifying its fairness.

North Korea, under the threat of possible sanctions, received Carter but refused to issue visas to Senators Nunn and Lugar, whom the administration had asked to travel to Pyongyang. The North Korean decision raises an interesting problem, more relevant to the Carter Center than to other NGOs. Someone knowledgeable about the US political process could argue that the North Koreans should have perceived the two senators to be in better position to influence the policy of the Clinton White House than Carter. Nonetheless, Kim Il Sung placed great importance upon having a former US president come to North Korea to talk with him, particularly one with whom his officials had been in periodic communication for years. Kim made clear during the visit that he expected Carter to be able to influence Washington policy towards his country. Kim Il Sung's expectation does not form an isolated phenomenon. Other disputants have sought the Carter Center as a mediator because they believe, sometimes without good foundation, that Carter can positively affect Washington's attitudes and policies in their case.

Second, the Carter Center and other well-established NGOs can afford to try and fail. They can undertake missions that have a low probability of success because a 'failure' does not necessarily undermine their reputations or erode support of relevant constituencies to the degree that it might for governments. Indeed, the Carter Center has deliberately chosen to seek involvement in mediation roles in situations that seem intractable. As long as the Center enjoys the reputation as a useful channel and can maintain the support of its principal funding sources, it does not have to keep a scorecard that measures its efforts solely in terms of short-term outcomes. In some cases – the Carter initiative to resolve the Ethiopian–Eritrean situation, for example – an effort considered a short-term failure may create opportunities where governments or IGOs finally decide they have sufficient interest and/or legal authority to act.

Third, long-term success in mediation depends upon approval or follow-on action by governments or IGOs. At the very least, success depends upon the neutrality of players with an interest in the outcome. NGOs act as starters and facilitators. The attributes that make NGOs attractive mediators also mean they lack the resources to directly support the activities necessary to carry out agreements. The efforts of the Carter Center (and others) would have had far less impact if the US government had refused to accept the result of the elections in Nicaragua or the specifics of the agreement reached with North Korea.[30] To draw from another arena, the Center's Global Development Initiative (GDI), which evolved out of the mediation experience with elections and conflict resolution in Guyana, depends not only upon the active support of local government but upon acceptance by donors and international financial institutions as well.[31]

Fourth, the Carter intervention in North Korea dealt solely with international issues. In other situations where such contact has involved interaction with regimes or individuals of questionable reputation, the commitment to high-level dialogue has provoked controversy. In Liberia, for example, where domestic human rights issues vie with those raised by transborder conflict, critics have raised questions about the utility and desirability of Track I½, fearing that the process itself may confer a modicum of legitimacy on individuals and regimes that have engaged in egregious violations of human rights.[32] There is no inherent conflict between the two. One of the strengths of the Center has been its ability to combine high-level access with human rights initiatives at other societal levels even though at times the two approaches may have worked at cross purposes.[33]

Finally, normative leverage normally works best in cases where the parties foresee little possibility of winning militarily, or where they clearly perceive that continuing a current course augurs future disaster. William Zartman and Saadia Touval describe these two situations as 'hurting stalemates'.[34] The skilful mediator will seek to become involved when these conditions apply. The parties in Nicaragua had reached such a point, but North Korea sought Carter's involvement for still a different reason. Kim Il Sung wanted respect, treatment as an equal, and by someone whom he considered a senior American with influence in Washington. In his mind then, if not that of anyone currently in Washington, Carter fit the bill. Had a senior administration official been willing to go to Pyongyang in 1994, that person, rather than Carter, would probably have received the invitation from Kim Il Sung.

NOTES

1. Associated with Emory University since its inception, The Carter Center entered into a legally defined partnership arrangement with the university in 1995.
2. See the Carter Center home page at www.cartercenter.org.
3. For example, the breakdown of sources of spending by the Peace Program in FY00/01 was approximately 60 per cent private contributions and 40 per cent contributions from governments and IGOs. These figures can obviously vary from year to year, but the proportions have remained fairly stable over the last few years.
4. Most NGOs tend to concentrate on a single issue set or a set of issues grouped about a particular topic (such as AIDS). See, Leon Gordenker and Thomas G. Weiss, 'Pluralizing Global Governance: Analytical Approaches and Dimensions', in Weiss and Gordenker (eds.), *NGOs, the UN and Global Governance*, Boulder, CO: Lynne Rienner, 1996, pp.36–40. See also Pamela Aal, 'Nongovernmental Organizations', in Pamela Aal, Daniel Miltenberger and Thomas G. Weiss (eds.), *Guide to IGOs, NGOs and the Military in Peace and Relief Operations*, Washington, DC: United States Institute of Peace, 2000, pp.121–80.
5. Dayle E. Spencer and William J. Spencer, 'The International Negotiation Network: A New Method of Approaching Some Very Old Problems', Working Paper, The Carter Center of Emory University, November 1992, p.29; Columbia International Affairs Online (CIAO), www.ciaonet.org/wpsfrm.html.
6. 'The Conflict Management Toolkit: Practice', School of Advanced International Studies, The Johns Hopkins University, www.sais-jhu.edu/CMtoolkit/index.php?/name=dip-track2.
7. For a discussion of the differences between principal and neutral mediators see, Thomas Princen, *Intermediaries in International Conflict*, Princeton, NJ: Princeton University Press, 1992, pp.18–31.
8. See, Jacob Bercovitch, J. Theodore Anagnoson and Donnette L. Wille, 'Some Conceptual Issues and Empirical Trends in the Study of Successful Mediation in International Relations', *Journal of Peace Research*, Vol.28, No.1, 1991, p.8.
9. Robert A. Pastor, 'Mediating Elections', *Journal of Democracy*, Vol.9, No.1, Jan. 1998, p.156. Under the auspices of the Carter Center, the Council of Freely Elected Heads

of Governments pioneered the mediation approach in the 1989–90 Nicaraguan elections. See also, Robert A. Pastor, 'The Role of Electoral Administration in Democratic Transitions: Implications for Policy and Research', *Democratization*, Vol.6, No.4, winter 1999, pp.1–27. For a comprehensive analysis of roles played by mediators and various international organizations in critical elections see, Henry F. Carey, 'Electoral Regimes and Democratic Transitions in Less Developed Countries', unpublished PhD thesis, Columbia University, New York, 1997.

10. Another lesson that the Center learned by experience is that for elections to lead to sustainable democracies, there must be more than a smooth transition. Economic progress and good governance must follow if the new democracy is to endure. The development effort can be scuttled by political disputes unless these potential conflicts can be resolved relatively quickly. Consequently, the Center now includes conflict resolution experts on its economic development teams.

11. Pastor, 'Mediating Elections' (n.9 above), p.156. Mediation does not include active supervision or the running of an election, which is always the province of governments.

12. According to Gordon Streeb, Associate Executive Director of the Peace Program at the Carter Center, intergovernmental organizations have recently been more willing to undertake these tasks. In 2000 the OAS strongly condemned the fraudulent election in Peru by which President Fujimori tried to remain in power. In December of the same year, the European Union played an active mediating role in the Zambian presidential election. Personal conversation with Marion Creekmore, 30 July 2002.

13. The following discussion on Carter Center activities in Nicaragua draws freely from The Council of Freely-Elected Heads of Government, *Observing Nicaragua's Elections, 1989–1990*, The Carter Center, May 1990, pp.12–35, Columbia International Affairs Online (CIAO), www.ciaonet.org/wpsfrm.html. Unless noted otherwise, direct quotes in this section come from this source.

14. Richard Boudreaux, 'Latin Leaders Agree on Disbanding Contras: Will Devise a Plan in 90 Days to Demobilize Rebels, Remove Them From Honduras Bases', *The Los Angeles Times*, 15 Feb. 1989, p.1. It also agreed to free more than 1,600 political prisoners and give opposition parties equal access to state-run broadcast media.

15. Christopher Thomas, 'Bush Cuts Funds for Contras in Switch to Diplomatic Path: Nicaragua', *The Times* (London), 30 Mar. 1989 (Lexis-Nexis).

16. Monitoring the Nicaraguan elections was not the first time the Council of Freely Elected Heads of Government had accepted the challenge to serve as election monitors. The Council had been part of an earlier attempt to assure fair elections in Panama. 'The Election That Wasn't', *The Economist*, 13 May 1989, p.47.

17. Lee Hockstader, 'Deal at Hand on Miskitos, Says Carter: Indian Leaders Could Return to Nicaragua', *The Washington Post*, 19 Sept. 1989, p.A22.

18. Carter visited Nicaragua three times before election day to check on the electoral campaign. Each of his visits resulted in an accord with the government: one, as noted above, to allow Nicaraguan Indians to return from exile; one to ensure against campaign violence; and one to release stalled US funds for the opposition. 'Carter Says Sandinistas Are Trying to Smear Foes', *The New York Times*, 15 Nov. 1989, p.11A.

19. Shelley A. McConnell, 'ONUVEN: Electoral Observation as Conflict Resolution', in Tommie Sue Montgomery (ed.), *Peacemaking and Democratization in the Western Hemisphere*, Miami: University of Miami North–South Center Press, 2000, p.119.

20. Lee Hockstader, 'Carter Played Pivotal Role in Hours After Polls Closed', *The Washington Post*, 27 Feb. 1990, p.A19. UNO's majority in the national assembly (51 of 92) fell short of the 2/3 majority needed to amend the constitution. As a result, the UNO could carry through its programme if it could hold together, but constitutional changes could only be effected with the support of the FSLN.

21. Don Oberdorfer, *The Two Koreas*, Reading, MA: Addison-Wesley, 1997, pp.317, 320–22.

22. Carter also consulted with the Rev. Billy Graham who had travelled to North Korea in January, and Tom Johnson and Eason Jordan, CEO of CNN and President of CNN

International, respectively. Jordan had headed the CNN delegation that covered the 82nd birthday celebration of Kim Il Sung in Pyongyang in April. This coverage would lead to CNN being the only Western news organization permitted by the North Koreans to cover the Carter visit.

23. These included Ambassador Laney, General Gary Luck, who commanded American forces in Korea, and South Korean President Kim Young Sam as well as other US and South Korean officials.

24. The South Korean officials probably remembered that as US President, Carter had wanted to withdraw US troops from South Korea. This history may have reinforced their concern that Carter's involvement would prove detrimental to their interests.

25. Carter's delegation included his wife Rosalynn; Carter Center Program Director Marion Creekmore; a former US diplomat, Richard Christenson; a State Department officer fluent in Korean; Carter's appointment secretary, Nancy Konigsmark; and several secret service agents.

26. After the meeting with the foreign minister, Carter decided to prepare a letter for President Clinton asking for authorization to advise the North Koreans that the United States would agree to an early third round of talks if such a move would facilitate resolving the nuclear stalemate. He would not send the letter, however, until after his talk with Kim Il Sung. Since secure communication with Washington was only possible south of the DMZ, Carter dispatched Marion Creekmore with the letter back across the DMZ to await instructions as to whether or not to send it. Creekmore was subsequently advised to return to Pyongyang without sending the letter.

27. Oberdorfer (n.21 above), pp.330–32

28. Kim Il Sung's death from a heart attack in early July prevented the summit, which finally occurred in 2000 with the meeting of South Korean president Kim Dae Jung and Kim Il Sung's son, Kim Jong Il.

29. See, Melanie C. Greenberg, John H. Barton and Margaret E. McGuinness, 'Introduction: Background and Analytical Perspectives', in Greenberg, Barton and McGuinness (eds.), *Words Over War: Mediation and Arbitration to Prevent Deadly Conflict*, Lanham, MD: Rowman & Littlefield, 2000, p.7.

30. Gordenker and Weiss, 'NGO Participation in the International Policy Process', in Weiss and Gordenker (n.5 above), p.210.

31. For a brief description of the origins of the GDI, its goals and current status, see, www.worldbank.org/poverty/strategies/newsletter/gdi.pdf.

32. See, David Backer and David Carroll, 'NGOs and Constructive Engagement: Promoting Civil Society, Good Governance and the Rule of Law in Liberia', *International Politics*, Vol.38, No.1, March 2002, pp.22–3.

33. Ibid., p.22.

34. William Zartman and Saadia Touval, 'Mediation: The Role of Third-Party Diplomacy and Informal Peacemaking', in Sheryl Brown and Kimber M. Schraub (eds.), *Resolving Third World Conflict: Challenges for a New Era*, Washington DC: United States Institute of Peace, 1992, p.51.

Conclusion:
NGO Dilemmas in Peace Processes

HENRY F. CAREY

Scholarly infatuation with international advocacy networks, government networks and 'networked networks' of NGOs and IGOs continues.[1] But as this volume illustrates, much ambivalence pervades assessments about the effects of NGOs on peace processes. On the one hand, pessimism arises because some NGOs may exacerbate conflict. And while peace processes include NGOs as never before, there are few visible signs of success. According to traditional realists, state-dominated geopolitics and international anarchy will always limit what NGOs might achieve. Amnesty International and Human Rights Watch, for example, have only indirect influence on governments and their reports are often ignored. Other critics warn that NGOs put security above values of justice, equity and need, making Faustian pacts with external or internal military forces for their own protection, whether or not these forces engage in abuses.[2]

On the other hand, optimism derives from the spawning of soft law (such as UNHCR's adoption of NGO recommendations after its year-long 'global consultations') or hard treaty law (including NGO influence in the making of conventions regulating landmines, burning carbon fuels, and the establishment of the International Criminal Court – ICC). NGOs have also provided vital services in complex humanitarian emergencies in Somalia, Bosnia, Kosovo, Sierra Leone and Eastern Congo, during and after wars. NGOs continue taking unpopular stands and seeking to meet human needs. Opportunities have emerged for them to address injustices, promote norms and provide practical solutions to peacebuilding problems. For example, UNHCR increasingly acts in conjunction with a growing number of NGOs, such as the International Rescue Committee, CARE and Catholic Relief, to assist refugees and internally displaced persons. Space for NGOs has also emerged when states see that cooperation with NGOs is in their enlightened self-interest. For their part, NGOs may have socialized state elites towards humanitarian values.

Indeed peace processes (encompassing preventive diplomacy,

peacemaking, peacekeeping and peacebuilding) have a demonstrable need for civil society participation. This is particularly true where local polarized forces are unwilling to cooperate directly with each other, but may permit NGOs to provide neutral services. Even at higher levels of counsel, reaching the grassroots seems to be particularly important in peacekeeping and peacebuilding. Thus, NGO participation in preventive or Track-II diplomacy also has great potential.

The essays in this volume address several key themes, which set the agenda for NGO contributions to peace processes. These include the mixing (and overlap) of NGO roles and subsequent problems of coordination, the trade-off between short-run and long-run NGO objectives and strategies, and the tension between neutrality and politically-driven approaches to NGO involvement. The following discussion summarizes the key findings of in the context of these themes.

NGO Roles and Humanitarian Coordination

NGOs involved in the environment, human rights and the humanitarian support of peacekeepers often report that they are being asked to substitute for the UN in a variety of ways. It is impossible to imagine these efforts succeeding if civil society is not assisted by effective international and domestic NGOs. But will the appropriate NGOs be selected or enabled to participate? There is such a broad variety of NGOs that the outcome of missions can be seriously affected by the kinds of NGOs involved and resources allocated. The wrong kind of NGOs, co-opted or compromised by peripheral or parochial concerns, may doom these efforts.

There is much debate about the coordination of NGOs in this volume. Evans-Kent and Bleiker argue that multilateral, state-based and geopolitical approaches to post-conflict reconstruction often restrict the surviving strengths of civil society. Instead of contracting services by NGOs, states should utilize NGOs to connect to those who need assistance, and to listen to their concerns and respect the desire to help themselves. Monshipouri emphasizes the need to incorporate human rights protection into the development of state and civil society. Given the range of post-conflict contexts, local NGOs can help provide adaptation strategies to promote long-term development in a variety of circumstances. Monshipouri's depiction of Afghanistan puts into stark relief the need for localized NGO approaches rather than the prevalent 'one size fits all' tendency of donor-driven and large INGO relief projects. He argues that political rehabilitation and social reconstruction must be approached concurrently, though it remains to be seen if NGOs can manage such disparate tasks to sustain reconstruction in Afghanistan. A picture of confusion, competition and overlap among NGOs is evident in many peacekeeping missions. In Afghanistan, an Agency Coordinating Body for Afghan Relief (ACBAR) has been established as the central NGO coordinating mechanism, though as of mid-2002 it had failed to respond fully to the scale of the problems of famine and homelessness.

Okumu argues in his essay that humanitarian international NGOs run the enormous risk of being manipulated by warlords and state elites who steal or misdirect aid for their own purposes. Yet, there have been enough success stories in Africa to suggest that successfully targeted aid by humanitarian NGOs can occur when military and civilian police agencies allow NGOs autonomy. Even in the horrific conflicts in Liberia and southern Sudan, where aid prolonged the war, a few NGOs helped victims of state abuses. In Liberia, 13 humanitarian NGOs resorted to using 'locally available equipment', limited their food relief to the starving and stopped bringing new resources into Liberia that could fuel the 'war economy'. Similarly, the largest NGOs in southern Sudan agreed not to cooperate with the 'humanitarian' front of the main rebel faction and allied themselves with those humanitarian groups not directly involved in conflict.

Short- and Long-term NGO Objectives and Strategies

Most peace processes aim to establish or re-establish democratic regimes. In contributing to these processes, NGOs must deploy complex capabilities – from monitoring to active consultation and implementation. This requires not only resources but also the will to avoid the 'briefcase temptation' to focus on professional status and future contracts rather than on service delivery to the most needy. Peace processes that lack foreign resources may be free from a scourge of briefcase NGOs, but often suffer a capability gap.

NGOs have increasingly demanded long-term roles to ensure that peacemaking is not ephemeral. Legal problems arise, however, because the new humanitarian NGOs make their claim on ethical grounds, not on positivist legal principles derived from state consent as expressed in treaties.[3] At the same time, some conflict-resolution NGOs pursue short-term peace settlements while human rights NGOs demand that individual leaders be held legally accountable. Often citing UN missions where tribunals have been established without amnesties, human rights NGOs assert that there is no conflict between peace and justice for *crimes genocidaires*. Armed peace support missions enable NGOs promoting peace and justice to enjoy the advantage of an external military presence under which they can conduct research. International judicial intervention, backed by NGO forensic research, is then feasible and assists in reducing impunities for grave breaches of the 1949 Geneva Conventions.

Aggestam asks whether NGOs are able to be people-centred in the areas of economic development and democratization. She views NGOs as politicized and oriented towards funding requirements rather than addressing real needs. Long-term development assistance may not be focused on conflict prevention and may bring about unjust or economically inappropriate settlements. Humanitarian NGOs focus on providing relief and social services, and typically engage in ad hoc peacebuilding rather than seeking to address long-term, economic and territorial causes of conflict. NGOs could also play a role in early warning and prevention,[4] but, as Aggestam argues, they are too divided and short of resources to look beyond short-term efforts.

Schloms also argues that long-term considerations are sacrificed to the imperatives of short-term pragmatic concerns. In practice, peacebuilding cannot be coherent or integrated when NGOs attempting to resuscitate a state are threatened by disruption and violence. Specialized NGOs are often too apolitical to thrive in contexts which require linkages with political actors. Yet too much cooperation with governmental and political actors, in order to enhance local political coordination, also runs the risk of being co-opted into a partisan cause.

One deterrent against the long-term resumption of violence is prosecution and punishment. Pilch analyses the evolving norms of international humanitarian law in the long-neglected area of sexual violence. The new norms against sexual violence and other violations of civilian immunity would not have been possible in two ad hoc tribunals if NGOs had not adduced the evidence from victims' communities.

Political/Ideological Bias versus Neutral/Legalistic Approaches

NGOs, both international and domestic, must be mobilized to counter state violations of human rights without countering the legitimacy of state power per se (which is needed by legitimate courts to enforce the rule of law). Since one part of a state must prosecute the state violators of human rights, NGO criticism should be focused on the part that violates human rights. The difficulties of politicizing human rights

NGOs on matters of humanitarian law can be seen at the preparatory commissions of the ICC and the proposed treaties prohibiting enforced disappearances and terrorism. While human rights NGOs lobbied very effectively to establish the Rome statute in July 1998, they have contributed to dissensus in defining the elements of the core crimes, especially aggression. Part of the explanation may lie in Gaer's contention that INGOs are focusing on critiques through report-writing and policy evaluations of peacekeeping goals. In peace processes, NGOs such as Amnesty International and Human Rights Watch complain that human rights components of peacekeeping missions are not designed by the Office of the High Commissioner for Human Rights and human rights NGOs. This removes the effective monitoring of humanitarian law violations from peace support missions. The exclusion of human rights NGOs may result from perceptions that they are partisan, even though they may be neutral in asserting that governments respect international law.

Conflict-resolution NGOs may attempt mediation in neutral terms, though they might be viewed as partisan in citing legal violations, in trying to constructively engage a party that may be recalcitrant or in having links with a disputant. Creekmore and Taulbee admit that few mediators can overcome perceptions of bias. Although former President Jimmy Carter's mediation efforts have benefited from relatively easy access to heads of state, corporate executives and religious leaders, there are other former leaders such as Finnish President Martti Ahtisaari and Costa Rican President Oscar Arias who have also remained peacemakers out of office. Such mediation can help change the terms of disputes – though issues concerning democratic processes lend themselves to such third-party involvement whereas conflicts over identity and territory are less prone to mediation.

Concern about NGO neutrality pervades debates about humanitarian relief as well. While legal neutrality has been fundamental to the identity and protection of the ICRC, which provides both humanitarian relief and monitoring, several contributors question the perverse incentives which led the ICRC to maintain neutrality during the massacres of World War II and former Yugoslavia. While it did withdraw from Burundi in the face of repeated violations of humanitarian law, the ICRC's assertion of neutrality and confidentiality, through private constructive engagement, has at least allowed it to gain the confidence of many state regimes. Ku and Cáceras remind us, however, that the ICRC's work is complemented by NGOs that monitor humanitarian law more overtly and provide relief to those who are considered victims. Nevertheless, at the risk of attracting charges of hypocrisy, the ICRC takes explicit political positions on some issues, particularly in criticizing alleged violations of humanitarian law by the larger powers, such as the United States, whose citizens are less likely to be receiving ICRC humanitarian relief.[5] The UNHCR is supposed to be similarly apolitical in helping Internally Displaced Peoples (IDPs), and if necessary directly confronting repressive governments on the issue. Yet it is difficult to see how apolitical the UNHCR, and all humanitarian NGOs, can be in pursuing humanitarian norms in the face of so many conflicting demands. Perhaps what is needed is new international law, which assumes that sovereignty no longer prevents them from becoming 'political' by confronting core matters violated by states. Otherwise, NGOs will face 'moral hazards' preventing them from acting responsibly. For example, NGOs need to be deployed to assist those excluded from the ICRC regime on POWs and the UNHCR regime on refugees. These include not only internally displaced peoples, but also those fleeing war who cannot prove their *de jure* status based on persecution as either refugees, POWs or IDPs.

Conclusion

The coordination of peacekeeping and peacebuilding cannot be easily reconciled with the very different tasks extant during a conflict. Furthermore, the short-term goals of NGOs and IGOs are often at odds with long-term goals. Finally, legally-mandated neutrality for NGOs under international humanitarian law may have to be renounced to limit the sovereignty of rights-violating states which perpetuates armed injustice and impunity. One function of NGOs is to render these apparent tradeoffs less stark. Instead, the interstices between these paradoxes and dilemmas can be partly, though not completely served by a greater reliance on the varying roles and capabilities of NGOs.

NGOs have complemented traditional conflict management but have not diminished the influence of states. In war and in polarized societies, NGOs are sometimes complicit in augmenting partisanship. Human rights NGOs have been more political than humanitarian NGOs, which may have been too apolitical and subservient to governments. However, the case of the ICRC suggests the need to occasionally forgo legality in pursuit of morality. A similar dilemma exists with humanitarian interventions by states and NGOs to stop mass murder and ethnic cleansing without UN Security Council authorizations. Such intervention may be illegal, but morally necessary, however paradoxically and incoherent that may seem. Yet, the move to incorporate NGOs into institutional peacebuilding has moved the so-called 'international community' beyond traditional security concerns and conceptions of peace by increasing the plurality of approaches. The potential for progress seems to lie in an increased willingness of states and IGOs, perhaps with legal backing, to consult and utilize NGOs more effectively.

The desire for peace can be quixotic, where states, NGOs and IGOs cannot agree on what kind of peace is appropriate. Moreover, the means of effecting, maintaining and building peace is fraught with conflicting incentives, interests and definitions. Pursing one version of peace and justice can be the basis for consensus. Yet peace NGOs may be the only voices for justice and support for victims, particularly when consensus is misguided or misdirected. As two critics of NGO naïveté concede: 'Humanitarianism as an expression of concern for the victims of armed conflict and political disorder has traditionally been spearheaded by non-state actors.'[6]

NGOs, ranging from formal, small professional units to more broad-based social movements, encompass non-state actors outside of political and economic society. Whether international or domestic in orientation and resources, INGOs and NGOs have the potential of ensuring that society will not be brutalized. Yet, they usually represent a particular set of interests, whether enlightened or not. Peace processes, whether dominated by states and IGOs or oriented towards alternative tracks managed by civil society, can also take on interests of their own. The dynamics of peace processes involve different sets of NGO, INGO and state interests, each seeking the moral high ground but resorting to the realities of power and position, and NGOs and INGOs have had their diverse, often paradoxical effects on peace, whether based on order or justice. NGOs are perhaps the last, best hope to ensure that the legal and symbolic institutions established by peace processes do not become a façade.

NOTES

1. On advocacy networks see, Margaret E. Keck and Kathryn Sikkink, *Activists Beyond Borders: Advocacy Networks in International Politics*, Ithaca: Cornell University Press, 1998; on government networks and networked networks, see Anne-Marie Slaughter, 'Governing the Global Economy through Government Networks', in Michael Byers (ed.), *The Role of Law in International Politics: Essays in International Relations and International Law*, Oxford: Oxford University Press, 2001, pp.177–205. For a critique of NGOs, see Annelise Riles, *The Network Inside Out*, Ann Arbor: University of Michigan Press, 2000.

2. David Chandler, 'The Road to Military Humanitarianism: How the Human Rights NGOs Shaped A New Humanitarian Agenda', *Human Rights Quarterly* Vol.23, No.3, 2001, p.678; Mary B. Anderson, 'Humanitarian NGOs in Conflict Intervention', in Chester Crocker and Fen Hampson with Pamela Aall (eds.), *Managing Global Chaos: Sources of and Responses to International Conflict*, Washington DC: United States Institute of Peace Press, 1996; Amir Pasić and Thomas G. Weiss, 'The Politics of Rescue: Yugoslavia's Wars and the Humanitarian Impulse', *Ethics and International Affairs*, Vol.11, 1997, pp.105–31.

3. Henry F. Carey, 'Naturalism vs Positivism: Debates over Coercive Protection of Human Rights in Haiti, Bosnia and Kosovo', *Civil Wars*, Vol.5, No.2, summer 2002, pp.25–76.

4. See the essays in Robert I. Rotberg (ed.), *Vigilance and Vengeance: NGOs Preventing Ethnic Conflict in Divided Societies*, Washington DC: Brookings Institution Press, 1996.

5. David P. Forsythe, *Humanitarian Politics: The International Committee of the Red Cross*, Baltimore: Johns Hopkins University Press, 1977.

6. Pasić and Weiss (n.2 above), p.105.

Abstracts

Conflict Prevention: Old Wine in New Bottles? *by Karin Aggestam*

This essay examines the extent to which scholarly work offers new insights into the *problematique* of conflict prevention and whether there are any significant alterations in the international management of conflict. The existing literature generally exhibits a number of methodological and theoretical weaknesses, which makes conflict prevention less useful as an analytical concept. In practice, states and IGOs tend to dominate conflict prevention, but NGOs are increasingly important actors since most contemporary conflicts concern unstable state–society relations. (Inter)governmental–NGO relations in conflict prevention are characterized by cost-benefit calculations, shared normative concerns as well as competing understandings of peace. As a way of bridging the gap between theory and practice, the author argues for a stronger emphasis by academics on diagnosis and cumulative knowledge of contemporary conflicts rather than endeavours to predict them.

NGO–Military Relations in Peace Operations *by Francis Kofi Abiew*

The dimensions of peace operations in the post-Cold War era have tended to reflect comprehensive attempts at settling conflicts rather than simply policing ceasefires. As a result, international humanitarian NGOs and multinational military forces are increasingly working closer together in the same theatre of operations than ever before due to a strong demand for coherence of approach. However, these actors have not always necessarily acted jointly, or in concert, to achieve the desired goals of sustainable peace. This article examines the various factors impeding effective NGO–military cooperation, and offers suggestions for improvement of the relationship. It argues that given the complex nature of contemporary conflict management and resolution, involving military and non-military activities, only a well-planned and coordinated combination of civilian and military measures can create the conditions for durability of peace in divided societies.

Humanitarian NGOs in Peace Processes *by Michael Schloms*

From a peacebuilding perspective, the inclusion of humanitarian aid in peace processes appears to be a promising strategy. It is argued that aid, when carried out in close cooperation with international and governmental actors, and when embedded in a broader peacebuilding strategy, can help to implement peace. The implementation of this concept faces three sets of problems: the tension between peacebuilding and humanitarian objectives, the value accorded by aid agencies to independence from political and governmental actors, and the limited capacity of humanitarian agencies to analyse the political context of aid. This essay concludes that these obstacles reflect fundamental characteristics of humanitarianism that cannot easily be overcome within the context of peacebuilding as an integrated approach. However, humanitarian action and peacebuilding clash precisely in conflict situations where immediate, massive humanitarian needs coincide with structural, political breakdown.

Neutrality and the ICRC Contribution to Contemporary Humanitarian Operations by *Charlotte Ku and Joaquín Cáceres Brun*

The International Committee of the Red Cross is one of the most widely recognized NGOs operating today. The important role played by the ICRC in developing and monitoring international humanitarian law is often overlooked in the midst of discussions on the controversial issue of neutrality. This essay considers these debates about the viability of neutrality as a guiding principle in contemporary relief operations, concluding that although other approaches to relief and victim assistance are important, the ICRC effort to work with all parties can provide a useful bridge between pre- and post-conflict situations prior to achieving a longer term solution.

Human Rights NGOs in UN Peace Operations by *Felice D. Gaer*

As UN peace operations expanded in size, number and complexity from the early 1990s, human rights NGOs have had increasing success in advocating that the UN system include a valid human rights component in peace operations, before, during or after conflict. The goal of 'mainstreaming' human rights into the field also under-girded their advocacy for the position of a High Commissioner for Human Rights. Ensuring that such mandates –either through peace agreements or in UN Security Council resolutions – were then actually implemented in effective, sustainable field operations, was monitored through reports by human rights NGOs. Personnel from NGOs have played a leading role in recommending the design of human rights operations and have helped provide leadership and other staff in many of these programmes. These groups have thus added a key new function to their role in the development and refinement of relevant norms and the development of legal systems that protect them.

Sexual Violence: NGOs and the Evolution of International Humanitarian Law by *Frances T. Pilch*

This essay explores the efforts of selected NGOs with a human rights focus, especially women's advocacy groups, in raising public consciousness, providing expert opinion and information, supporting prosecutions and influencing the development of legal jurisprudence on sexual violence in armed conflict. Their growing interdependence, their use of technology, and their application of legal expertise to influence the work of contemporary international and domestic courts is examined in relation to the revolution that has taken place concerning the attainment of justice for victims of sexual violence.

Peace beyond the State? NGOs in Bosnia and Herzegovina *by Bronwyn Evans-Kent and Roland Bleiker*

By examining the work of several NGOs in the context of post-conflict reconstruction in Bosnia and Herzegovina (BiH), this essay scrutinizes both the potential and limits of NGO contributions to peace-settlements and long-term stability. While their ability to specialize and reach the grassroots level is of great practical significance, the contribution of NGOs to the reconstruction of war-torn societies is often idealized. NGOs remain severely limited by ad hoc and project-specific funding sources, as well as by the overall policy environment in which they operate. Unless these underlying issues are addressed, NGOs will ultimately become little more than extensions of prevalent multilateral and state-based approaches to post-conflict reconstruction.

Humanitarian International NGOs and African Conflicts *by Wafula Okumu*

This essay analyses how humanitarian international NGOs (HINGOs) have been manipulated into participating in war economies and how they are enhancing the military objectives of warring parties in African conflicts. Following a basic definition of a HINGO, it proceeds to discuss how HINGOs became involved in, and then prolonged, African conflicts. It also reviews the specific criticisms levelled at HINGOs, before making recommendations and a conclusion that HINGOs can continue providing relief without fuelling or prolonging conflicts by working within a comprehensive framework of a peace-support partnership with development, democratization and human rights agencies, the military, and civilian police operations.

NGOs and Peacebuilding in Afghanistan *by Mahmood Monshipouri*

As a post-conflict society, Afghanistan faces numerous difficulties. Attempts to simultaneously reconstruct the country and build the capacity of people to provide for their basic needs are crucial. Central to building peace in Afghanistan are combatting the sources of insecurity affecting people and communities on the one hand, and advancing nation building on the other. Three central themes guide this study: (1) order and stability are necessary conditions for nation building in Afghanistan; (2) peacebuilding is inseparable from the broader context of reconstruction; and (3) conflict resolution must be seen as a central goal of development policy. NGOs, national and international, must seek equilibrium and coherence among different facets of reconstruction. Because their role in coping with humanitarian crisis is critical, NGOs' involvement need not be made contingent on any particular political solution. Beyond that, their legitimacy lies in an ability to provide the most viable ways of meeting the country's new challenges, especially as they relate to the building of human skills and integrating human rights concerns into developmental schemes.

NGO Mediation: The Carter Center *by James Larry Taulbee and Marion V. Creekmore, Jr.*

The Carter Center occupies a unique niche among NGOs in the contemporary political environment. Though active across a broad spectrum of issue areas, the Carter Center has been most noted for its high-profile mediation efforts. Beginning with the Nicaraguan election in 1990, the Center sought to develop election mediation as a particular technique of conflict resolution for states making the transition to democracy. In the North Korean mediation of 1994, the Center intervened to provide an alternate channel for discussion of important outstanding issues. The two cases illustrate the symbiotic relationship between NGOs, IGOs and governments. In both cases, the active participation of former US president Carter provided high-level access to relevant decision makers and focused media attention on the issues. Government and IGO actions set the context for both initiatives. Government and IGO approval were necessary for legitimizing and implementing the agreement reached.

Notes on Contributors

Henry F. Carey is Assistant Professor of Political Science at Georgia State University, where he teaches international law and organizations, as well as East European Politics. He has published on women in peacekeeping and NGOs, and he is editor of *National Reconciliation in Eastern Europe* (Columbia University Press, 2003*), Politics and Society in Post-Communist Romania* (Lexington Books, 2003), and a special issue of the *Journal of Human Rights* on NGOs and the rule of law (2003).

Oliver P. Richmond is Lecturer at the University of St Andrews, Scotland, and specializes in conflict theory. He has published on aspects of the role of UN peacekeeping, international mediation, conflict resolution, NGOs, ethnic conflict and conflict theory. His most recent publication is *Maintaining Order, Making Peace* (Palgrave, 2002).

Francis Kofi Abiew is Postdoctoral Fellow and Coordinator, Centre for Security and Defence Studies at the Norman Paterson School of International Affairs, Carleton University, Canada. He is the author of *The Evolution of the Doctrine and Practice of Humanitarian Intervention* (Kluwer Law International, 1999), and has published articles on humanitarian intervention, NGOs and Peacebuilding.

Karin Aggestam is research fellow at the Department of Political Science, Lund University, Sweden. She is author of *Reframing and Resolving Conflict. Israeli-Palestinian Negotiations 1988-1998* (Lund University Press, 1999). She is a member of the *Forum for Conflict Prevention*, which holds regular meetings between Swedish academics and diplomats at the Swedish Foreign Office.

Roland Bleiker is Reader in Peace and Conflict Studies, University of Queensland, Australia and currently a Humboldt Fellow at the Institut für Sozialwissenschaften, Humboldt Universität zu Berlin (2002–2003). His recent publications include *Popular Dissent, Human Agency and Global Politics* (Cambridge University Press, 2000).

Joaquín Cáceres Brun teaches public international law at the Colegio Universitario de Segovia 'Domingo Soto', Spain, and is a member of the Spanish Red Cross Centre for Studies on International Humanitarian Law. He has published articles on international humanitarian law and human rights.

Marion V. Creekmore, Jr. has been Distinguished Visiting Professor for History and Political Science at Emory University, USA, since 2000. A former career diplomat, he served in policy level positions in Washington and abroad, including as US Ambassador to Sri Lanka and Republic of Maldives. Between 1993 and 2000, he was Program Director at The Carter Center, Emory's Vice Provost for International Affairs, and Director of Emory's Halle Institute for Global Learning.

Felice D. Gaer directs the Jacob Blaustein Institute for the Advancement of Human Rights. Nominated by the US, she was elected to serve on the Committee Against Torture in Geneva, the UN expert body which monitors state compliance with the Torture Convention. Her recent articles address UN human rights programmes, women's human rights, non-governmental organizations and UN policy in the Balkans.

Bronwyn Evans-Kent is research scholar and doctoral candidate in the School of Political Science and International Studies at the University of Queensland, Australia. She has undertaken extensive research in Bosnia and Herzegovina, focusing in particular on the role of NGOs in peacebuilding efforts. She coordinated an international conference on 'Rethinking Humanitarianism'.

Charlotte Ku is Executive Director and Executive Vice President of the American Society of International Law. She is co-editor with the late Harold K. Jacobson of *Democratic Accountability and the Use of Force in International Law* (Cambridge University Press, 2003).

Mahmood Monshipouri is Chair of the Political Science Department at Quinnipiac University, Connecticut. He is author of *Democratization, Liberalization, and Human Rights in the Third World* (Lynne Rienner, 1995) and *Islamism, Secularism, and Human Rights in the Middle East* (Boulder, CO: Lynne Rienner Publishers, 1998). He is editor, along with Kavita Philip, Neil Englehart and Andrew J. Nathan, of a volume entitled *Constructing Universalisms: Human Rights in an Age of Globalization* (M.E. Shape, 2003).

Wafula Okumu is Academic Programme Associate in the Peace and Governance Programme at the United Nations University, Tokyo. He has conducted research and published in the areas of democracy and human rights in Africa and is currently co-editing a book on democratic transitions in East Africa.

Frances T. Pilch is Associate Professor of Political Science, United States Air Force Academy. Her publications have included articles on the crime of rape in international law, the concept of rape as constituting genocide, and the genocide conviction of Radislav Krstiæ by the International Criminal Tribunal for the former Yugoslavia.

Michael Schloms is an associate fellow at the Research Unit 'International Politics' at Wissenschaftszentrum Berlin für Sozialforschung (Social Science Research Center) in Berlin. He is completing a PhD on the dilemmas of humanitarian action in famine situations and is a member of a multilateral research team analysing humanitarian assistance for North Korea. He has published articles on North Korea and humanitarianism.

James Larry Taulbee is Associate Professor of Political Science at Emory University in Georgia. His written work has addressed questions on the legal control of terrorism, the use of mercenaries and private military companies, the effectiveness of human rights initiatives, the International Criminal Court and the utility of non-conventional defence strategies.

Index